An Introduction to Audio Description

An Introduction to Audio Description is the first comprehensive, user-friendly student guide to the theory and practice of audio description, or media narration, providing readers with the skills needed for the effective translation of images into words for the blind and partially-sighted.

A wide range of examples, from film to multimedia events and touch tours in theatre, along with comments throughout from audio description users, serve to illustrate the following key themes:

- the history of audio description
- the audience
- the legal background
- how to write, prepare and deliver a script.

Covering the key genres of audio description and supplemented with exercises and discussion points throughout, this is the essential textbook for all students and translators involved in the practice of audio description. Accompanying film clips are also available at: https://www.routledge.com/products/9781138848177 and on the Routledge Translation Studies Portal: http://cw.routledge.com/textbooks/translationstudies/.

Louise Fryer is a teaching fellow at University College London and describes for the National Theatre of Great Britain and VocalEyes. For many years, she presented *Afternoon on 3, Live in Concert* and *Proms* for BBC Radio 3.

Translation Practices Explained
Series Editor: Kelly Washbourne

Translation Practices Explained is a series of coursebooks designed to help self-learners and students on translation and interpreting courses. Each volume focuses on a specific aspect of professional translation practice, in many cases corresponding to courses available in translator-training institutions. Special volumes are devoted to well consolidated professional areas, to areas where labour-market demands are currently undergoing considerable growth, and to specific aspects of professional practices on which little teaching and learning material is available. The authors are practicing translators or translator trainers in the fields concerned. Although specialists, they explain their professional insights in a manner accessible to the wider learning public.

These books start from the recognition that professional translation practices require something more than elaborate abstraction or fixed methodologies. They are located close to work on authentic texts, and encourage learners to proceed inductively, solving problems as they arise from examples and case studies.

Each volume includes activities and exercises designed to help learners consolidate their knowledge (teachers may also find these useful for direct application in class, or alternatively as the basis for the design and preparation of their own material.) Updated reading lists and website addresses will also help individual learners gain further insight into the realities of professional practice.

Titles in the series:

Translating Children's Literature
Gillian Lathey

Localizing Apps
Johann Roturier

User-Centered Translation
Tytti Suojanen, Kaisa Koskinen, Tiina Tuominen

Translating for the European Union Institutions 2e
Emma Wagner, Svend Bech, Jesús M. Martínez

Revising and Editing for Translators 3e
Brian Mossop

Audiovisual Translation
Frederic Chaume

Scientific and Technical Translation Explained
Jody Byrne

Translation-Driven Corpora
Federico Zanettin

Subtitling Through Speech Recognition
Pablo Romero-Fresco

Translating Promotional and Advertising Texts
Ira Torresi

Audiovisual Translation, Subtitling
Jorge Diaz-Cintas, Aline Remael

Medical Translation Step by Step
Vicent Montalt, Maria González-Davies

Notetaking for Consecutive Interpreting
Andrew Gillies

Translating Official Documents
Roberto Mayoral Asensio

Conference Interpreting Explained
Roderick Jones

Legal Translation Explained
Enrique Alcaraz, Brian Hughes

Electronic Tools for Translators
Frank Austermuhl

Introduction to Court Interpreting
Holly Mikkelson

For more information on any of these titles, or to order, please go to www.routledge.com/linguistics

An Introduction to Audio Description
A practical guide

Louise Fryer

LONDON AND NEW YORK

First published 2016
by Routledge
2 Park Square, Milton Park, Abingdon, Oxon OX14 4RN

and by Routledge
711 Third Avenue, New York, NY 10017

Routledge is an imprint of the Taylor & Francis Group, an informa business

© 2016 Louise Fryer

The right of Louise Fryer to be identified as author of this work has been asserted by her in accordance with sections 77 and 78 of the Copyright, Designs and Patents Act 1988.

All rights reserved. No part of this book may be reprinted or reproduced or utilised in any form or by any electronic, mechanical, or other means, now known or hereafter invented, including photocopying and recording, or in any information storage or retrieval system, without permission in writing from the publishers.

Trademark notice: Product or corporate names may be trademarks or registered trademarks, and are used only for identification and explanation without intent to infringe.

British Library Cataloguing-in-Publication Data
A catalogue record for this book is available from the British Library

Library of Congress Cataloging-in-Publication Data
Names: Fryer, Louise, author.
Title: An Introduction to audio description : a pratical guide / by Louise Fryer.
Description: Milton Park, Abingdon, Oxon ; New York, NY : Routledge, [2016] |
    Series: Translation Practices Explained
Identifiers: LCCN 2015046903| ISBN 9781138848153 (hardback : alk. paper) |
    ISBN 9781138848177 (pbk. : alk. paper) | ISBN 9781315707228 (ebook : alk. paper)
Subjects: LCSH: Translating and interpreting—Technological innovations. | Multimedia
    systems—Research. | Audio-visual equipment—Technological innovations.
Classification: LCC P306.93 .F79 2016 | DDC 418/.020871—dc23
LC record available at http://lccn.loc.gov/2015046903

ISBN: 978-1-138-84815-3 (hbk)
ISBN: 978-1-138-84817-7 (pbk)
ISBN: 978-1-3157072-2-8 (ebk)

Typeset in Times New Roman
by Swales & Willis Ltd, Exeter, Devon, UK

Contents

List of tables — xiii
How to use this book — xiv
Acknowledgements — xvi
Glossary and abbreviations — xvii

1 Introducing audio description — 1

   1.1 What is audio description? 1
   1.2 Audio description within audiovisual translation 2
   1.3 AD within AVT 3
   1.4 Meaning making in AD 4
       1.4.1 AD, access and equivalence 4
   1.5 AD and presence 6
   1.6 Definitions of AD 7
   1.7 Conclusion 9
   1.8 Exercises and points for discussion 10
   1.9 Suggested reading 10
   References 11

2 A brief history, legislation and guidelines — 15

   2.1 Introduction 15
   2.2 A brief history 15
   2.3 The legal background 19
   2.4 Non-broadcast TV 20
   2.5 AD in practice 21
       2.5.1 Screen-based AD 21
       2.5.2 Live AD 21
   2.6 Guidelines 22
   2.7 Conclusion 23
   2.8 Exercises and points for discussion 23
   References 23

3 Putting the audio into audio description — 26

3.1 Introduction 26
3.2 The visual information stream 26
3.3 The auditory information stream 27
    3.3.1 Exercises and points for discussion 27
    3.3.2 Dialogue 28
    3.3.3 Exercises 29
3.4 Cognitive load 29
3.5 Sound effects 30
3.6 Exercises and points for discussion 30
3.7 Translating music 31
    3.7.1 Describing live musical events 31
    3.7.2 Visual dominance and music 32
3.8 Finding the 'gaps' 33
3.9 The *When* of AD 34
    3.9.1 The When *of live AD 36*
    3.9.2 Touch tours 37
    3.9.3 Sound and live events 37
    3.9.4 Exercises and points for discussion 39
3.10 Conclusion 39
3.11 Suggested reading 39
References 39

4 The audience for audio description — 42

4.1 Introduction 42
4.2 What is blindness? 42
4.3 Age and blindness 43
4.4 A model of visual processing 44
    4.4.1 mental models, schemata and scripts 44
4.5 A cognitive model of AD 47
4.6 Exercises and points for discussion 48
    4.6.1 An extract from the AD script for Notes on Blindness *49*
    4.6.2 Notes on Blindness *49*
4.7 What do AD users want from AD? 49
4.8 Conclusion 50
4.9 Exercises and points for discussion 51
4.10 Suggested reading 51
References 51

5 Audio description skills: writing — 54

5.1 Introduction 54
5.2 The *What* of AD 55

5.3 Word choice 58
    5.3.1 Need to know versus nice to know:narration and description 58
    5.3.2 Cultural references 61
    5.3.3 Ambiguity 62
    5.3.4 Pronouns 63
    5.3.5 Tense 63
    5.3.6 Articles 65
5.4 Sound symbolism 66
    5.4.1 Rhythm and rhyme 66
5.5 Sight-specific references 68
    5.5.1 Verbs of vision 68
    5.5.2 Colour 68
5.6 Creative use of language 70
    5.6.1 Repetition 70
    5.6.2 Structure, word order, literary constructions 70
    5.6.3 Punctuation 70
5.7 Cues and notes 70
5.8 Conclusion 71
5.9 Exercises and points for discussion 71
References 72

6   Audio description skills: script preparation   75

6.1 Introduction 75
6.2 Screen software 75
    6.2.1 How it works 75
    6.2.2 Timecode 77
    6.2.3 Speech rate 77
    6.2.4 Creating the script 78
    6.2.5 Freely available software 79
6.3 Live scripting strategies 80
    6.3.1 By hand 80
    6.3.2 Electronic scripts 80
6.4 Common scripting faults 81
6.5 Exercises 83
    6.5.1 Exercises using software 83
    6.5.2 Exercises by hand 84
6.6 Discussion points 84
6.7 The process 84
    6.7.1 Screen AD 84
    6.7.2 Live AD 84
    6.7.3 The process for the AD user at live events 85

x *Contents*

    6.8 Conclusion 85
    References 85

7 Audio description skills: delivery   87

    7.1 Introduction 87
    7.2 Delivery and prosody 87
        7.2.1 Accent, gender and emotion 88
        7.2.2 Stress and segmentation 90
        7.2.3 Tone 92
        7.2.4 Pace, pitch, segmentation 93
        7.2.5 Authenticity, the I-voice and delivery of
            live AD 94
        7.2.6 Pronunciation 95
        7.2.7 Fluency 96
    7.3 Preparing the voice 96
        7.3.1 Warming up 96
        7.3.2 Microphone technique 96
    7.4 Recording 97
        7.4.1 Recording strategies 97
        7.4.2 Listening back 97
    7.5 Live delivery 98
    7.6 Conclusion 99
    7.7 Exercises and points for discussion 99
    7.8 Suggested reading 99
    References 99

8 Beyond the basics: audio description by genre   102

    8.1 Introduction 102
    8.2 Genre and suitability of AD 102
    8.3 Movie genres 104
        8.3.1 Spectacle 105
        8.3.2 Horror 106
        8.3.3 Historical films and costume dramas 107
    8.4 Intertextuality 108
        8.4.1 Intertextuality and historical films 108
    8.5 Factual programmes 109
        8.5.1 Sport, news and current affairs 109
        8.5.2 Documentaries 110
        8.5.3 Nature documentaries 110
    8.6 Soaps and serials 112
    8.7 Children's programmes 114
    8.8 Genre and live performance 115
    8.9 Conclusion 116

8.10 Exercises and points for discussion 116
References 116

9   Beyond the basics: text on screen 119

9.1 Introduction 119
9.2 Tops and tails 119
   9.2.1 Title sequences 119
   9.2.2 Logos 121
9.3 Text on screen and delivery 122
   9.3.1 Audio subtitles 122
9.4 AD and voice-over 124
9.5 Text and live events 125
9.6 Multilingualism 126
9.7 Simultaneity and asynchrony 126
9.8 End credits 127
9.9 Conclusion 127
9.10 Exercises and points for discussion 128
References 128

10 Beyond the basics: accessible filmmaking and describing camerawork 130

10.1 Introduction 130
10.2 The language of cinema 130
10.3 Cinematic audio description 132
10.4 AD and the artistic team 136
10.5 Auteur description 137
10.6 Conclusion 138
10.7 Exercises and points for discussion 138
References 139

11 Audio description and censorship 141

11.1 Introduction 141
11.2 Language 142
   11.2.1 Expletives 143
11.3 Sex and AD 144
   11.3.1 AD of porn 146
11.4 Blood and gore 148
   11.4.1 Blood, gore and live events 149
11.5 Positive aspects of censorship 150
11.6 Political correctness: describing race and disability 150
11.7 Conclusion 152
11.8 Exercises and points for discussion 153
References 153

12 Audio introductions — 155

12.1 Introduction 155
12.2 Audio introductions and timing 155
12.3 Sensitive material 158
12.4 The *What* of audio introductions 158
    12.4.1 Technical language 159
12.5 The process 159
12.6 Cross referencing 161
12.7 Synopses 161
12.8 Conclusion 162
12.9 Exercises and points for discussion 162
References 163

13 Contentious issues and future directions in audio description — 164

13.1 Introduction 164
13.2 Objectivity and subjectivity 164
13.3 Describing facial expression 166
13.4 Reinforcement, repetition and redundancy 169
13.5 AD and persistence 170
13.6 Topics for future research 170
13.7 Conclusion 172
13.8 Exercises and points for discussion 172
References 172

14 Afterword — 175

14.1 What is audio description, revisited 175
14.2 Conclusion 176

Appendix 1: Answers to Chapter 1, exercise 3 — 177
Appendix 2: Like Rabbits *AD script* — 178

Index — 184

Tables

2.1	Differences between AD for live events and screen AD	18
5.1	Number of respondents by sight status in response to the question: 'Do you build up an image in your mind?'	57
6.1	Marking checklist	82
7.1	Common recording faults	98
10.1	Qualitative responses to the cinematic description of *Brief Encounter*	134

How to use this book

Gower: 'What's dumb in show, I'll plain with speech.'
(W. Shakespeare, *Pericles*, Act III, Prologue)

Audio description (AD) is increasingly recognised as a constituent part of audio-visual translation studies (AVT), complementing subtitling for the deaf and hard of hearing (SDH) by providing access to media for blind and partially sighted people. Although many academic articles and a number of books have been published on AD in recent years, to the best of the author's knowledge, there is no practical manual for students combining the results of such research with practical advice. This book aims to fill the gap, targeting the growing readership in AVT at universities. This includes students and researchers and those responsible for delivering AD courses. This book may also be of interest to the general public and anyone with an interest in linguistics, psycholinguistics, visual perception, media, film or disability. Although it focuses on AD in the UK, as that is the location of my own experience, attempts have been made to refer to description across Europe, the United States and elsewhere whenever possible.

Most of this book's content draws on actual postgraduate AD courses taught by the author at City University, Imperial College and University College London (on-campus) and the University of Macerata in Italy (online) and delivering training courses for broadcast media in the UK and abroad. As AD began in theatre, at least in the UK, this book also draws on practical courses I have delivered with the Audio Description Association (ADA UK) and VocalEyes (a UK arts and access charity) concentrating on AD of live performance, such as theatre, opera, dance and open-air festivals. Although occasionally the boundaries between 'screen' AD and AD for live events are blurred with live AD provided for film screenings, there are distinct differences between writing and delivering AD for audiovisual (AV) media and for live performance, and I will discuss both types. Rather than giving you a set of hard and fast rules to follow, I intend to help you discover what questions to ask yourself when presented with an AV 'text' to describe, so that you can create your own solutions to the unique set of challenges presented each time, while keeping in mind what the (at times contradictory) guidelines in different countries propose and keeping the needs of the users uppermost.

How to use this book xv

This book is designed to be read sequentially, as each chapter builds on the previous one. The opening chapters are largely theoretical and are aimed at embedding the reader in the perceptual and meaning-making questions at the heart of AD. AD is largely discussed from a cognitive perspective. Chapter 4 introduces the reader to the AD audience so that AD students understand both why AD is necessary and the heterogeneous nature of those who use it. Chapters 4–7 are the practical core of the book, with exercises and checklists to help guide students and teachers.

Chapters 8–14 go beyond the basics to explore additional elements, such as audio introductions (Chapter 12), which complement the dynamic AD, freeing it of many of its time constraints. They take a broader perspective, looking at areas of challenge and contention such as description of camerawork (Chapter 10) and AD and censorship (Chapter 11). AD is still evolving and the final chapter looks ahead to areas ripe for future research.

Acknowledgements

I would not have been able to write this book without the influence of (and late night discussions with) the many describers I have worked with over the years. Particular contributions have come from Veronika Hyks, Bridget Crowley and Roz Chalmers, who have given me access to scripts reproduced in part here. I am also grateful to the National Theatre of Great Britain and VocalEyes, the Almeida Theatre, Archer's Mark, Lost Dog Productions and Rocket House Productions for allowing me to draw on scripts that I wrote for them. Thanks, too, to the directors who have given me access to their films used as examples to accompany this book: Vito Palmieri, Pablo Romero Fresco, and Peter Middleton and James Spinney. I thank Gian Maria Greco for transcribing *Matilde* for me. He is just one of the AVT academics who have inspired and encouraged me. I thank the many blind and partially sighted people who have taken part in my research, who have informed my thinking and who give me an audience. You will read their words in the following pages. I thank my family for their patience and practical assistance. Finally, I thank Andrew Holland, who suggested I become a describer in the first place and who has never been satisfied with the status quo.

Every effort has been made to contact copyright holders. Please advise the publisher of any errors or omissions, and these will be corrected in subsequent editions.

Glossary and abbreviations

AB	adventitiously blind (losing sight through illness or accident)
AD	audio description
ADA	Audio Description Association (UK)
ADC	Audio Description Coalition (USA)
AI	audio introduction
ARSAD	Advanced Research Seminar on Audio Description
AST	audio subtitles
ATVOD	Authority for Television on Demand
AUDETEL	audio description of television
AV	audiovisual
AVT	audiovisual translation
BBC	British Broadcasting Corporation
BPS	blind or partially sighted
CB	congenitally blind
DDA	Disability Discrimination Act
HBB4All	Hybrid Broadband Broadcasting for All
HBBTV	hybrid broadband television
HVAD	human voice audio description
ITC	Independent Television Commission
ITV	Independent Television
MA	Master of Arts
Ofcom	the communications regulator in the UK
POV	point of view
RNIB	Royal National Institute of Blind People
SDH	subtitling for deaf and hard of hearing people
SFX	sound effects

S/S	syllables per second
ST	source text
TT	target text
TTS	text-to-speech
TV	television
VOD	video on demand
WM	working memory
WPM	words per minute
WYSIWYS	What You See Is What You Say

1 Introducing audio description

1.1 What is audio description?

At the moment, the stage is screened from view by a black gauze. The house lights fade – all is darkness [whispering] a single beam of light picks out a young woman in a white slip. She stands, hair loose, skin pale, eyes wide and anxious. She shrouds herself in a black chador, only her face is visible. She raises one arm in front of her, concealing all but her eyes. A flash [sfx]. The gauze falls – the girl is gone.

This is how a recent production of Federico García Lorca's *The House of Bernarda Alba*, updated and translocated to Iran, began at London's Almeida Theatre (dir. Sheibani, 2012) if you were a blind member of the audience, listening to the audio description (AD). AD (also known as video description in the USA) is a verbal commentary providing visual information for those unable to perceive it themselves. AD helps blind and partially sighted people access audiovisual media and is also used in live settings such as theatres, galleries and museums (e.g. Díaz-Cintas et al., 2007; Vocaleyes.com) as well as in architectural tours, football and cricket matches (RNIB.org.uk) and to help blind people enjoy holidays (TravelEyes-International.com).

Radio description is a recent and unusual application of AD, intended to illustrate images referred to in a radio programme and that none of the audience can see. Description has always been a feature of radio programmes but was first included specifically under the term AD in BBC Radio 4's news follow-up programme *iPM* in November 2013, when an audio describer was asked to paint a couple of verbal portraits of the programme's presenters as an auditory alternative to webcam. Although this was a tongue-in-cheek initiative, further descriptions soon followed (Fryer, 2013; 2014). Although most of these descriptions have more in common with AD of visual art than with what Sabine Braun (2007) terms 'dynamic AD', the AD for an early film, *A Daring Daylight Burglary* (Mottershaw, 1908), that was incorporated into the radio documentary *The First Action Movie* (Byrnes, 2014) was dynamic in that it was timed to synchronise with the changing shots of the film as well as to capture the camera points-of-view. Description of camera shots is controversial in AD and this will be returned to in Chapter 10. Why did a radio producer feel the need to ask an audio describer to make the pictures better on radio? It is hoped that the following pages will make it clear that the way a describer thinks about image, sound and words equips them with particular skills that benefit a purely auditory medium.

In the UK, around 2 million people out of a population of around 64 million rely more on sound than most people do because they have impaired vision (RNIB, 2015a). There are thought to be 30 million blind and partially sighted people in Europe as a whole (European Blind Union, 2015), 21 million in the USA and 285 million globally (World Health Organization, 2014). Precise figures are hard to come by. This is not surprising, as in many countries there is no legal obligation to register as blind and there are widely varying definitions of blindness. The diverse characteristics of the AD audience are discussed in Chapter 4.

Agnieszka Szarkowska (2011: 142) points out that 'audio description can refer to both product and process'. This book includes discussion of both; however, it will refer to the finished product as the description and the process as describing. Those who carry out the process are called audio describers, or just describers for short. This term may embrace the person who writes the AD script or the person who reads it. Sometimes these persons are one and the same. At other times they are two different people, with one person writing the script and the reading part being given to a professional voice-over artist, or a machine using text-to-speech software (TTS). However, those writing the description must always bear in mind that the script will be delivered orally, even if it is read out by an electronic voice. Unlike most translation texts, AD is always written for a listener, not a reader. This is discussed more fully in Chapters 5, 6 and 7, as the way AD is received affects the way the AD script is both written and delivered.

In the UK, the practice of AD in theatre and for AV media proliferated during the late 1980s and 1990s. AD for TV is now a legal requirement in the UK and has been since 1996 (Broadcasting Act, 2003; Communications Act, 1996; Equality Act, 2010). In that time, its methods have evolved and they are still evolving. In 2007, Elaine Gerber believed them to be still largely untested (Gerber, 2007). This is changing as a result of academic interest and an increasing number of reception studies. As an emerging discipline, AD is taught most commonly at postgraduate level in university departments of translation.

1.2 Audio description within audiovisual translation

AD is increasingly recognised as a constituent part of audiovisual translation (AVT) and complements subtitling for people who are deaf, deafened or hard of hearing (SDH) by providing access to AV media for people who are blind or partially sighted (BPS). AVT refers to the translation of *all* audiovisual products, including feature films, documentaries, television (TV) programmes and online content – in other words, the corpus of source material covered under the umbrella term 'screen translation' (Karamitroglou, 2000: 3). Karamitroglou cites Gambier's list of AVT products, which comprises subtitling, simultaneous subtitling (e.g. respeaking), dubbing, interpreting (pre-recorded and consecutive), voice-over, narration, commentary, multilingual broadcast, surtitles and supratitles, and simultaneous translation – to which access practices such as signing for the deaf and AD should be added. According to Maszerowska et al. (2014: 5), 'Audio description in Europe is a media access practice still lacking critical mass in terms of terminology, practice and training', and they call AD 'one of the younger siblings of AVT' (ibid., 2014: 3). There is still much that scholarship around AD can learn from its older brothers and sisters, especially strategies used in interpreting, dubbing and subtitling.

1.3 AD within AVT

AVT students are generally surprised by audio description. Unlike subtitling, dubbing or voice-over, AD does not come with a pre-existing text that needs translating from one language to another. Rather, it has been identified by Braun (2008: 2) as 'intersemiotic, intermodal or cross-modal translation or mediation' (e.g. Benecke, 2004; Bourne and Jiménez Hurtado, 2007). The term 'intersemiotic' was coined by Jakobsen (1959) to describe types of translation in which part of the context comes from information outside the translated channel. 'Modal' in this context refers to modes of meaning. These include spoken, written, music and sound effects (SFX). Yet modal can also be thought of as relating to different sensory modes: namely, information received through one sense (vision) must be translated into information that can be received through another sense (audition). Joel Snyder has neatly coined the phrase 'the visual made verbal' (Snyder, 2014) to sum up AD. Jan-Louis Kruger also points out: 'Audio description or narration is substantially different from other AVT modes like dubbing and subtitling, primarily because the focus in other modes is on dialogue' (Kruger, 2012: 232). Describers must generate their script from scratch. Many translation and interpreting students find this taxing. However, others find this to be an exciting challenge, and the linguistic creativity required explains the fascination exerted by AD. Like all creative exercises, AD is governed by many constraints – which will be illuminated in the coming pages – leading Benecke (2014) to refer to it as partial or constrained translation, as the translator has only partial control over the source text (ST). The description must be fitted around the existing soundtrack, which, although its volume may be lowered for recorded media, will otherwise remain unchanged and should not be obliterated by the AD. The importance of sound is the focus of Chapter 3.

Although AD is commonly linked to subtitling, as both are means to improve access for people with a sensory impairment, potentially much stronger links have been overlooked with interpreting studies and dubbing, which, like AD, share an interest in oral delivery as the principal means of the communicative act. AD contains a performance element that has at times been overlooked by scholars in favour of the words of the AD text. Charlotte Bosseaux (2015) has attempted to correct this omission in the field of dubbing. In this book it is hoped to take such a step on behalf of AD. Delivery is discussed in Chapter 7. In contrast to AD for recorded media, AD of live events (see Chapter 2) in particular shares a similar set of factors that govern the exchange for interpreting as described by Wadensjö (1999);

4   *Introducing audio description*

namely constraints provided by the technology; the field or subject matter; the tenor – role and relationships; and the mode or communication channel (Tebble, 1999). The audio describer, specifically the screen describer (at least in some countries) like the Swedish dialogue interpreter described by Wadensjö, enjoys 'professional status, and ... work regulated by an official code'. Wadensjö goes on to say: 'The Codex states, in short, that the dialogue interpreter should only interpret i.e. relay everything said and relay what was said the way it was said ... It follows along with an official principle of the interpreter's neutrality' (Wadensjö, 1993: 105). Metzger has debunked what she refers to as the 'myth of neutrality' (Metzger, 1999) for interpreting. This has yet to be done fully for AD, and the exact parameters of the subjective/objective spectrum have been an area of fierce debate. This is a debate that refuses to go away, and it will be alluded to throughout this book, and discussed more fully in Chapter 13.

1.4 Meaning making in AD

One principal concern of translation is how meaning carried through the words of one language or sign system can be conveyed through the words or signs of another (e.g. Gorlée, 1994; Remael, 2010). In AVT multiple channels or systems interact. For Gottlieb (2004), for example, multilingual subtitling is 'diasemiotic', requiring the translation of a verbal auditory channel (words that we hear) into a visual (verbal) channel (words that we see). SDH presumably could be seen as trisemiotic, adding in a third channel, translating from the verbal and non-verbal auditory channels to a verbal (visual) channel with the addition of visually expressed sound effects. Dubbing, being consistently auditory, is 'isosemiotic'. Orero and Szarkowska (2014) agree with Gambier (2006) that AD should be thought of as 'multisemiotic', translating the visual (both verbal, such as sub-titled speech or the headline of a newspaper, and non-verbal, such as an action sequence of two protagonists fighting) into spoken words.

In a recent development, AD scripts have begun to be directly translated from one language to another. So an AD script for an English source programme may be translated directly into Polish, for example, without a Polish describer having to reinvent the wheel (Jankowska, 2015). This means that the place of AD within AVT is no longer always inter-semiotic but sometimes simply interlingual. However, it is important that the translator of AD scripts is still aware of the basic principles that underlie AD in order to create a translation that is fit for purpose.

1.4.1 AD, access and equivalence

AD assumes that a verbal commentary can successfully translate visual information. However, different systems of information transfer do not necessarily equate. Equivalence is problematic in translation. Alluding to Shakespeare's *The Merchant of Venice*, Derrida asks 'Can a pound of flesh equate to a sum of money?' He concludes: 'in every translation, there is also ... an incalculable equivalence, an impossible but incessantly alleged correspondence between the pound of flesh and money, a required but impractical translation between the uniqueness of a proper body and the arbitrariness of a fiduciary sign' (Derrida, 2002: 431). Adamou and Knox (2011: 1) argue that 'inherent in this idea of equivalence are problematic assumptions that the text has a single "correct" meaning, which can be "correctly" read by viewers (or at least "competent" ones), and, somewhat contradictorily, that textual identity is stable'. This book will make clear the weakness of those assumptions, as all members of an audience 'read' a text differently, regardless of sensory loss. This does not mean that describers should not aim at equivalence, just that uniformity of reception even by the sighted audience (including describers) cannot be guaranteed.

Gambier (2006) distinguishes between accessibility and usability. He argues that 'The goal of usability is a better experience for the user; the goal of accessibility is equality of access.' Perhaps, then, usability is the best AD can aim for. The author's research would suggest otherwise. Comments from AD users suggest that the information given in the AD compensates for lack of direct sensory information by providing visual details in verbal form. Studies suggest that, in blind people, perceptual and linguistic processing may be intrinsically linked. Neuroscience reveals that blind people process language in their visual cortex (e.g. Merabet and Pascual-Leone, 2009). If the brain is plastic enough to rewire cross-modal connections, surely it is not too far-fetched to suggest that it might do the same with language processing, such that language replaces sight as an external reference frame within which incoming sensory information is interpreted?

Such linguistic compensation may be explained developmentally. An ongoing study into the development of blind infants (Dale, 2013) shows that, at around the age of 18 months, when a normally developing child is exploring the world by crawling and reaching out for objects, a blind baby sits motionless, unless another individual interacts. This interaction usually takes the form of verbal encouragement from the parent or carer, who will simultaneously present an object for the infant to explore through sound and touch. For sighted infants, congruent information from different modalities can be matched implicitly: a sighted baby hearing a mewing sound can turn its head to see a furry cat. In the next encounter, on seeing a cat, the child will expect to hear it mew and will put out their hand to stroke it. A blind child relies on being told explicitly that the creature is called a cat in order to build up the same auditory or tactile expectation when they are next told a cat is present. Similarly, for a sighted child, much of the shared experience of the external world can remain implicit, relying on pointing or eye-gaze. Shared interaction for the blind child necessarily involves language.

Even for an adult with late-onset sight loss, everyday interactions are likely to be accompanied by a greater exchange of verbal information than is usual between those who can perceive that information for themselves. When a sighted person is brought a cup of tea, for example, the tray may be simply set down with an instruction to 'help yourself'. For a blind person, the arrival of the tray is likely to be accompanied by a description of where the tray is, how many cups are on it, how full a particular cup is, whether or not milk has been added, which way the handle is facing, etc. Arguably, then, in the absence of sight, speech is essential to the integration of sensory input and therefore to perception. In this sense, speech replaces visual input. The model of description advanced in this book is based on the evidence that speech is an effective replacement for directly experienced visual input and that equivalence of response as much as usability is an achievable goal.

1.5 AD and presence

From the earliest studies, AD was shown to make a difference to blind people's comprehension of AV media, making it more usable (e.g. Schmeidler and Kirchner, 2001; Pettitt et al., 1996). Fryer and Freeman (2013: 16) argue that research into AD reception:

> has tended to rely on AD-specific questionnaires, that are often evaluating recall and comprehension. Yet, people generally watch TV or a film to be entertained, rather than as a memory test. AD is at its best when the user is unaware of it: 'When', as one blind theatre-goer puts it 'the describers are invisible, when I'm not consciously aware of the vital contribution they're making to my theatrical experience.' Such a perceptual illusion of non-mediation . . . is one definition of 'presence' that Biocca (1997: par. 5.3) calls 'the illusion of being there'. Biocca also argues that, at any one time, individuals can feel present in one of three environments: the physical, non-mediated environment; the virtual environment; or the environment of the imagination that is dependent on the user's internally-generated imagery.

The term 'telepresence' was coined over thirty years ago to describe human interaction with remote-access technology (Minksy, 1980). Since then the concept of presence has been extended to embrace the psychological sense of immersion and engagement in any mediated environment, such that it appears unmediated (Lombard and Ditton, 1997).

Jones (2007: 123) suggests that presence is the 'response to a mental model of an environment that takes shape in the mind of the individual based upon a combination of cues that originate both externally and internally'. Mental models are explored in Chapter 4. Those new to AD may especially question the ability of AD to provide an experience for blind and partially sighted people that comes anywhere close to being equivalent to that of sighted audiences. Equivalence of meaning can be assessed through measures of comprehension. However, presence makes it possible to measure equivalence of experience directly, comparing people with and without sight. Research shows that 'levels of presence for those with visual impairments can exceed those of the sighted audience when an audiovisual stimulus is accessed via AD of an appropriate style' (Fryer and Freeman, 2013: 1). This apparent paradox is not dissimilar to what Gysbers et al. (2004) called 'the book problem': that presence can as readily be induced by reading a novel as by all-singing, all-dancing immersive technologies such as virtual environments or Imax cinema. Presence researchers have shown that levels of presence do not share a linear relationship with direct sensory experience, so presence does not increase according to the number of stimulated modes. This might explain why AD users report a strong sense of presence, despite receiving AV information through a single, auditory channel. For illustrative purposes comments from the many blind or partially sighted people who participated in the author's research are included throughout this book. It is important to be aware of the needs and opinions of the target audience when translating images into words, and also of our own sighted biases (see Chapters 3 and 11). Hannah Thompson (2015), a reader in French at Royal Holloway, University of London, who has impaired sight, points out the problematic irony that AD is designed to help give blind users independence, yet 'blind cinemagoers are reliant on choices made by sighted describers'. As Venuti has stated, 'Translating can never simply be communication between equals because it is fundamentally ethnocentric' (Venuti, 1998: 4), but the issue is heightened in AVT because of the combination of semantic and sensory modes. It can be hard for a sighted person to understand blind culture, even if the language used to express meaning is one's own.

Sabine Braun (2007) points out that meaning is deduced from AV texts through a combination of explicit and implicit information. This in turn relates to the two main channels of information in AV texts, namely the visual (pictures show rather than tell) and the auditory (verbal storytelling tells you what to think). In deciding which visual details to include and how explicit to make the description of them, Sabine Braun (2007) turns to Sperber and Wilson's relevance theory (1995). She suggests: 'The differences between propositional representations (created from verbal utterances) and depictive representations (created from visual input) would be an important topic for further research in the context of AD' (Braun, 2007: 365). This calls to mind the debate between philosopher Bryan Magee and his congenitally blind colleague Martin Milligan (Magee and Milligan, 1995). When Magee suggested that congenitally blind people can have no real comprehension of the world, as their limited sense experience inhibits access to certain types of sensory data, Milligan's riposte was that 'nature (fortunately) makes available to human beings a great deal of redundant information through more senses than one' (Magee and Milligan, 1995: 43). Milligan stressed that language can convey all necessary meaning. He argued that it is just as useful to be told that around the corner is a staircase that descends twenty steps, as to see it for oneself.

Braun, capturing the state of the art in 2008, argued: 'As a practice rooted in intermodal mediation, i.e. "translating" visual images into verbal descriptions, [AD] is in urgent need of interdisciplinary research-led grounding' (Braun, 2008: 14). Since then great strides have been taken, grounding AVT in narrative theory and cognitive models. Elena di Giovanni, Pilar Orero and Rosa Agost argue that AVT has emerged as 'a truly multi-disciplinary research field' (di Giovanni et al., 2012: 10). This book takes a cognitive approach.

1.6 Definitions of AD

Although AD has been a feature of the European cultural landscape since the 1990s, Aline Remael (2014: 135) can still describe it as an 'AVT newcomer', while at the Advanced Research Seminar on Audio Description (ARSAD) held

8 *Introducing audio description*

by the Autonomous University of Barcelona in 2015, Alicia Rodríguez (2015) could still usefully ask, 'what is audio description?' She provided a selection of possible answers: A type of translation? An altruistic activity? A product or a service? In truth it is all of these, although AD scholars and lobby groups are themselves not united behind a single definition.

The website of the Audio Description Coalition (ADC) in the USA suggests:

> AD uses the natural pauses in dialogue or narration to provide descriptions of the essential visual information.
>
> (Audio Description Coalition, n.d.)

This in itself raises questions. Given that every movie soundtrack has been constructed, what are *natural* pauses? And which visual information is *essential*? How do you decide? Making that selection and then finding the best words with which to capture it form the core of this book.

The Royal National Institute for Blind People (RNIB) formerly gave this definition:

> Like a narrator telling a story, audio description (AD) is an additional commentary describing body language, expressions and movements. AD gives you information about the things you might not be able to see, meaning that you can 'keep up with the action' based on the visual images in the source material.

In line with the allusion to narration, Gert Vercauteren (2012) and others (e.g. Kruger, 2010; Vandaele, 2012) have highlighted the link between AD and structuralist narratology, based on the ideas of Mieke Bal (1997), whereby stories are composed of different basic building blocks that present a series of (chrono) logically ordered events performed or experienced by actors in a specific spatiotemporal setting. AD provides the context that enables blind and partially sighted people (BPS) to follow the dialogue and the rest of the soundtrack. In their definition, the RNIB seems deliberately vague about exactly who benefits from AD. Chapter 4 aims to familiarise you with the characteristics of the principal group of target users – those with a visual impairment – although it is suggested that AD is also useful to other groups, such as those learning a foreign language. It is also believed that AD can facilitate language learning by visually impaired children (Lopéz, 2008) and guide the attention of sighted children (Szarkowska et al., 2011).

Recently, the RNIB (2015b) changed its definition to this:

> AD is commentary that describes body language, expressions and movements, making the programme clear through sound.

This seems to me to sum up the essence of AD, while still leaving the choice as to exactly what you describe unexplained. That is where this book comes in.

In addition to explaining the mechanics of AD, this book will also explore where and what you describe. Although description of the visual arts tackles many of the same issues and uses some of the same strategies, these are not directly addressed in this book because there are many practical issues, such as guiding and orientation information used in AD of visual arts, that are not necessary in the AD of AV media. AD of the visual arts deserves a book of its own. AD of sport is also not addressed here, although there is more information about it on the RNIB website.

At the risk of adding yet another definition, we can think of AD as using speech to make AV material accessible to people who might not perceive the visual element themselves.

Although the majority of those people will have a visual impairment, this definition also covers those sighted people in the USA mentioned by Anna Jankowska who 'turn to the Narrative Television Network when they want to "watch" TV at the same time as completing other tasks' (Jankowska, 2015: 29). This type of 'Audio Description for All' was an early goal of the AUDETEL project, which ran a pilot AD service for UK TV in the early 1990s (Lodge, 1993) – but the present author is unaware of any other successful examples, and that aspect of AUDETEL did not come to fruition. More research is also needed into how AD might benefit elderly viewers who need help in following TV programmes or films. This research question was also addressed in the AUDETEL experiment. According to Peli et al. (1996: 378–9):

> Rabbitt and Carmichael (1995) examined the comprehension by older adults with normal vision of short segments of programs, as well as of an entire 30-minute program, presented to half the subjects with AUDETEL, a British AD service, and to half without AUDETEL. They tested the subjects' comprehension of each segment by asking them to identify characters and locations that appeared in the segment and to elaborate on their descriptions. They also measured the subjects' overall comprehension of the program using 20 true–false questions. Rabbitt and Carmichael found that comprehension of the segments (but not overall comprehension) was greater for the group that was exposed to the AD and surmised that AD helped cue the subjects to features of the program that were the focus of the open-ended questions. The primary impetus for their study was to determine whether the AUDETEL descriptions were disruptive to elderly viewers. On the basis of their data, they concluded that AUDETEL descriptions did not detract from the enjoyment or interfere with the comprehension of the program by elderly viewers with normal vision.

1.7 Conclusion

This chapter has presented an overview of audio description, looked at some pre-existing definitions and presented one of the author's own. It has explained the ways in which AD is related to other modes of AVT.

1.8 Exercises and points for discussion

1. Have you listened to any AD? (You can access examples via the product page for this book: https://www.routledge.com/products/978-1-138-84817-7) If so, what did you notice about it? Think about the writing style of the spoken text and what was mentioned and what was omitted. What (if anything) did you find surprising?
2. What is your experience of blindness? Do you know anyone who has a visual impairment?
3. Here are some questions about the visually impaired population. Although they are taken from the website of the RNIB and National Health Service statistics (2011) and apply to the UK, there is little reason to suppose that they are not generally applicable. You will find the answers in Appendix 1.

    1. What percentage of people with sight problems are aged over 65?
        a. 10%   b. 50%   c. 66%
    2. How many children in the UK have sight problems?
        a. 10,000   b. 25,000   c. 50,000
    3. How many people in the UK use Braille regularly?
        a. 1 million   b. 500,000   c. 25,000
    4. What percentage of blind or partially sighted people have other health problems or disabilities?
        a. 15%   b. 33%   c. 70%
    5. Women are twice as likely as men to experience sight loss.
        True or false?
    6. People who experience sight loss have better hearing.
        True or false?
    7. Most people who are blind or partially sighted can read some form of print.
        True or false?

4. Discuss any answers to the above questions that you found surprising.
5. Find out if the answers are similar for the blind population in your country.

1.9 Suggested reading

As primers to the art of AD, the following two books are recommended. The first gives an overview of topics in AVT: Jorge Díaz-Cintas, Pilar Orero and Aline Remael (eds), *Media for all: subtitling for the deaf, audio description, and sign language*, Amsterdam and New York: Rodopi, 2007. The second discusses all the issues that should be considered when creating AD, based around the example of Quentin Tarantino's film *Inglourious Basterds* (1997): Anna Maszerowska, Anna Matamala and Pilar Orero (eds), *Audio description: new perspectives illustrated*, Amsterdam: John Benjamins, 2015.

References

Adamou, Christina and Simone Knox (2011). 'Transforming television drama through dubbing and subtitling: sex and the cities'. *Critical Studies in Television: An International Journal of Television Studies* 6, no. 1: 1–21.
Audio Description Coalition (n.d.). Retrieved from www.audiodescriptioncoalition.org/ [accessed 24.08.15].
Bal, Mieke (1997). *Narratology: introduction to the theory of narrative*. Toronto, ON: University of Toronto Press.
Benecke, B. (2004). 'Audio-description'. *Meta: Journal des traducteurs/Meta: Translators' Journal* 49, no. 1: 78–80.
Benecke, B. (2014). *Audiodeskription als partielle Translation – Modell und Methode*. Berlin, Münster: LitVerlag.
Biocca, Frank (1997). 'The cyborg's dilemma: embodiment in virtual environments'. *Journal of Computer-Mediated Communication* 3, no. 2. Retrieved from http://onlinelibrary.wiley.com/doi/10.1111/j.1083–6101.1997.tb00070.x/full#ss6 [accessed 11.08.15].
Bosseaux, Charlotte (2015). *Dubbing, film and performance: uncanny encounters*. Oxford: Peter Lang.
Bourne, Julian and Catalina Jiménez Hurtado (2007). 'From the visual to the verbal in two languages: a contrastive analysis of the audio description of *The Hours* in English and Spanish'. In Díaz Cintas Jorge, Orero Pilar and Aline Remael (eds) *Media for all: subtitling for the deaf, audio description, and sign language*. Approaches to Translation Studies, vol. 30. Amsterdam: Rodopi, pp. 175–188.
Braun, Sabine (2007). 'Audio description from a discourse perspective: a socially relevant framework for research and training'. *Linguistica Antverpiensia, New Series – Themes in Translation Studies* 6. Peter Lang. Available from: http://epubs.surrey.ac.uk /303024/1/ fulltext.pdf.
Braun, Sabine (2008). 'Audiodescription research: state of the art and beyond'. *Translation Studies in the New Millennium* 6: 14–30.
Broadcasting Act (1996). Chapter 21. Retrieved from www.legislation.gov.uk/ukpga/1996/55/ contents [accessed 22.12.15].
Byrnes, Frances (producer) (2014). 'The first action movie'. BBC Radio 4. Rockethouse Productions. Retrieved from www.bbc.co.uk/programmes/b041vvw [accessed 08.08.15].
Communications Act (2003). Chapter 21. Retrieved from www.legislation.gov.uk/ukpga/ 2003/21/contents [accessed 22.12.15].
Dale, N. (2013). 'Infants with visual impairment and their parents – how they engage with each other'. Mary Kitzinger Trust workshop. Lecture conducted from UCL Institute of Child Health, London.
Derrida, J. (2002). 'What is a "relevant" translation?' In L. Venuti (ed.) *The translation studies reader*, 2nd edn. New York and London: Routledge, pp. 423–446.
Díaz Cintas, Jorge, P. Orero and A. Remael (eds) (2007). *Media for all: subtitling for the deaf, audio description, and sign language*. Amsterdam: Rodopi.
Di Giovanni, Elena, Pilar Orero and Rosa Agost (2012). *Multidisciplinarity in audiovisual translation*, Monographs in Translation and Interpreting, Vol. 4. Alicante: University of Alicante Press.
Equality Act (2010). Chapter 15. Retrieved from www.legislation.gov.uk/ukpga/2010/15/ pdfs/ukpga_20100015_en.pdf [accessed 22.12.15].
European Blind Union (2015). Retrieved from www.euroblind.org/resources/information/ [accessed 24.08.15].

Fryer, Louise (2013). 'Boy at Belsen'. Radio description for *iPM*, BBC Radio 4. Retrieved from https://audioboom.com/channel/pm?cursor=1409024009&masonry=1&page=5 [accessed 9.08.15].

Fryer, Louise (2014). 'Orchids'. Radio description for *iPM*, BBC Radio 4. Retrieved from http://www.bbc.co.uk/programmes/b03sb7wy [accessed 9.08.15].

Fryer, Louise and Jonathan Freeman (2013). 'Visual impairment and presence: measuring the effect of audio description'. In H. Witchel (ed.) *Inputs–Outputs Conference Proceedings: Interdisciplinary approaches to causality in engagement, immersion and presence in performance and human-computer interaction, Brighton, June 2013*. New York: ACM. Available from http://dl.acm.org/citation.cfm?id=2557599.

Gambier, Yves (2006). 'Multimodality and audiovisual translation'. In *MuTra Conference Audio Visual Translation Scenarios, Copenhagen (May 1–5, 2006)*. Retrieved from www. euroconferences. info/2006_abstracts. php# Gambier [accessed 24.08.15].

Gerber, Elaine (2007). 'Seeing isn't believing: blindness, race, and cultural literacy'. *The Senses and Society* 2, no. 1: 27–40.

Gorlée, Dinda L. (1994). *Semiotics and the problem of translation: with special reference to the semiotics of Charles S. Peirce*. Approaches to Translation Studies, vol. 12. Amsterdam: Rodopi.

Gottlieb, Henrik (2004). 'Subtitles and international Anglification'. *Nordic Journal of English Studies* 3, no. 1: 219–230.

Gysbers, A., C. Klimmt, T. Hartmann, A. Nosper and P. Vorderer (2004). 'Exploring the book problem: text design, mental representations of space, and spatial presence in readers'. Presented at *PRESENCE 2004 – 7th Annual International Workshop on Presence 13–15 October, Valencia, Spain*. Available from http://astro.temple.edu/~lombard/ISPR/Proceedings/2004/Gysbers,%20Klimmt,%20Hartmann,%20Nosper,%20Vorderer.pdf.

Jakobson, Roman (1959). 'On linguistic aspects of translation'. In R.A. Brower (ed.) *On translation*. Cambridge, MA: Harvard University Press, pp. 232–239.

Jankowska, Anna (2015). *Translating audio description scripts: translation as a new strategy of creating audio description*, trans. Anna Mrzyglodzka and Anna Chociej. Frankfurt am Main: Peter Lang.

Jones, Matthew T. (2007). 'Presence as external versus internal experience: how form, user, style, and content factors produce presence from the inside'. In *Proceedings of 10th International Workshop on Presence*, pp. 115–126. Available from: http://astro.temple.edu/~lombard/ISPR/Proceedings/2007/Jones.pdf.

Karamitroglou, Fotios (2000). *Towards a methodology for the investigation of norms in audiovisual translation: the choice between subtitling and revoicing in Greece*. Approaches to Translation Studies, vol. 15. Amsterdam: Rodopi.

Kruger, J. L. (2010). 'Audio narration: re-narrativising film'. *Perspectives: Studies in Translatology* 18, no. 3: 231–249.

Kruger, Jan-Louis (2012). 'Making meaning in AVT: eye tracking and viewer construction of narrative'. *Perspectives* 20, no. 1: 67–86.

Lodge, N. K. (1993). 'The European AUDETEL project – enhancing television for visually impaired people'. In *IEE Colloquium on Information Access for People with Disability*, pp. 7–1. Available from http://ieeexplore.ieee.org/xpl/login.jsp?tp=&arnumber=241325&url=http%3A%2F%2Fieeexplore.ieee.org%2Fxpls%2Fabs_all.jsp%3Farnumber%3D241325.

Lombard, Matthew and Theresa Ditton (1997). 'At the heart of it all: the concept of presence'. *Journal of Computer-Mediated Communication* 3, no. 0: doi 10.1111/j.1083-6101.1997.tb00072.x.

Lopéz, A.P. (2008). 'Audio description as language development and language learning for blind and visual impaired children'. In Hyde Parker and Guararrama Garcia (eds) *Thinking translation: perspectives from within and without*. Conference proceedings, Third UEA Postgraduate Translation Symposium. Boca Raton, FL: BrownWalker Press, pp. 114–133.

Magee, Bryan and Martin Milligan (1995). *On blindness: letters between Bryan Magee and Martin Milligan*. Oxford: Oxford University Press.

Maszerowska, Anna, Anna Matamala, Pilar Orero and Nina Reviers (2014). 'From source text to target text: the art of audio description'. In Anna Maszerowska, Anna Matamala and Pilar Orero (eds) *Audio description: new perspectives illustrated*. Amsterdam: John Benjamins, pp. 1–8.

Merabet L. B. and A. Pascual-Leone (2009). 'Neural reorganization following sensory loss: the opportunity of change'. *Nature Reviews Neuroscience* 11, no. 1: 44–52.

Metzger, Melanie (1999). *Sign language interpreting: deconstructing the myth of neutrality*. Washington, DC: Gallaudet University Press.

Minsky, Marvin (1980). 'Telepresence'. *Omni Magazine*, June, pp. 45–51.

Orero, Pilar and Agnieszka Szarkowska (2014). 'The importance of sound for audio description'. In Anna Maszerowska, Anna Matamala and Pilar Orero (eds) *Audio description: new perspectives illustrated*. Amsterdam: John Benjamins, pp. 121–140.

Peli, Eli, Elisabeth M. Fine and Angela T. Labianca (1996). 'Evaluating visual information provided by audio description'. *Journal of Visual Impairment and Blindness* 90: 378–385.

Pettitt, B., K. Sharpe and S. Cooper (1996). 'AUDETEL: Enhancing telesight for visually impaired people'. *British Journal of Visual Impairment* 14, no. 2: 48–52.

Rabbitt, P.M.A. and Carmichael, A. (1995). 'Designing communications and information-handling systems for elderly and disabled users'. In J. Snel and R. Cremer (eds) *Work and Aging: A European Prospective*. London: Taylor & Francis, p. 173.

Remael, A. (2010). 'Audiovisual translation'. In Yves Gambier and Luc van Doorslaer (eds) *Handbook of translation studies* 3. Amsterdam: John Benjamins, pp. 12–17.

Remael, A. (2014). 'From audiovisual translation to media accessibility: live-subtitling, audio description and audio-subtitling'. In *AUSIT 2012: Proceedings of the 'JubilaTIon 25' Biennial Conference of the Australian Institute of Interpreters and Translators*. Newcastle-upon-Tyne: Cambridge Scholars Publishing, p. 134.

RNIB (2015a). https://help.rnib.org.uk/help/newly-diagnosed-registration/registering-sight-loss/statistics [accessed 22.12.15].

RNIB (2015b). Retrieved from www.rnib.org.uk/information-everyday-living-home-and-leisure-television-radio-and-film/audio-description?gclid=CJD806qzwccCFYLnwgod P1YKb [accessed 24.08.15].

Rodríguez, Alicia (2015). 'Quality in AD'. Paper presented at *Advanced Research Seminar on Audio Description (ARSAD) 2015*, Barcelona (March).

Schmeidler, E. and C. Kirchner (2001). 'Adding audio description: does it make a difference?' *Journal of Visual Impairment and Blindness* 95, no. 4: 197–212.

Snyder, Joel (2014). *The visual made verbal: a comprehensive training manual and guide to the history and applications of audio description*. Arlington, VA: American Council of the Blind.

Sperber, Deirdre and Dan Wilson (1995). *Relevance: communication and cognition*. Oxford: Blackwell.

Szarkowska, Agnieszka (2011). 'Text-to-speech audio description: towards wider availability of AD'. *Journal of Specialised Translation* 15: 142–163.

Tebble, H. (1999). 'The tenor of consultant physicians: implications for medical interpreting'. *The Translator* 5, no. 2: 179–200.

Thompson, Hannah (2015). 'How the arts can help change attitudes to blindness'. *Guardian*. Retrieved from www.theguardian.com/culture-professionals-network/2015/aug/03/arts-change-attitude-blindness-blind-creations [accessed 10.08.15].

Vandaele, J. (2012). 'What meets the eye: cognitive narratology for audio description'. *Perspectives* 20, no. 1: 87–102.

Venuti, Lawrence (1998). *The scandals of translation: towards an ethics of difference*. New York: Taylor & Francis.

Vercauteren, Gert (2012). 'A narratological approach to content selection in audio description: towards a strategy for the description of narratological time.' In Rosa Agost, Pilar Orero and Elena di Giovanni (eds) *Multidisciplinarity in audiovisual translation. MonTI* 4: 207–231. Retrieved from http://roderic.uv.es/bitstream/handle/10550/37094/26948.pdf?sequence=1&isAllowed=y [accessed 7.01.2016].

Wadensjö, Cecilia (1993). 'The double role of a dialogue interpreter'. *Perspectives: Studies in Translatology* 1, no. 1: 105–121.

Wadensjö, Cecilia (1999). 'Telephone interpreting and the synchronization of talk in social interaction'. *The Translator* 5, no. 2: 247–264.

World Health Organization (2014). Visual Impairment and Blindness, Fact Sheet No. 282. Retrieved from www.who.int/mediacentre/factsheets/fs282/en.

Film reference

A Daring Daylight Burglary, F. Mottershaw (1908).

Reference to live event

The House of Bernarda Alba, dir. B. Sheibani (2012). Almeida Theatre, London. AD by VocalEyes (describers Louise Fryer and Julia Grundy).

2 A brief history, legislation and guidelines

2.1 Introduction

This chapter examines the formal side of AD, namely the legislation that governs it and its development in different countries. It also contrasts the two forms with which this book is concerned: AD for screen and AD for live events. It stresses that BPS people have often been instrumental in fostering the development of AD. Although legislation has also been crucial, the practice is unregulated in many contexts, leaving the specifics open to evolution and debate. This has been to the advantage of (unregulated) live AD, allowing it to be more creative and adventurous.

2.2 A brief history

Although many believe that the history of AD can be traced back to the United States, Díaz Cintas et al. (2007) claims its first reported use was in Spain in the 1940s. More recent research has uncovered an article from 1917 in the RNIB's journal *The Beacon* (ADA, 2014) reporting how Eleanor, Lady Waterlow, wife of the English watercolour painter Ernest Waterlow, enabled soldiers blinded during the First World War to enjoy a 'cinematograph lecture' about Scott's expedition to the Antarctic by describing the images. The same article also reports that 'experiments at theatrical performances had already met with success', so the origins of AD may date back further and be more diverse than previously thought. The first AD transmission on TV was in 1983 by NTV a commercial broadcaster in Japan (ITC, 2000). Japanese benshi (live performers) had been adding a verbal commentary to make silent films accessible from the dawn of cinema (Washburn and Cavanaugh, 2001). The art of the film explainer was not limited to Japan (Marcus, 2007) but also included Germany, the Netherlands and Scotland. Arguably, these lecturers did not actually explain films but made them accessible to audiences who were not sufficiently literate to read the intertitles or to understand the 'language of cinema'. With the advent of talking cinema, film explainers gradually became redundant.

AD, in the sense of a sighted person painting a verbal picture for a friend or family member with impaired vision, has taken place informally for hundreds if not thousands of years. But as American AD pioneer Margaret Pfanstiehl has pointed out, 'doing it in a prepared scheduled way is of course quite another matter' (Pfanstiehl and Pfanstiehl, 1985: 92). Margaret Pfanstiehl had a direct impact on live AD in the UK, although AD for screen in the UK arguably owes its existence to another American, Gregory Frazier. He was a professor at San Francisco State University who developed what he called 'television for the blind' for his Master's thesis in the 1970s. In the early 1980s, Margaret Ptfanstiel applied Frazier's ideas and began a live service for the Arena stage in Washington, extending the reading service she had established for the blind, called The Washington Ear. The first play to be audio described was *Major Barbara* by George Bernard Shaw. In England, Monique Raffray, who worked for the South Regional Association for the Blind, was on the editorial board of the *British Journal of Visual Impairment*, and who was herself blind, read about The Washington Ear in the bulletin produced by a BBC radio programme *In Touch* that deals with matters of blindness. Together with her colleague Mary Lambert, Monique determined to bring AD to the UK and they corresponded with the Pfanstiehls. Mary visited the Pfanstiehls in Washington in 1987, attending an audio-described performance of Andrew Lloyd Webber's musical *Cats*. The previous year, the RNIB had set up a working party on AD. An informal described performance of *A Delicate Balance* by Edward Albee took place at the Robin Hood theatre in Averham, near Newark, in 1986. Although this is sometimes cited as the first audio description in the UK, in an email sent to the author on 16 April 2015 Mary Lambert stressed the description's informal nature, as the describers did not have proper equipment: 'I seem to remember we had a box on our laps, and obviously some headphones. I remember the describer . . . saying at the appropriate time, "Mary and Monique, it's time to leave for your train" and we had to "creep" out of the theatre and get our cab!'

Mary Lambert states that the first UK description was of the musical *Stepping Out* at the Theatre Royal, Windsor, in November 1987. Over the next five years, theatre AD proliferated in the UK, coming to the Duke of York Theatre in London in February 1988 and the West Yorkshire Playhouse in Leeds in September 1991. Other early adopters were the Chichester Festival Theatre; the Churchill Theatre, Bromley; The Octagon Theatre, Bolton; The Citizens Theatre, Glasgow; The Sherman Theatre, Cardiff; and the Derby Playhouse. The development of AD was supported and fostered by the RNIB's Working Party on Audio Description, energetically championed by Marcus Weisen (incorrectly named as Marcus Weiss in some sources, e.g. Orero [2007]).

At first, all describers in the UK were volunteers, until the National Theatre of Great Britain decided to train a group of professional actors, believing that an understanding of the medium was essential for AD quality. Training at the National Theatre of Great Britain was carried out by Diana Hull and Monique Raffray. Diana had been on a study visit to the USA with a particular focus on training. Forty-five visually impaired people attended the first description at the National Theatre of Great Britain of *Trelawney of the Wells* in March 1993. Currently, theatre AD in the UK is delivered by a mixture of volunteer and professional describers. Some theatres offer little more than an honorarium, others pay a more reasonable freelance rate. Fees vary not only from theatre to theatre but even within the same venue, taking into account the number of described performances in a show's run and the fact that some shows take longer to prepare than others. The process is outlined in Chapter 6.

After AD for theatre, AD for screen soon followed. In the USA in 1987, the broadcasting station WGBH in Boston set up its 'descriptive video' service. In Europe the pilot TV audio description service AUDETEL was organised in the early 1990s by a conglomerate of European broadcasters, academics and the RNIB (Lodge, 1993). In 1994, the RNIB established its home video service. This was a library of videos with audio description mixed onto the soundtrack.

Just as with subtitles or captions, there are two methods of delivering AD: it can be 'open', so that everybody hears it, or it can be 'closed', i.e. carried on a separate sound channel accessed by headset only by those who need it. In the theatre the AD content may be delivered to a headset on a short-range radio frequency or via an infrared signal in the auditorium while users listen to the dialogue either on the same headset or direct from the stage. There are pros and cons. Listening to the show sound on the headset means that it can be heard at an enhanced volume, if required; however, the AD user can feel cut off from the rest of the audience. It is essential that the volume of the AD can be controlled independently from the volume of the show sound. Otherwise, in a loud show, it is not possible to make the AD sufficiently loud that it can be heard over the top. On DVD, AD (where available) can be selected, commonly from the languages menu. On digital TV, AD can usually be accessed via the audio button on the remote control.

The quantity of live AD in the UK increased in 1998 with the arrival of VocalEyes, founded by one of the National Theatre of Great Britain describers, Andrew Holland, together with James Williams, who was the Executive Director of the theatre company Method & Madness. VocalEyes was funded by Arts Council England, and its aim was to describe touring productions so that the AD would not have to be reinvented for each venue. From this beginning, VocalEyes expanded into descriptions for West End Theatre, of dance and ballet and of the visual arts. By the summer 2013, VocalEyes had described over 1,500 performances at over 100 different venues around the UK.

Currently around ninety-nine theatres in the UK regularly provide audio described performances (RNIB, 2015). This number is hard to confirm because there is little consensus as to what constitutes a theatre. Impromptu 'fringe' venues, for instance, may spring up for short periods only. Also the frequency of described performances varies: there may be just one described performance or several in a production's run. For long-running shows in the West End of London, such as *The Lion King* (dir. Taymor, 2000) or *Billy Elliot* (dir. Daldry, 2005) for example, a couple of performances may be described each year. Although the AD is in some senses repeated, the describers always deliver the description live to accommodate slight variations in performance. While they are expected to write a script (covered in detail in Chapter 5), they must also be prepared to improvise when, for example, an actor forgets his or her lines, mislays a prop or introduces a spontaneous piece of stage business, or some feature of a complex set breaks down. In Spain and in the USA there have been some

18 *A brief history, legislation and guidelines*

attempts to use pre-recorded AD, accessed via a mobile phone app (Snyder and Padro, 2015). This is easier for shows with a pre-recorded soundtrack, such as Cirque du Soleil, so that the AD can be kept in synch. Apps are also being trialled to help more people receive AD in cinemas (RNIB, 2015) via their tablet or mobile phone. In France, pre-recorded AD for live shows is the norm.

Table 2.1 sets out some of the main differences between describing for live events and screen AD. One key difference between the two is that a film or TV programme has been directed and the camera shots determined, so that the audience all share a single point of view (POV). In the theatre the describer is free to select which part of the stage picture they will describe. In addition, the duration and location or 'gaps' where an audio-descriptive utterance might be inserted is fixed for AV media, but the length and position of those 'gaps' may change from one live performance to another. In situations where apps have been trialled, the AD is synchronised with a show's recorded soundtrack (Snyder and Padro, 2015). In such cases, the AD is synchronised with a show's recorded soundtrack (Snyder and Padro, 2015). Alternatively, AD for live events is pre-recorded but triggered live, its delivery cued by a member of the stage crew, such as the stage manager. The variability of this 'window' in which AD can be delivered has implications for the way in which AD script is constructed (see Chapter 6). Often, and in

Table 2.1 Differences between AD for live events and screen AD

Live events	Screen
Sense of occasion	Conveyor-belt process
Audience response influences AD choices	Possibly watched alone, so little thought given to audience response
Can have a longer preparation time (not in repertory theatre)	Fast turn-around
Repeat performances allow for the script to be refined. Delivery has to be right first time	Usually one-off, although opportunity for delivery to be refined via retakes. In theory the AD should not need revision, as the AV product is fixed
Live delivery, technical quality variable	Recorded delivery, studio-quality sound
Collaboration with audience/company	Contact possible, but rare
Multiple viewpoints	Fixed viewpoint determined by director/camera POV
Need/room for improvisation	Fully scripted
Opportunity for some direct engagement with audience	Limited opportunity for engagement with audience
Unregulated	Regulated by guidelines
Uses some volunteer describers	Fully professional
Timing variable	Timing fixed
Audio Introduction is standard	Currently no Audio Introduction
Touch Tour possible	Touch Tour not possible
Action prone to variation, due to unforeseen events or casting restrictions	Action fixed, only variation due to last-minute editing

accordance with the original model disseminated by the Pfantstiels, two describers will prepare and deliver the live description. In smaller venues there may be only one describer. Wherever possible, best practice involves feedback from at least one BPS person during the preparation process. In TV AD, Bayerische Rundfunk in Germany and Italy's Sensa Barriere, consistently involve blind people at the preparation stage, while some AD scripts in Poland are also created by a mixed team (one sighted and one blind describer) (Mazur and Chmiel, 2012).

2.3 The legal background

The growth of AD in the UK has been significantly assisted by legislation. The Disability Discrimination Act (DDA, 1995; updated 2005) made it unlawful for any organisation or business to treat a disabled person less favourably than an able-bodied person. Businesses were required to make 'reasonable' adjustments, such as installing wheelchair ramps or altering working hours. For BPS people, reasonable adjustments included providing information in an audio format or Braille or offering an AD service for films, plays and exhibitions. This provision was carried over into the Equality Act, which replaced the DDA in 2010. In the wake of AUDETEL, the Communications Acts (1996, 2003) required digital terrestrial broadcasters to audio describe a prescribed percentage of their programmes. While the quota for programmes to be subtitled for people who are deaf or hard of hearing (SDH) was set at 60 per cent after five years of a digital terrestrial channel's coming into service, for AD the quota was only 10 per cent. This reflected the paucity of affordable technology available to receive the service. The arrival of digital platforms has improved this, yet the quota has remained unchanged. Several channels in the UK voluntarily exceed the legal quota: Sky, for example, currently describes around 20 percent of its programmes (Sky, 2015). A few channels are exempt, for example BBC News. The effects of programme genre on AD are discussed in Chapter 8. Since 2001, the Canadian Radio Television and Telecommunications Commission has made it compulsory for an AD commitment to be made before it renews broadcasting licenses.

It remains to be seen whether media laws have teeth. In Australia, in July 2015, a blind woman launched 'a case of unlawful discrimination against the Australian Broadcasting Corporation (ABC) for their failure to provide audio description as part of their regular programming' (Blind Citizens Australia, 2015).

In Europe, the Audiovisual Media Directive 2007/65/EC acknowledges that:

> Cultural activities, goods and services have both an economic and a cultural nature, because they convey identities, values and meanings, and must therefore not be treated as solely having commercial value ... regulatory policy in that sector has to safeguard certain public interests, such as cultural diversity, the right to information, media pluralism, the protection of minors and consumer protection and to enhance public awareness and media literacy, now and in the future.

Article 7 specifies that:

> Member States shall encourage media service providers under their jurisdiction to ensure that their services are gradually made accessible to people with a visual or hearing disability. Sight- and hearing-impaired persons as well as elderly people shall participate in the social and cultural life of the European Union. Therefore, they shall have access to audiovisual media services. Governments must encourage media companies under their jurisdiction to do this, e.g. by sign language, subtitling, audio-description . . .

In addition to the European Union, legally enshrined responsibilities for AD also exist in the USA (21st Century Communications and Video Accessibility Act, 2010), which prescribes four hours of described programmes per TV channel per week. Within Europe numerous countries have their own legal obligation to provide AD, including Germany (Rundfunkstaatsvertrag), Poland (Polish Radio and Television Act), Spain (2009 Ley general audiovisual) and Flanders in Belgium (Mediadecreet, 2013). Portugal's Television law (2011) is no longer in effect, although its public broadcasters have long been required to fulfill quotas for subtitling and AD. Legislation was introduced in Finland at the start of 2014. Bayerischer Rundfunk (BR) was the first public radio and TV broadcaster in Germany to introduce a regular description service. There is more information about the development of European AD services on the following website: http://hub.eaccessplus.eu/wiki/Audio_description_in_Europe.

Increasingly, AD is expanding beyond Europe and North America, reaching Iceland, Thailand and Korea. Dawning Leung (2015) states that, in the last few years, AD services haves been regularly provided in Hong Kong and on Mainland China, although in the latter 'AD services seem to be very limited, and restricted only to films'.

Although AD has developed at different rates and been applied to different art forms at different times in different countries, a common theme in its instigation has been lobbying by user groups or by an individual describer, or when individuals involved in the relevant production company have a particular interest such as having a family member who is blind. From this, we might conclude that the concept of AD is mystifying in the abstract (as Jankowska (2015: 52) says, 'a blind viewer sounds like an oxymoron') but its benefits are self-evident to anyone with direct experience of visual impairment.

2.4 Non-broadcast TV

European legislation distinguishes between linear and non-linear services, with the latter referring to non-traditional services where the user can 'pull' programmes of their choice (on demand) and the former being more traditional services that are 'pushed' to viewers. Non-linear services have recently become more accessible, following the decision of Netflix to caption all of its content by the end of 2014 (Nikul, 2015). This was the result of legal action on the part of the American National Association of the Deaf, and a commitment to audio-describe selected titles was announced in April 2015. The director of content operations at Netflix,

A brief history, legislation and guidelines 21

Tracy Wright (2015), stated that, 'Over time, we expect audio description to be available for major Netflix original series, as well as select other shows and movies. We are working with studios and other content owners to increase the amount of audio description across a range of devices including smart TVs, tablets and smartphones.' It's a fast-changing scene. According to a report into video on demand (VOD) by Media Access Australia,

> The only VOD providers to currently provide audio description are the BBC's iPlayer, 4oD (which provided audio description on 15% of programmes in 2014), Channel Entertainment (7% of programs in, 2014) and Sky (which did not provide comprehensive figures to the regulator, the Authority for TV on Demand (ATVOD). Channel 5 and ITV have expressed an intention to introduce the service. ATVOD states that encouraging the provision of audio description will be a particular focus for it in 2015.
>
> (Nikul, 2015: 8)

The importance of VOD services is that they are less constrained than traditional broadcast services, allowing, for example, for the provision of extra information such as audio introductions (see Chapter 12). This is being trialled for hybrid services by the HBB4All (Hybrid Broadband Broadcasting for All) project (http://www.hbb4all.eu/).

2.5 AD in practice

2.5.1 Screen-based AD

Despite the dual focus of this book – both on-screen and live description – in practice the bulk of AD is produced for screen media, in particular film and TV. It is in these industries that graduates from programmes in AVT are most likely to find employment. In the UK, the first commercial AD units were formed in London in 2000, and the first-audio described cinema releases in the UK followed in 2002. Currently, AD in the UK is produced by translation bureaux and facilities houses, including Deluxe, Ericsson, IMS, ITFC, Red Bee Media and SDI Media. These companies also produce multilingual subtitles and SDH. In fact, some companies switch subtitlers to AD duties when they have a tight AD deadline to meet. Some of them also provide sign language translation.

2.5.2 Live AD

Live AD refers to the AD of live events. While the AD for such events is almost always delivered live, it is usually prepared in advance. Venues offering live AD may also be employing professionals, although payment is generally very low relative to the large amount of time it takes to prepare a live description. The process is set out in Chapter 6. In the UK, some production houses such as the National Theatre of Great Britain and the Royal Shakespeare Company use their own in-house teams; others buy in services from individual freelance describers or small, independent companies such as VocalEyes, Mind's Eye and Sightlines.

There is a very small market for script exchange between these companies. However, it is rare that another person's AD script can be used with no changes. In addition to variation in writing and delivery style from one describer to another, the production might move to a different-sized venue, and a character reaching his position more quickly on a smaller stage leaves less time for description. In a larger venue, more may be said. Alternatively, a production might stay in the same theatre and be recast. One major dance sequence in the musical *Billy Elliot*, for example, is specifically choreographed around the dance skills of the particular boy playing the role of Billy, and hence may change quite radically from one child star to the next (Fryer, 2009).

Variation is not limited to recasting; three different boys may play Billy in a single week – not accounting for illness or injury. This is a particular issue with shows involving children, whose work, at least in the UK, is restricted by law. Similarly, although not legally regulated, opera singers may insist in their contract that they do not appear at every performance, in order not to strain their voice. While theatre describers in the UK are encouraged to write a script, they must also be prepared to improvise, for the reasons outlined here. In addition, some of the best actors are the most difficult to describe, as they like to keep each performance 'fresh' rather than replicate their gestures and expressions from one performance to the next. In screen AD a script will always be written, as, in addition to fixing the words, the script also provides the cues to trigger the recording process. This is explained further in Chapter 6.

2.6 Guidelines

There is no regulation of AD in live settings. However, UK legislation requires the broadcasting regulator (now Ofcom, formerly the Independent Television Commission (ITC)) to draw up and 'from time to time review a code giving guidance as to how digital programme services should promote the understanding and enjoyment of programmes by sensory impaired people including those who are blind and partially-sighted . . . ' (ITC, 2000). The original code (ibid.) was developed in the wake of AUDETEL, providing guidelines that have been the basis of AD practice for screen media in the UK and elsewhere ever since. According to Anna Jankowska 'the guidelines or standards existing in many countries . . . are often established with reference to the personal experience of their creators or to similar guidelines used on foreign markets which are often derivative of other sources' (Jankowska, 2015: 24). Gert Vercauteren (2007: 147) complains: 'The current guidelines in Flanders, Germany, Spain and the United Kingdom are . . . little more than a starting point since they remain rather vague on some issues, whereas in other instances they lack structure and even miss some basic information.' Since the year 2000, European scholars have been researching the grey areas and exposing flaws, false assumptions and cultural differences. The RNIB's comparative survey (Rai et al., 2010: 6) concludes that: 'Though, in principal [*sic*] the guidelines and/or standards studied in this paper are very similar in nature, there are minor differences in a few of the recommendations.' The authors show that differences emerge in advice on naming characters; in the use of adjectives that are regarded by some as subjective; and in including mention of colour. However, it is important to note that the ITC Guidance (ITC, 2000) specifies that 'these notes are presented in the form of guidelines only, with no absolute rules'. The advantage is that this should allow the art of AD to change and develop; the disadvantage is that it leaves areas of AD practice open to debate and to Vercauteren's accusation of 'vagueness'. This can be regarded as a positive rather than a failing. This book, refers to the results of reception studies to inform the advice given where it departs from the ITC Guidance. As stated, there are no official guidelines for the AD of live events, perhaps because there is no official body to police these descriptions; or perhaps because it is not clear whether the responsibility for provision of AD lies with the venue or the production company. Perhaps it is assumed that AD users will 'vote with their feet', choosing not to attend theatres that provide what they regard as description of poor quality. The author believes that, because of the lack of guidelines, AD in theatre is often more adventurous and less hidebound than screen AD. This is one reason why many examples of live AD are included to illustrate points in the chapters that follow.

2.7 Conclusion

This chapter has outlined the development of AD, expanding from its earliest origins in the UK to its recent emergence in China and elsewhere. It has pointed out the important role played by pioneers in America such as the Pfanstiehls and Gregory Frazier. It has stressed differences in the process of AD for screen and for live events. The situation is fluid, owing to new ways of accessing AV media. Although legislation has often been crucial for the development of AD, the practice is unregulated in many contexts, leaving the specifics open to evolution and debate.

2.8 Exercises and points for discussion

1 Does audio description happen in your country? Is there a legal framework or guidelines governing the provision of AD where you live? If so, find out what they say.
2 Should AD be regulated? Discuss the advantages and limitations.
3 In what way does AVT differ from any other form of translation?

References

21st Century Communications and Video Accessibility Act, 2010. Retrieved from https://www.fcc.gov/guides/21st-century-communications-and-video-accessibility-act-2010 [accessed 24.08.15].
Audio Description Association (ADA) (2014). 'Commemorating the Great War'. *Notepad* (December), 107–112.
Audiovisual Media Directive 2007/65/EC. Retrieved from http://ec.europa.eu/archives/information_society/avpolicy/reg/tvwf/access/index_en.htm [accessed 9.08.15].

Blind Citizens Australia (2015). Press release retrieved from https://wordpress.bca.org.au/media-release-audio-description-abc-sued-for-unlawful-discrimination/ [accessed 11.08.15].

Communications Act (2003). Retrieved from www.legislation.gov.uk/ukpga/2003/21/pdfs/ukpga_20030021_en.pdf [accessed 24.08.15].

Díaz Cintas, Jorge, Pilar Orero and Aline Remael (2007). *Media for all: subtitling for the deaf, audio description, and sign language*. Approaches to Translation Studies, vol. 30. Amsterdam: Rodopi.

Disability Discrimination Act (2005). Retrieved from www.legislation.gov.uk/ukpga/2005/13/contents [accessed 24.08.15].

Fryer, L. (2009). *Talking dance: the audio describer's guide to dance in theatre*. Apt Description Series, 3. ADA Publications, ISBN 978-0-9560306-2-7.

ITC (2000). ITC guidance on standards for audio description. Retrieved from www.ofcom.org.uk/static/archive/itc/itc_publications/codes_guidance/audio_description/index.asp.html [accessed 22.12.15].

Jankowska, Anna (2015). *Translating audio description scripts: translation as a new strategy of creating audio description*, trans. Anna Mrzyglodzka and Anna Chociej. Frankfurt am Main: Peter Lang.

Leung, D. (2015). 'Audio description in Hong Kong: gauging the needs of the audience'. Paper presented at the *Advanced Research Seminar in Audio Description (ARSAD) 2015*, Barcelona (March).

Lodge, N. K. (1993). 'The European AUDETEL project – enhancing television for visually impaired people'. In *IEE Colloquium on Information Access for People with Disability*, London: IEEE, pp. 7/1–7/7. Retrieved from http://ieeexplore.ieee.org/stamp/stamp.jsp?tp=&arnumber=160418 [accessed 7.01.2016].

Marcus, Laura. (2007). *The tenth muse: writing about cinema in the modernist period*. Oxford: Oxford University Press.

Mazur, Iwona and Agnieszka Chmiel (2012). 'Audio description made to measure: reflections on interpretation in AD based on the Pear Tree Project data'. In Aline Remael, Orero Pilar and Mary Carroll (eds) *Audiovisual translation and media accessibility at the crossroads*. Media for All 3. Amsterdam and New York: Rodopi, p. 173.

Nikul, Chris (2015). 'Access on demand: captioning and audio description on video on demand services'. In Media Access Australia report series, available from www.mediaaccess.org.au/latest_news/international-policy-and-legislation/video-on-demand-access-builds-up.

Pfanstiehl, Margaret and Cody Pfanstiehl (1985). 'The play's the thing – audio description in the theatre'. *British Journal of Visual Impairment* 3, no. 3: 91–92.

Rai, Sonali, Joan Greening and Leen Petré (2010). 'A comparative study of audio description guidelines prevalent in different countries'. London: RNIB, Media and Culture Department.

RNIB (2015). Retrieved from www.rnib.org.uk/audio-description-app [accessed 24.08.15].

Sky (2015). Accessibility page. Retrieved from http://accessibility.sky.com/faqs/why-not-audio-describe-all-sky-programmes [accessed 25.08.15].

Snyder, Joel and Simon Padro (2015). 'Audio description and the Smartphone: AD access in the future'. Paper presented at *Advanced Research Seminar on Audio Description (ARSAD) 2015*, Barcelona (March).

Vercauteren, Gert (2007). 'Towards a European guideline for audio description'. In J. Díaz Cintas, P. Orero and A. Remael (eds) *Media for all: subtitling for the deaf, audio description and sign language*. Amsterdam: Rodopi, pp. 139–150.

Washburn, Dennis and Carole Cavanaugh (2001). *Word and image in Japanese cinema*. Cambridge: Cambridge University Press.
Wright, Tracy (2015). Netflix blog. Retrieved from http://blog.netflix.com/2015/04/netflix-begins-audio-description-for.html [accessed 24.08.15].

References to live performances

Billy Elliot, dir. S. Daldry (2005–2016), Victoria Palace Theatre, London.
The Lion King, dir. J. Taymor (2000–ongoing), Lyceum Theatre, London.

3 Putting the audio into audio description

3.1 Introduction

Evidently two main information streams combine to convey the information in AV media: the visual (essentially implicit) and the auditory (generally, but not always, explicit). While visual information is at the core of the source material for the describer it is super-abundant, meaning that often it is the auditory information that narrows down what should be described. This chapter dissects the auditory information stream and analyses how it influences the editorial choices of the describer.

3.2 The visual information stream

The role of a describer is to convey or summarise the visual information. The way in which sighted people perceive such information has already been discussed. One glance is usually enough to tell us: *who* is in a scene, *where* they are located, *what* they are doing and the way in which they are doing it (*how*). Vision overrides information pick-up from other modalities such as hearing. When presented with bimodal (auditory and visual) stimuli, sighted people respond more quickly to the visual component than to the auditory one (Koppen and Spence, 2007). However, each influences the other. Michel Chion et al. (1994) refer to the audio-visual contract. They point out that we never see the same thing when we also hear; we do not hear the same thing when we also see.

The art of ventriloquism relies on prioritising the visual stimulus of the dummy's moving mouth over the auditory stimulus (the words coming from the operator), such that the dummy appears to be speaking. We experience a similar effect in the cinema, attributing words to the characters on the screen in front of us, even though the voices are relayed via speakers placed around the side and back walls of the auditorium (Murray et al., 2005).

Visual information is generally considered to be continuous, with everything in our field of vision instantly (and repeatedly) accessible. Auditory information, by contrast, is linear. It is generally thought of as an intermittent sequence of sounds and 'gaps' where there is no sound. This is not necessarily true – for either sense. Our eyes constantly dart from one point of fixation to the next in a series of jumps or saccades, with our brains filling in the missing detail and ensuring that an image persists while new information is added, so that the picture is fleshed out. We learn to watch film so that, rather than a series of static shots, we perceive it as a moving image, untroubled by changing points of view and perspective.

3.3 The auditory information stream

There are a number of sound sources in AV media that convey information. The most directly informative is dialogue in a drama or commentary in a documentary. There is also ambient sound, music and/or SFX. Dialogue tells us who is in a scene, so long as the characters all speak or are addressed by name; their voices might also give clues as to their age, cultural or educational background and whether they are friend or foe. Dialogue, like description, is made up of two elements: *what* is said and *how* it is said. Kreifelts et al. (2013: 225) state that 'when judging their social counterpart's emotional state, humans predominantly rely on non-verbal signals'. The majority of these are visual, such as facial expressions, gestures and posture, but also include non-verbal vocalisations (e.g. coughs, sighs or screams). The rhythm, emphasis and intonational aspects of speech are termed 'prosody'. In an fMRI (functional magnetic resonance imaging) study Kreifelts and colleagues (2007) showed that, for people with unimpaired vision and hearing, a combination of auditory and visual information led to higher success in classifying emotions than either the auditory or visual component alone. Furthermore, emotional signals in one modality affect processing of emotional signals in the other. For example, Maiworm et al. (2012) showed that the ventriloquism effect was weakened when preceded by a threatening auditory stimulus (syllables spoken in a fearful voice).

This raises a question for the describer: does our sensitivity to prosody negate the need to describe, for example, bursts of emotion-laden visual stimuli such as gloomy lighting or an alarmed facial expression, or, as Smith (1999) describes it, the shadow of a villain looming, moments before the character himself appears? These are elements that, for the sighted audience, help to create what film critic Tom Sutcliffe calls 'the delicious interlude between suspicion and confirmation' (Sutcliffe, 2000: 115). The auditory equivalents include sounds arising from the action (e.g. heavy breathing, footsteps, floorboards creaking); SFX (both environmental sounds such as the howling of a wolf and non-naturalistic sounds such as an amplified heartbeat); and music that underscores a scene. Such auditory prompts lead the audience to interpret the visuals according to one schema or another (see Chapter 4). In a horror movie, for example, scary music leads us to expect that a door, slowly opening, will swing wide to reveal a murderer rather than a person collecting on behalf of a charity.

3.3.1 Exercises and points for discussion

One of the best ways of discovering which aspects of the visual information stream are important is to 'watch' a film with your eyes closed. See what you can tell from the soundtrack to the clip called *Matilde*, which you can find on the product

28 *Putting the audio into audio description*

page for this book: https://www.routledge.com/products/978-1-138-84817-7. While you listen ask yourself the following questions:

> Where are we?
> Who is in the scene?
> What time of day is it?
> How many changes of location are there?
> What is going on?

Note down your responses and compare them with those of a colleague. To what extent did you agree?

As you listen you will find that some noises are easily identifiable: you'll hear a door shutting, chair legs scraping, the thwack of a tennis racquet, balls bouncing, a man talking authoritatively in Italian, feet on stairs and lots of rummaging sounds. Is it possible to assemble them into a coherent story? Some of the sounds you hear later may confirm suspicions you had earlier on. There is also music. But the music is non-diegetic, meaning that it does not arise from the action. It is simply there to provide atmosphere; there is no guitarist or accordion-player in the scene. You will also probably feel that the clip is very long. In fact it is about ten minutes, but without vision to hold our attention it is easy for the mind to wander and our attention to drift. In a study (Fryer and Freeman, 2012) in which BPS people were required to watch a seven-minute clip of *Brief Encounter* (Lean, 1946) with no AD, one reported 'without the AD my mind wandered in and out. I needed it to get back on track.'

3.3.2 Dialogue

Matilde (Palmieri, 2013) contains little dialogue, so there are few clues as to the characters. We are aware of the teacher, and we hear him question Matilde, who is presumably a pupil, but whether this is the same girl as the one we hear counting we cannot be sure. We also hear the gentle voice of a middle-aged woman. Even in a film with more plentiful dialogue, it would be the task of the audio describer to identify who was talking. This is especially important at the beginning of a film, as there are often lots of characters and we have yet to work out their relationship to each other or their roles in the narrative.

Sometimes there is an assumption that blind people are better than sighted people at identifying voices. However, as one congenitally blind man expressed it:

> I think faces are easier to recognise than voices . . . So where you have a play or film or a soap [opera] with twenty or thirty different characters, you don't always know who is speaking. Because [the describers have] told you once who is speaking at the beginning when they've identified each character that probably is enough for a sighted person who's clocked their face. But it isn't enough either for a new listener to a soap or, if it's a one-off, a play or film. You may very well need two or three introductions.

Putting the audio into audio description 29

In AD guidelines in, for example Germany, Greece and France (Benecke, 2014), describers are discouraged from naming a character before their name is revealed in the script. In the UK, the ITC Guidance (ITC, 2000) warns against naming too early if it will ruin the plot. However, it is usual in the UK to try to name the characters as soon as they appear. This is for convenience, to avoid having to repeatedly describe a character by their physical appearance, which is cumbersome and time consuming. The ideal, where space and time allows, is to both name and describe a character, such that the name acts as a tag, to remind the AD user of what the character looks like, whenever they reappear. Ideally, the name is inserted immediately before a character speaks, as though you are cueing them. If there is no room, because the dialogue follows on quickly, you might need to insert the name in a gap in the middle of their speech, or at the end. From the content of their speech, and especially through the prosody of their delivery, we know whether that character is sad or happy, menacing or scared. As this information is audible, a character's emotional state need not be explicitly stated.

3.3.3 Exercises

Watch *Matilde* again, this time looking at the screen. While you watch, think about what you did not know from simply listening to the soundtrack, as well as what you did. It is important not to over-describe by saying too much. Blind people can find it patronising, irritating or laughable to be given redundant information, as the following comment illustrates:

> The ones that make me laugh are 'There's a knock at the door' and you hear 'bang bang bang' and you think that was quite obvious. Maybe who's at the door would be nice to know, but not that there's going to be a knock at the door.

AD is designed to fit around the dialogue and significant sound effects. Although blind people have been shown to perform better than sighted people on tasks requiring divided auditory attention (e.g. Occelli et al., 2008; Hötting and Röder, 2004), anecdotal reports suggest that AD increases cognitive load.

3.4 Cognitive load

Cognitive load theory was originally conceived by Miller (1956) and developed, largely in relation to learning, by Sweller (1988). Cognitive resources can be thought of as limited, such that the more we use for processing information, the less remains available. De Rijk et al. (1999) suggest that complex detail leads to sensory overload, destroying presence through fatigue. The load theory of attention (Lavie and De Fockert, 2005) proposes that strain on working memory reduces ability to focus on the task in hand, making it harder to distinguish between relevant and irrelevant stimuli. Knowledge and experience help to screen unnecessary or redundant data, freeing up as many cognitive resources as possible in pursuit of particular goals.

30 *Putting the audio into audio description*

Ng et al. (2013) argue that a dynamic medium (a film, as compared with static images, for example) is essentially transient, constantly presenting the viewer with new information. This needs to be processed while, at the same time, information it has superseded must be held in working memory (WM) long enough that connections between the two information states may be made. WM must not be overstretched and, according to cognitive load theory, the perfect balance (germane load) is dependent on intrinsic load (the complexity of the message), extrinsic load (the complexity of the medium or the way the message is communicated) and the expertise of the individual: individual characteristics (e.g. familiarity with and interest in the content) will dictate how much load a person's WM can bear. Too much (but equally too little) intrinsic or extrinsic load will upset the balance. Ng et al. (2013) suggest that novel information can quickly overwhelm WM, whereas familiar information can be dealt with via schemas within long-term memory, which is virtually limitless (e.g. Sweller, 2010).

3.5 Sound effects

People with unimpaired vision and hearing use sound for confirmation. In addition to sound that naturally occurs through the action, there are also sound effects. These have been specially added to draw our attention and to make us feel that we are really 'there'. Foley is 'the term for everyday sounds such as squeaky shoes or cutlery jangling in a drawer' (Kisner, 2015). Foley artists have long since realised that images seem more real when accompanied by sound, even though real sounds are not necessarily used. For example, watching a head being chopped off seems more realistic when accompanied by the sound of somebody slicing through a melon (clearly the real sound is not readily available and few of us have experience of it).

Realistic sounds often amplify information given not only through vision but also through the dialogue. However, a constructed sound track also uses evocative effects (Crook, 1999). These are sounds that are not dependent on dialogue but create a general atmosphere or sense of place. Blind people are used to establishing their location using audio cues (Strelow and Brabyn, 1982), and it is a skill they are likely to have developed more effectively than sighted people (Schenkman and Nilsson, 2010). They will know whether they are in a large building or a small apartment either from sounds coming from their environment or through the reverberation (or lack of it) when speaking or clicking their tongue or finger, through a process known as 'echolocation'. Although television is rarely sophisticated enough to give such a detailed aural picture, sound can be an important cue for AD users. However, sound can also be ambiguous.

3.6 Exercises and points for discussion

Have a listen to the first few seconds of *Joining the Dots* on the accompanying website. The surging sound you hear could be the sea, or perhaps the wind. However, as soon as the pictures begin you reinterpret the sound as the rattle of a train. This is clarified for blind users by just a few simple words in the AD. Watch the rest of this film for more evidence of how useful AD can be for blind people like Trevor, as he participates in a 'touch tour' before an audio-described theatre performance. Touch tours are discussed in more detail below (3.9.2).

3.7 Translating music

Approaches to translating music have recently been attracting scholars' attention (see translatingmusic.com), whether it be surtitling at the opera (Weaver, 2011), cover versions of punk anthems (Caschelin, 2015), or the choice between subtitling, dubbing or omitting the translation of songs in American musical films such as *Grease* (Kleiser, 1978) and *Singin' in the Rain* (Donen and Kelly, 1952) (Mateo, 2015).

Although most guidelines suggest AD should not mask important elements of the soundtrack, that advice is generally disregarded when it comes to music. The exception is describing over lyrics. The RNIB, in its guidelines for describing for children (2009), suggests that 'wherever possible songs remain intact without description over them'. By 'song', it is implicit that the guidelines are referring to lyrics, as they go on to say:

> If there is important plot information to convey, this should be fitted in later in the song, during repetitions in the song or during instrumental passages. There may be occasions when there is important plot information to convey during the first chorus. In this case the second chorus should be left free of description. The most important thing is to make sure that children have the opportunity to learn the tune and the words, and to enjoy the song.

Similar advice is given in the ITC Guidance with reference to describing musicals:

> The main challenge for the describer is where to place the description. Many film songs come from stage shows and are well known and viewers want to listen to them without the describer talking over them. The describer must either try to pre-empt a song with a brief description of a dance or costumes, or, must judge carefully when to intervene and when to stay silent during a song, to cause least offence. The third option is to let the music play and say nothing at all.
> (ITC, 2000: para. 4.2)

Particular difficulties arise if the song lyrics are in a foreign language and have been subtitled. This is explored in Chapter 9.

3.7.1 Describing live musical events

Making music accessible to BPS through AD may sound unnecessary. Surely blind people can hear music? Leaving aside the issue that, as we have noted, most blind people are elderly and may have additional disabilities including hearing loss, just think for a moment about elements of live musical performance that most sighted people take for granted. You arrive at a concert hall. You take in the grand façade of the venue, say, the Royal Albert Hall. You mingle with other people in the foyer, noting the type and number of people the performance attracts. You collect a programme, skim through the notes about the pieces, the list of performers, photographs. You enter the auditorium and look towards the stage, where a few players wander on. You are impressed by all the percussion – the tam-tam, the tubular bells. You note two harps, a celeste, a piano. More players drift on. It is a big orchestra. There is an unusual gender balance. Most of the players are young. They are dressed in black suits, not formal white tie and tails. They seem to have tracksuit tops over the backs of their chairs. The violins are split, the firsts on one side of the conductor, the seconds on the other. You notice the audience crushed at the front of the arena tense a little. The lights dim in the auditorium and brighten on stage. The conductor bounds on, his hair a mop of dark curls that will in a few moments flop forwards, accentuating every down beat of his baton. The British composer George Benjamin (2013), writing about Stravinsky's ground-breaking work, *The Rite of Spring*, said: 'One of the most thrilling aspects of a good performance . . . is how it looks: few things on a concert platform can rival the display of so many musicians executing such jagged and unpredictable rhythmical shapes in perfect unison.' Some venues in the UK, such as London's Southbank Centre, have begun to train their hosts (front-of-house staff) in AD so they can fill in this type of information for blind audience members when no full AD service is available. The importance of the visuals is underlined by the increasing use of screens at large concert venues, especially for pop and rock concerts. These types of live events have yet to be made accessible.

3.7.2 Visual dominance and music

A study by Chia-Jung Tsay (2013) with 1,000 participants showed that although 'People consistently report that sound is the most important source of information in evaluating performance in music . . . People reliably select the actual winners of live music competitions based on silent video recordings, but neither musical novices nor professional musicians were able to identify the winners based on sound recordings or recordings with both video and sound.' Fryer et al.'s (2014) study comparing BPS users' response to film clips designed to elicit particular emotional responses from sighted people was intended to test reactions to AD delivered by a human voice, as compared with AD delivered by computer-generated text-to-speech. However, the comparison with listening to the same film clip with no AD established clearly that participants listening to scary music in films such as *The Shining* (Kubrick, 1980) reported feeling significantly less scared with no AD than when listening with description provided by a human voice (HVAD). Even though they were aware that the clip was intended to elicit fear, the music was unable to induce this sensation on its own. All this suggests that, while talking over instrumental music has become an established practice in AD that has received little research interest, the instinctive assumption that it is

Putting the audio into audio description 33

not too intrusive or counter-productive to do so is probably correct. Much work has been done in the field of Computational Auditory Scene Analysis (e.g. Tallal and Gaab, 2006) exploring the way in which the human ear (and brain) is skilled at filtering competing audio signals to be able to analyse and preferentially attend to some sounds or types of sound more than others.

Music is more important in some film genres than in others. Paula Igareda (2012: 1889) points out: 'Music has been an integral part of films from as far back as the silent movie era, where a piano accompaniment was used to build the narrative and an orchestra was used to drown out the sound of the projector.' Polly Goodwin (2015) has recently suggested that one way of providing AD for silent movies without ruining the soundtrack is by giving BPS a written description in large print or Braille, although the issue of synchrony has still to be addressed.

3.8 Finding the 'gaps'

You may remember one of the first definitions of AD presented in Chapter 1: 'AD uses the natural pauses in dialogue or narration to insert descriptions of the essential visual elements' (Audio Description Coalition, n.d.). Natural pauses are construed as silence, yet silence is often deliberate, carefully constructed as a constituent part of the soundtrack. As Kisner (2015) explains:

> Consider the scene at the end of *No Country for Old Men* when Javier Bardem's character has a car accident. After the crunch of impact, there are a few moments of what might be mistaken for stillness. The two cars rest smoking and crumpled in the middle of a suburban intersection. Nothing moves – but the soundscape is deceptively layered. There is the sound of engines hissing and crackling, which have been mixed to seem as near to the ear as the camera was to the cars; there is a mostly unnoticeable rustle of leaves in the trees; periodically, so faintly that almost no one would register it consciously, there is the sound of a car rolling through an intersection a block or two over, off camera; a dog barks somewhere far away. The faint sound of a breeze was taken from ambient sounds on a street like the one depicted in the scene. When Javier Bardem shoves open the car door, you hear the door handle stick for a moment before it releases. There are three distinct sounds of broken glass tinkling to the pavement from the shattered window, a small handful of thunks as he falls sideways to the ground, his laboured breathing, the chug of his boot heel finally connecting with the asphalt – even the pads of his fingers as they scrabble along the top of the window. None of these sounds are there because some microphone picked them up. They're there because [the sound editor, Skip] Lievsay chose them and put them there, as he did for every other sound in the film.

In *Joining the Dots*, silence has an emotive function. As a describer, you would not want to interrupt Trevor's words by speaking during his pauses, for fear of disrupting the poignancy of his meaning. You might think this is also a danger

34 *Putting the audio into audio description*

when speaking over music. However, Fryer and Freeman's study exploring emotion elicited by films showed that the 'addition of verbal information did not lead to a reduction in presence or in levels of elicited emotion, despite AD partially masking the soundtrack' (Fryer et al., 2014: 99). All guidelines concur that speaking over dialogue is not an option. The alternative, over the music, is not ideal but is probably the 'least worst' option.

3.9 The *When* of AD

In the context of AD, *when* refers not only to the timing and location of your utterance but also the temporal setting of the ST. The visual evidence for this is often given by clothing and objects or, in live AD, by the set and costumes. For example, we can tell by Matilde's clothes that this film is contemporary, meaning that it is set either in the present or in the recent past. However, there are also sometimes written textual clues. There may be a caption specifying the date, a clock or a calendar on the wall. It is clear from video artist Christian Marclay's *The Clock* (2010), in which he splices together clips showing time references for every minute of a twenty-four-hour period that unfolds in real time, that such visual references are many and various. In addition to the general period, we can also tell the season; the quilted coat Matilde wears shows that it is late in the year, while the curling red and gold leaves on the ground specify the season: autumn. From the action, we know that it is a weekday, although the BPS audience will also be able to deduce this from the schoolroom setting. In the same way, the describer may prefer to mention the leaves on the ground, i.e. to give the visual evidence, rather than explicitly stating 'Autumn'. The light (both natural and artificial) tells us whether it is early or late in the day. As the light changes during the film, it gives a sense of time passing, so we know that when Matilde returns to school it is the following day and she has had time to dream up her scheme to overcome her noisy surroundings.

The next aspect of *When* is when to begin the AD. When does the film start? For your blind audience the film will start with your description. This is certainly true of *Matilde*, although other films may start with music, perhaps the title theme or the music that accompanies the distributor's logo. The opening seconds of *Matilde* show the logos for various film festivals against a black screen. On-screen text and logos are discussed in Chapter 9. You will notice that the sounds of the classroom and the voice of the teacher intrude over these images. If you simply say what you see, the sound will make no sense. Your audience will be lacking the necessary reference frame to interpret the teacher's words and the sounds of moving furniture. The standard convention in this case is to pre-empt the image of the classroom, the girl and her fidgeting classmates, and to introduce them and the teacher, ending your description just before his first line. In this way, the AD script will resemble a screenplay, with your opening words akin to an establishing shot, setting the scene where the action is to take place.

After that, small visual details such as the quick shot of chair legs scraping across the tiled floor (at 00:33) can be left undescribed. There is no space to insert a description here, without speaking either over the sound effect or over the teacher's words. Once the AD has outlined the basic information, the sounds can achieve their effect.

As well as when does an AD utterance start, an equally valid question would be when does it stop? How long should your description last? This will entirely depend on the content of your ST. Your description can last only until the beginning of the next burst of dialogue or the next important sound effect and you must wait for another quiet moment in the soundtrack before you talk again. Vercauteren (2012) suggests that a useful indicator of when to add in new descriptive information, as well as in deciding what are the key visual elements to describe, comes from frame changes. He cites Emmott (1997) and Herman (1997), who extended the psychological model of knowledge structures, namely mental schemas, scripts and frames, to the sphere of narratology. Herman (1997) points out that a key difference between knowledge structures and stories is that stories unfold in time, whereas frames represent only a single point in time. The same is true of a film narrative. The description needs to summarise that point and need not add anything else until the frame changes. Vercauteren has identified three possibilities for different types of frame modification and how they inform the decision as to the key visual element for your next AD insertion. For these he relies on the Assumption of Normality, citing Brown and Yule (1983: 62) – who themselves cite Toolan (2010: 13) – whereby 'a speaker or writer can be assumed to be continuing to speak or write of the same spatiotemporal setting and the same characters, unless a change is explicitly signalled' (Vercauteren, 2012: 221). Cues for explicitly signalling such a change in the AD comprise the following, with the descriptive focus as shown:

1   *Frame modification*: new characters within the same contextual frame key visual information: characters.
2   *Frame switch*: one contextual frame replaces another key visual information: spatiotemporal setting.
3   *Frame recall*: re-activation of an earlier contextual frame AD of one or more elements from that earlier frame.

In *Matilde* the frames are as follows:

   Frame 1: the classroom

   Frame 2: the school grounds

   Frame 3: Matilde at the window

   Frame 4: the school grounds viewed through the window.

Using Vercauteren's system of analysis, the classroom frame is modified at approximately 01.07 by the addition of the title. This in turn is switched at approximately 01.10, replaced by a shot of children playing Chinese Whispers in the school grounds. At 01.17 the frame switches back to Matilde, modified such that

Matilde is at the window on her own. Only now can we deduce the chronological sequence of events: for the second frame we have jumped forwards a few minutes in the chronology of the story, the lesson is over. It is break time. The frame modification that brings the camera behind Matilde to show us her point of view as she watches the other children playing makes it clear that these two events are happening at the same time. Matilde's location is unspecified. Only when she turns to look at the female teacher or teaching assistant can we know that Matilde is no longer in the classroom, but in another part of the school building.

It is good practice for a describer to watch a film or a production all the way through before attempting to describe it. The describer is left to decide whether to keep the AD user in the same degree of uncertainty or to use the benefit of hindsight, and clarify each new location or character as they appear. Interestingly, most guidelines are inconsistent, arguing that it is wrong to name a character before they have been named in the script, while stipulating no such constraint for location. Clearly, as with a character, if a setting is deliberately mysterious, it should not be named if that would pre-empt a later reveal in the plot. Otherwise, as settings are more likely to be recalled visually than aurally (the exception in *Matilde* being the tennis court), standard UK practice is to use the describer's omniscient overview to name a setting when it is first shown.

3.9.1 The **When** *of live AD*

The starting point of a live event is usually visual: a curtain raised, or lights dimming in the auditorium and brightening on stage. This is often accompanied by an aural cue: music, perhaps, or the audience falling quiet with an expectant hush. The visual cues will need to be verbalised, as in the example from *The House of Bernarda Alba* at the start of Chapter 1. Yet sometimes the opening moment is deliberately blurred, with actors on stage for some minutes before the dialogue begins. The describer of live events is usually busy at this point reading the audio introduction (AI). This is a separate piece of prose which summarises the visual design of the production (see Chapter 12). But, as this pre-show, on-stage action might contribute to our understanding of the play later on and is visible to the sighted audience, the describer should at the very least mention that it happens, perhaps referring to it in the AI or interrupting the AI to describe key moments in more detail. One AD user, the theatre director Maria Oshodi, who is blind and who attended the 'dry run' and gave feedback, refers to the description of this pre-show business as 'Badger Watching'. 'Dry run' is the term used for the process whereby you test out your script in real time with no AD audience except for a colleague listening in who can pick up any problems and help you to fill in any missing details. Video or no video, a dry run is essential to check details, and the closer to the date of the described performance, the better, as changes to timing and stage business are likely to evolve over time, with less variation between contiguous performances than between performances more widely spaced. It is at the 'dry run' stage that feedback from one or two blind people can be most usefully incorporated, and consistency of style ensured between the two halves of the script. To Maria's mind, the description of pre-show business resembles the hushed style of narration used by the presenter of a nature documentary when he stands close to the animal subjects of one of his programmes. Although these pre-show moments appear to be improvised, once the actors have developed a sequence of movements they feel comfortable with, the pattern will often be repeated for several performances, so the AD can be scripted as normal, with appropriate moments found to insert it during the live AI.

3.9.2 Touch tours

It could be argued that the AD for a show begins even before the AD user arrives at the theatre, if they choose to listen to the AI in advance. In many UK venues they are also invited to attend a touch tour. As the National Theatre of Great Britain states on its website:

> It's a chance to visit the set, feel the props, and enhance your enjoyment of the show. The tour is free and lasts about half an hour.

It usually begins an hour or so before curtain up. The exact format of a touch tour varies from show to show, but in general the describers will give an overview of the set, in situ, before inviting BPS audience members and their sighted companions to explore it themselves. Members of the company (the cast and production crew) are often in attendance. Actors are asked to describe their character and costumes. *Joining the Dots* shows Trevor at a touch tour at London's Almeida Theatre. It will give you a good idea of how the company interacts with blind patrons, allowing the verbal description to be fleshed out by the use of other senses. At times, features of a moveable set are demonstrated. People with residual vision can sometimes use that vision effectively when they can get close to something, under working lights, rather when trying to see from the auditorium under stage lighting. The describers work closely with the stage manager to identify the most important props to get to grips with. It can be important to liaise so that not all stage secrets are divulged too soon.

3.9.3 Sound and live events

In screen AD, describers have some control over the existing soundtrack, as its volume can be faded, if necessary. This luxury is not available for live AD. There may be times where description, although desirable, is not possible because the volume of music or the SFX is simply too loud for the AD to be heard comfortably, even through headphones. On these occasions, scenes or actions may need to be pre- or post-described. Leakage from headsets can occasionally be problematic, causing the AD to be heard by members of the sighted audience, especially when a loud scene changes to one that is very quiet. On rare occasions this has led to a decision not to provide a full description for a particular show. Instead, only an AI is provided, for fear of disturbing the sighted audience.

38 *Putting the audio into audio description*

Another sound that will contribute to the *When* of AD is any audible response from the sighted audience. Feeling part of the audience is an important aspect of AD for BPS users. Asked by VocalEyes what AD means to them, one AD user said:

> Audio description means that, as a blind person, I can watch a film with my friends and laugh at the same time as they do. I can understand the story without having to pause the DVD so that they can describe the bit that I didn't understand. That my husband can relax beside me without having to make the big effort of describing the action to me.

Timing is also critical. Asked what characterises quality in AD, one partially sighted woman replied:

> P: I say one that gets as close to the right portion in the play as they can. It is very difficult sometimes because of the dialogue and you don't want to interrupt the dialogue – the audio describer is actually telling you that somebody is doing something before they've actually done it – and not everyone is going to know that but with my amount of sight I very often do.
> L: Right . . . and that's frustrating?
> P: No, it's irritating [laugh].
> L: [laugh] Especially if the actor doesn't then do it!
> P: Right, um, or if everyone goes 'ah' all around me, all the other blind people, and I'm going [sotto voce] 'they actually haven't died yet, they're still standing up' [laugh]. But I mean, that's very much determined by where the actual um, you know, dialogue's going to come in. Sometimes you have to say it beforehand.

It is clear, then, that the AD has to be sufficient that the user can interpret the audience response, and timed to provoke a simultaneous user response. Reactions such as laughter or sounds of disgust can alert the describer to the location where a description needs to be inserted. Occasionally this can be hard to predict, especially if the describer does not empathise with the response. For example, the dance piece *Like Rabbits* performed at London's Almeida theatre (Duke and Kirkwood, 2013) provoked laughter from some members of the audience, who giggled at the female dancer's rejection of the male when he attempted some sexually provocative moves. In feedback from BPS members of the audience one person asked that the laughter be explained. The describer was at a loss because, to her, the scene had been poignant rather than funny. Spontaneous moments of applause may also need interpretation if the AD users are not to feel they have missed out; for example, the impressive set of the Neverland emerging from the drum revolve in the National Theatre of Great Britain's production of *Peter Pan* (Caird, 1997) predictably drew 'oohs' and 'aahs'; the description of the set needed to be equally impressive, allowing the AD users to join in the response of the sighted audience.

3.9.4 Exercises and points for discussion

Take a short film clip (around two minutes) of your choice. Listen to the soundtrack (without watching the images) and analyse the type and function of the sounds. Are the sound effects instantly identifiable, such as a clock chime or a knock on the door? Or are they given context by the visuals? If so, do they need to be prefaced by a description for us to understand what they are? Can you find spaces where you might be able to insert a description?

Construct a skeleton script with just the timecodes for the ins and outs of your AD. At this stage, you don't need to fill in the 'gaps'; just find them. Notice if your decisions are being driven by the visuals, the sound or both. Should you need more detail on how a script is constructed, you will find it in Chapter 6.

3.10 Conclusion

In this chapter we have explored the contribution of sound to the AV partnership, how it might dictate where you insert a descriptive utterance and what you say. For many new to description, 'watching' the ST with your eyes closed or your back to the screen is the first step in the process of describing. Describers with more experience dispense with this as they learn to recognise the triggers from the soundtrack that make AD necessary and to identify the 'gaps' that make it possible. The absence of dialogue provides such gaps, although the describers need to be certain about the function of music, SFX or silence such that the AD is not intrusive and does not mask important aural information. Finally, this chapter has introduced the *When* and the *Where* of AD, referring to the spatiotemporal setting as well as the timing of the description.

3.11 Suggested reading

You can read more about the interaction between AD and the soundtrack in the following articles:

Agnieszka Szarkowska and Pilar Orero, 'The importance of sound for audio description'. In Anna Maszerowska, Anna Matamala and Pilar Orero (eds) *Audio description: new perspectives illustrated*. Amsterdam: John Benjamins, 2014, pp. 121–140.

Louise Fryer, 'Audio description as audio drama – a practitioner's point of view'. *Perspectives: Studies in Translatology* 18, no. 3 (2010): 205–213.

References

Audio Description Coalition (n.d.). Retrieved from www.audiodescriptioncoalition.org/ [accessed 24.08.15].

Benecke, Berndt (2014). 'Character fixation and character description: the naming and describing of characters in *Inglourious Basterds*'. In Anna Maszerowska, Anna Matamala and Pilar Orero (eds) *Audio description: new perspectives illustrated*. Amsterdam: John Benjamins, pp. 141–158.

Benjamin, George (2013). '"How Stravinsky's *Rite of Spring* has shaped 100 years of music'. Retrieved from www.theguardian.com/music/2013/may/29/stravinsky-rite-of-spring [accessed 23.12.15].

Brown, G. and Yule, G. (1983). *Discourse analysis*. Cambridge: Cambridge University Press.
Caschelin, Sylvain (2015). 'Translation trials: anarchy in the UK revisited'. Paper presented at *Translating Music Today Symposium*, Europe House, London, 15 July.
Chion, Michel, Claudia Gorbman and Walter Murch (1994). *Audio-vision: sound on screen*. New York: Columbia University Press.
Crook, T. (1999). *Radio drama: theory and practice*. London: Routledge.
de Rijk, A. E., K. M. Schreurs and J. M. Bensing (1999). 'Complaints of fatigue: related to too much as well as too little external stimulation?' *Journal of Behavioral Medicine* 22, no. 6: 549–573.
Emmott, C. (1997). *Narrative comprehension: a discourse perspective*. Oxford: Oxford University Press.
Fryer, L. and J. Freeman (2012). 'Cinematic language and the description of film: keeping AD users in the frame'. *Perspectives: Studies in Translatology*, doi:10.1080/0907676X.2012.693108.
Fryer, L., J. Freeman and L. Pring (2014). 'Can you feel what I'm saying? The impact of verbal information on emotion elicitation and presence in people with a visual impairment'. In A. Felnhoffer and O. Kothgassner (eds) *Challenging presence: Proceedings of the International Society on Presence Research, Vienna* (March), pp. 99–108. ISBN 978-3-7089-1081-9.
Goodwin, Polly (2015). 'The limits and possibilities of audio describing silent film'. Paper presented at *Blind Creations Conference*, Royal Holloway, London, 29 June.
Hötting, Kirsten and Brigitte Röder (2004). 'Hearing cheats touch, but less in congenitally blind than in sighted individuals'. *Psychological Science* 15, no. 1: 60–64.
Igareda, Paula (2012). 'Lyrics against images: music and audio description'. *MonTI. Monografías de Traducción e Interpretación* 4: 233–254.
ITC (2000). ITC guidance on standards for audio description. Retrieved from http://www.ofcom.org.uk/static/archive/itc/itc_publications/codes_guidance/audio_description/index.asp.html [accessed 22.12.15].
Kisner, Jordan (2015). 'Rain is sizzling bacon, cars are lions roaring: the art of sound in movies'. *Guardian*. Retrieved from www.theguardian.com/film/2015/jul/22/rain-is-sizzling-bacon-cars-lions-roaring-art-of-sound-in-movies [accessed 4.09.15].
Koppen, Camille and Charles Spence (2007). 'Audiovisual asynchrony modulates the Colavita visual dominance effect'. *Brain Research* 1186: 224–232.
Kreifelts, Benjamin, Dirk Wildgruber and Thomas Ethofer (2013). 'Audiovisual integration of emotional information from voice and face'. In P. Belin, S. Campanella and T. Ethofer (eds) *Integrating face and voice in person perception*, New York: Springer, pp. 225–251.
Lavie, N. and J. De Fockert (2005). 'The role of working memory in attentional capture'. *Psychonomic Bulletin & Review* 12, no. 4: 669–674.
Maiworm, Mario, Marina Bellantoni, Charles Spence and Brigitte Röder (2012). 'When emotional valence modulates audiovisual integration.' *Attention, Perception, & Psychophysics* 74, no. 6: 1302–1311.
Mateo, M. (2015). 'Translating musicals: from stage to film across the continents'. Paper presented at *Translating Music Seminar, 2015*, Europe House, London (July).
Miller, G.A. (1956). 'The magical number seven, plus or minus two: some limits on our capacity for processing information'. *Psychological Review* 63, no. 2: 81.
Murray, Micah M., Sophie Molholm, Christoph M. Michel, Dirk J. Heslenfeld, Walter Ritter, Daniel C. Javitt, Charles E. Schroeder and John J. Foxe (2005). 'Grabbing your ear: rapid auditory–somatosensory multisensory interactions in low-level sensory cortices are not constrained by stimulus alignment'. *Cerebral Cortex* 15, no. 7: 963–974.

Ng, H.K., S. Kalyuga and J. Sweller (2013). 'Reducing transience during animation: a cognitive load perspective'. *Educational Psychology* 33, no. 7: 755–772.
Occelli, Valeria, Charles Spence and Massimiliano Zampini (2008). 'Audiotactile temporal order judgments in sighted and blind individuals'. *Neuropsychologia* 46, no. 11: 2845–2850.
Schenkman, Bo N. and Mats E. Nilsson (2010). 'Human echolocation: blind and sighted persons' ability to detect sounds recorded in the presence of a reflecting object'. *Perception* 39, no. 4: 483.
Smith, Greg M. (1999). 'Local emotions, global moods, and film structure'. In C. Plantinga and G. M. Smioth (eds) *Passionate views: film, cognition, and emotion*. Baltimore, MD: Johns Hopkins University Press, pp. 103–126.
Strelow, Edward R. and John A. Brabyn (1982). 'Locomotion of the blind controlled by natural sound cues'. *Perception* 11, no. 6: 635–640.
Sutcliffe, Tom (2000). *Watching*. London: Faber & Faber.
Sweller, J. (1988). 'Cognitive load during problem solving: effects on learning'. *Cognitive Science* 12, no. 2: 257–285.
Sweller, J. (2010). 'Element interactivity and intrinsic, extraneous, and germane cognitive load'. *Educational Psychology Review* 22, no. 2: 123–138.
Tallal, Paula and Nadine Gaab (2006). 'Dynamic auditory processing, musical experience and language development'. *Trends in Neurosciences* 29, no. 7: 382–390.
Toolan, M. (2012). *Narrative: a critical linguistic introduction*. London: Routledge.
Tsay, Chia-Jung (2013). 'Sight over sound in the judgment of music performance'. *Proceedings of the National Academy of Sciences* 110, no. 36: 14580–14585. Retrieved from www.pnas.org/content/110/36/14580.full [accessed 21.07.15].
Vercauteren, Gert (2012). 'A narratological approach to content selection in audio description: towards a strategy for the description of narratological time.' Rosa Agost, Pilar Orero and Elena di Giovanni (eds) *Multidisciplinarity in Audiovisual translation. MonTI* 4: 207–231. Retrieved from http://roderic.uv.es/bitstream/handle/10550/37094/26948.pdf?sequence=1&isAllowed=y [accessed 7.01.16].
Weaver, Sarah (2011). 'Opening doors to opera: The strategies, challenges and general role of the translator'. *InTralinea* 12, www.intralinea.org/archive/article/Opening_doors_to_opera_.

Film references

Brief Encounter, D. Lean (1946).
Grease, R. Kleiser (1978).
Matilde, V. Palmieri (2013).
No Country for Old Men, J. Cohen and E. Cohen (2007).
Singin' in the Rain, S. Donen and G. Kelly (1952).
The Clock, C. Marclay (2010).
The Shining, S. Kubrick (1980).

References to live events

Like Rabbits, dirs B. Duke and L. Kirkwood (Lost Dog Productions http://lostdogdance.co.uk/) (2013). Almeida Theatre, London (describer Louise Fryer).
Peter Pan, dir. J. Caird (1997). National Theatre of Great Britain, London, AD by in house team (describers Louise Fryer and Andrew Holland).

4 The audience for audio description

4.1 Introduction

As you can tell from the exercise at the end of Chapter 1, and as Ofcom's Code on Television Access Services confirms, 'People using access services do not fall neatly into homogeneous groups. For example, many people using audio description have visual impairments, but by no means all are completely blind, and most have had some vision at some time . . . Those using access services range from the very young to older people, but a significant proportion of viewers using access services are older people, as the incidence of hearing and sight loss increases with age' (Ofcom, 2015: point A4.2).

This has implications for the kind of language you can use in your descriptions. The age characteristics of the blind population are discussed in more detail in Chapter 5. In practice, although a blind audience is as diverse as any sighted audience in terms of age and experience (in addition to their varied sight loss characteristics), audio describers largely work from the assumption that they are describing for a person with no sight. That said, it is important that the description is timed to coincide with the action as closely as possible, for the benefit of those (the majority) who have some residual vision. Timing is discussed in more detail in Chapter 6.

First, for whom are you describing?

4.2 What is blindness?

Literature relating to studies with BPS people uses an array of terminology to discuss those with a visual impairment. In the USA, for example, the term low vision is used in place of partially sighted (for a review of terms, see Cattaneo and Vecchi, 2011). In the UK, a person is legally blind when 'they cannot do any work for which eyesight is essential' (Palmer et al., 2007: 199). This is regarded as having between zero and 10 per cent of nominal visual acuity. This legal definition fails to distinguish between those who see nothing at all (totally blind) – which, incidentally, is only around 4 per cent of the blind population – and those with severe visual impairment, meaning that they have some light perception and can perceive the difference between light and shade. Blindness encompasses not only extremely poor visual acuity (less than 3/60, i.e. the inability to see at 3 metres what a person with 'nominal' visual acuity can see at 60 metres), but also poor visual acuity (3/60–6/60), combined with severe reduction in the visual field; and average visual acuity (6/60 or better) with extreme reduction in the visual field. Partial sight is legally defined in the UK as very poor visual acuity (3/60–6/60) combined with a full field of vision; moderate visual acuity (up to 6/24) and a reduced field of vision or blurred or cloudy central vision; or relatively good visual acuity (up to 6/18) but severe reduction in the visual field. The effect of this variation in residual vision, for AD, is that people may see some parts of the screen or stage more clearly than others. For example, they may be able to perceive a character's movement but not their facial expression. They may be able to perceive action but struggle to read captions or subtitles. In the USA the legal definition of blindness is uncorrected visual acuity of 20/200 or less in the better eye; or a visual field limitation such that the widest diameter of the visual field, in the better eye, is at an angle no greater than 20 degrees. In addition, a person is regarded as functionally blind when he or she has to use so many alternative techniques to perform tasks that are ordinarily performed with sight that his/her pattern of daily living is substantially altered. Such alternative techniques might include reading a newspaper by listening to it or using Braille to read a book. This may be a more helpful way of thinking about blindness than the medical definitions.

Another aspect of this broad spectrum is that only a very small number of people are born with no sight or lose it in early infancy, meaning that they have no visual experience. This explains many of the answers to the quiz at the end of Chapter 1 that you may have found surprising. For example, women are more likely than men to become blind simply because women tend to live longer. Sight problems commonly develop later in life, through accident or illness. Some eye conditions, such as retinitis pigmentosa, lead to gradual deterioration, so the impairment progresses from partial sight to total blindness over years or even decades. A few conditions, such as congenital cataracts, are reversible, so initial blindness is replaced by sight. Some acquired conditions can be reversed to a certain extent, e.g. one woman who suffered from diabetic retinopathy found that her sight improved following a kidney transplant (Jo Hopkins, personal communication). With medical and technical advances such as retinal implants it seems likely that the number of people whose visual impairment improves will increase.

4.3 Age and blindness

Most BPS people are elderly. Of the 143,385 people registered blind in England (HSCIC, 2014), 61 per cent are aged 75 or over, and only 0.5 per cent are aged 4 or under. The figures are similar for those who are registered with partial sight: 61 per cent aged 75 or over; 1 per cent aged 4 or under. Overall, as vision problems are mostly age related, and given the ageing population, the number of BPS people in the UK is expected to increase (RNIB online).

44 *The audience for audio description*

The AD audience is therefore diverse in terms of sight experience and circumstances. It might include a young person living independently who has been born blind or lost their sight in early infancy; an elderly relative who has recently lost their sight and is living with their sighted partner or family; the sighted or partially sighted parents of a sighted child and the sighted parents of a blind child. All might benefit from AD in some way. Some partially sighted people may rely more on AD in some circumstances than in others. As one occasional AD user who has partial sight explained:

> In action films that have very fast sequences I might have to say to someone sitting next to me, you know, what happened there? Um ... because I don't always see the fast action. [I find problems with] anything in black and white, because the contrast disappears. And I often use a strategy to identify my characters by remembering what they're wearing and what colour their clothes are, or I remember the colour of their hair or something like that and I know it's the same person. And in black and white movies you can't do that. And so I remember when I went to see *Schindler's List* (Spielberg, 1993), a movie that begins and ends in colour, but for most of the time is in black and white, just being totally lost because to me it looked like a whole series of disconnected frames um ... with no continuity, none of the characters seemed to be the same, it was just, completely disconnected.

4.4 A model of visual processing

At its most basic, the visual processing system is triggered by light entering the brain via photoreceptors at the back of the eyeball. Visual information is conveyed along the optic nerve leading from each eye to the optic chiasm where the optic nerves converge. One axon from each crosses over into the contralateral optic tract. From this point the optic tracts diverge, pass around the mid-brain (cerebral peduncle) and feed into the lateral geniculate nucleus (LGN) of the thalamus. The LGN axons radiate from here, through white matter of the brain, to the primary visual cortex (striate cortex or V1) of the occipital lobe at the back of the brain. The rest of the occipital lobe makes up the pathway of association (extra striate) cortex, concerned with recognition, colour, motion and depth (Crossman and Neary, 2014).

4.4.1 Mental models, schemata and scripts

However, perceiving with our eyes does not only involve the visual pathway. What we see is also influenced by our experience. The early twentieth-century theoretical biologist, Jakob von Uexkul, identified the *Umwelt*, i.e. 'the mass of knowledge that we carry around with us into every interaction'. Such knowledge is thought to be organised by the use of schemata (see section 4.6), a set of cognitive shortcuts whereby a simple trigger activates all that we know and have experienced from previous encounters with a particular object, action or environment. The word 'beach', for example, brings with it associations that may include yellow sand, blue sea, the call of gulls, children building sandcastles and adults playing beach ball. Each schema provides a reference frame for interpreting incoming sensory data and presents a likely script (Schank and Abelson, 1977). Schemata and, in turn, the *Umwelt* are continually updated, depending on new encounters and experiences, so that a visit to a volcanic island may create a revised schema for 'beach' that includes the possibility of black sand. Petrilli and Ponzio (2013) claim that human beings are able to model an indefinite number of worlds. Describers need to be aware of their own 'scripts' and mental models that 'blind' them to particular details. For example, a describer who grew up in the south-west of England described a barn in a production of Brian Friel's *Translations* (dir. J. Grieve, 2014), but without mentioning that it was built of stone. She felt that it went without saying because stone is the standard building material for barns in the South-West. However, the appearance of the barn was surprising to her colleague, who grew up in the east of England, where barns are traditionally built of wood. Having read the AI, this was what she was expecting. To her, the stone construction was a notable feature. We all see differently, depending on our interest and experience. As Tom Sutcliffe (2000) memorably expressed it, when an audience is watching Hitchcock's film *Psycho* (1960), there is always someone looking at the shower fittings. Pinchbeck and Stevens (2005) suggest that levels of presence are affected by the interaction between sensory data and a user's schemata. In particular, bottom-up information that is incongruent with a schema may delay processing and interrupt presence (see section 1.5).

For a low-immersive environment, namely books, Gysbers et al. (2004) showed that a minimal description that provided less specific information evoked a greater sense of presence than a text abundant in detail. The author Tracy Chevalier (Minshull, 2011) illustrates this in a discussion of Guy de Maupassant's short story 'The Necklace'. Although the necklace is central to the plot, Chevalier points out that de Maupassant limits his description to just four words: 'a superb diamond necklace'. This allows readers to imagine the necklace for themselves. It also allows that image to change over time. As Chevalier puts it in a radio essay broadcast by BBC Radio 3 (Minshull, 2011):

> As a teenager I'd pictured the necklace as a big net of diamonds that would cover most of your chest – something Elizabeth Taylor would wear, the sort of thing you need an impressive décolletage to display it on. Now, 30 years later when I imagine Mathilde's necklace, it is a simple strand of diamonds, very understated and elegant – Grace Kelly rather than Liz Taylor.

It is ironic that Chevalier's radio essay is illustrated on BBC iPlayer by a picture of a diamond necklace that allows for no ambiguity.

As a schema – shaped by an individual's own experience – influences what that person expects in terms of incoming information, it may also influence the allocation of their attention to reinforce those expectations. Bistricky et al. (2011) showed that depressed (sighted) individuals detected fewer words portraying people in a positive light (e.g. 'winner'), as compared both with negative words and with positive words that were unrelated to people (e.g. 'sunshine'). Participants with no history of depression showed no difference between word types.

This is why the oft-quoted American approach to AD, advocated by Snyder (2014), that describers should say what they see, or WSIWYS (What You See Is What You Say), is not necessarily helpful. Describers need to be aware that their own perception is likely to be biased. In her book about her experience of blindness, *Sight Unseen*, Georgina Kleege marvels at the ignorance of sighted people about sight: 'For the sighted seeing is both instantaneous and absolute. They apparently believe the brain stays out of it' (Kleege, 1999: 96). In the 1970s, the psychologist J. J. Gibson developed what he termed 'an ecological approach to visual perception' (1979). He took issue with the photographic analogy of vision, with its model of objects projected on the retina, like pictures projected on a screen. Gibson (1979) argues that we are not passive recipients of a static, snapshot view of the world. We look around and move around while we are looking. Gibson suggests that perception is not merely a response to a stimulus but, rather, a way of picking up information: 'Perception may or may not occur in the presence of information' (ibid.: 56). That is a phrase to remember when you are considering whether or not something in the background of the scene (a secondary object) should be mentioned.

Orero and Vilaró (2014) give a good example, comparing the eye-gaze of sighted viewers for a short sequence from the DVD of Danny Boyle's film *Millions* (2004) shown with and without AD. The DVD menu begins with the yellow cockerel mobile of the Pathé logo, its shadow projected on a white wall. Once the user presses 'play', the cockerel appears again, but now modified such that the shadow features a halo. Only the group watching with AD reported noticing the difference, and a heat map generated by an eye tracker showed that the eye-gaze of those viewers had shifted up to focus on the halo itself. This prompts the question, should the describer mention the halo? Or not? There are two reasons why the describer should do so. First, the director has deliberately chosen to include the halo. In the situation that even just one sighted person notices the halo it is important to describe it, otherwise you guarantee that no blind person will be able to. Second, the halo may subconsciously trigger a schema of saintliness and moral behaviour, which is what the film is about. It may make what follows easier to understand because it gives us the right context in which to interpret the information from the film dialogue and the AD, i.e. it stimulates retrieval of an appropriate script and schema.

4.5 A cognitive model of AD

Before we think about how visual impairment affects the way BPS people engage with audiovisual media, let us think about what happens when someone who does not have impaired sight watches a television programme or a film. These AV forms are both recognised as low-immersive, mediated environments. For the sighted audience direct perceptual information comes from a reduced number of senses, as compared with the real world. People with no sensory loss enjoy a stream of congruent information from two sensory modalities: sight and hearing. When they watch a bottle falling, for example, they also hear it shatter as it hits the ground. The two information streams support and complement each other, replicating the kind of environmental synchrony of auditory and visual stimuli in the real world that Bertelsen and de Gelder term 'valid co-occurrence' (2004). It is proposed that such perceptual information from two sources activates sensory and semantic associations shaped by the experience of the viewer, filling in absent sensory data, to create a sense of 'being there' (Biocca, 1997: 18). AD can itself be regarded as a form of mediation but the words can be so well chosen and placed that the user is unaware of the AD and it does not intrude on the user's conscious perception. Although visibility can be a contentious issue in translation, BPS people continually stress that they prefer the describer to remain invisible. They come to watch a film or see a show; not to listen to the AD. By adding a verbal commentary, woven around the existing dialogue, to capture the visual elements of a scene, AD creates what Piety (2004: 455) calls an 'audio amalgam'. In this way an AV medium is translated into pure audio, so that for the AD user a film or play in some ways comes to resemble an audio drama (Fryer, 2010). Words interacting with the existing sound track should stimulate a number of other senses in the user. That this is achievable is shown by users' comments in response to some of the early UK TV broadcasts with AD (Whitehead, 2005):

> [*Murder in the First* was] ... absolutely first class. I have visited Alcatraz and the AD on this film brought back the atmosphere, smells and everything. Superb!
>
> For *The Godfather*: the AD was stunning, absolutely amazing: I could actually smell the olive trees!

The semi-structured interviews carried out with BPS people as part of the author's doctoral research provoked many spontaneous comments, such as to suggest that people with visual impairment can immerse themselves in mediated environments such that they have a sense of 'being there'. One participant suggested that the experience of a blind person could even be enhanced, as compared with that of a sighted person, because, with no visual reminder of media form (such as wobbly scenery or the frame of the cinema or television screen), there was less need to suspend disbelief. However, most felt that without AD their sense of presence was

48 *The audience for audio description*

hindered by lack of access to visual information. Dialogue and non-verbal sound did not always enable a person with a visual impairment to follow the plot, let alone access the 'full picture'. This led to a sense of exclusion or general disengagement, i.e. the antithesis of presence.

Occasionally the audio and visual streams do not present consistent information but are deliberately incongruent so as to achieve a particular effect. In Hitchcock's *Psycho* (1960), for example, even though it is not natural to hear sharp, shrill violin shrieks as you are taking a shower, the mediated environment (the bathroom) is maintained through the visuals. For the blind user, non-diegetic music may lead to a temporary 'Break in Presence' (BIP) (Slater: 2002) because, with no ambient sound, the mediated environment ceases to persist for the duration of the scene. Similar BIPs may occur when a non-speaking character affects the action, or when the translated words of a character who speaks in a foreign language are subtitled rather than dubbed, resulting in an inability to follow the narrative flow. Nuances that are more subtle, as when the facial expression of a character belies their speech, may initiate a false schema in the mind of the blind user, affecting their interpretation of the drama. AD is specifically intended to address these problems.

4.6 Exercises and points for discussion

Watch *Notes on Blindness* (dirs Middleton and Spinney, 2014), which you can find on the product page for this book: https://www.routledge.com/products/978-1-138-84817-7. (The script is given below.) This film clip visualises an extract from the audio diary of John Hull, who recorded his experience as he gradually lost his sight. The filmmakers have used John's original tape recordings as the voice-over. This audio was originally intended to stand alone. However, the filmmakers felt it was important that the film be audio described so that their visualisations were available to blind and partially sighted audiences.

You will notice that this AD threads its way through John Hull's own narration. The describer has given herself cues of different types, so she knows when to speak. Those in bold are time cues taken from the film's timecode or elapsed running time. This is the most common type of cue in film and TV AD, and is usually listed like this: 00:00:00:00 in hours:minutes:seconds:frames, although in the above example only minutes and seconds are used, owing to the software the describer had available. Frame rate per second varies from country to country and format to format. In the PAL system that is used for analogue television in most of Europe, Eastern Africa and much of Asia and Australasia, the standard frame rate per second is 25. The NTSC standard used in North America, the northern countries of South America, the Philippines, Taiwan and Japan, has a frame rate of 26 per second. You will notice that great precision is necessary in identifying gaps to place the description. Those cues in *italics* are taken from the film dialogue (in this case John's narration). This is the most common type of cue in live AD contexts. You will also notice that some of these sound cues are not dialogue but SFX. It is also common to use visually apprehended actions or lighting effects as cues. If you are familiar with the practice or theory of subtitling you will notice that the AD continues across cuts and exceeds the duration recommended for on-screen captions. Reading speed is discussed in Chapter 7.

4.6.1 An extract from the AD script for Notes on Blindness

09:24 Rain stipples the frosted glass of John' workshop window. Moss grows in the rotting frame. John runs his hand along the wooden workbench.

09:37 He comes to stand facing the door, with its view of the garden. In his 40s, bearded, wearing glasses, John opens the door and inhales.He pauses on the threshold, listening.

Cue: ...*falling inside*. water teems down over crockery
Cue: ...*shape and dimension*. Splashing in the kitchen sink. John sits at his kitchen table, soaked. Rain falls around him. Blurry droplets bounce from every surface as he holds his cup of tea.
Cue: ...*addressed by a world*. Framed again in the doorway, in close-up - now in longshot from the end of the garden, our view of John expands.
Cue: ...*it is beautiful to know* a close-up of the cassette recorder. The depressed record button springs up. Darkness

4.6.2 Notes on Blindness

The AD for this clip is unusual in that it describes not only the action but also, on occasion, the camerawork. The filmmakers for *Notes on Blindness* were particularly concerned that people should be aware of the way their film was constructed. This is not the usual approach to audio description: usually, the camera POV and type of shot are ignored. Describing camerawork will be discussed in more detail in Chapter 10. The description for this particular film was written in collaboration with the filmmakers; it is an example of accessible filmmaking (Romero-Fresco, 2013). You may wonder why or whether blind people are interested in camerawork. This will also be addressed in Chapter 10. For now, we have a chance to find out more about what the users are hoping AD will provide.

4.7 What do AD users want from AD?

Many blind people value AD not only in order to follow the plot but also as a means of social inclusion. Here are some comments from AD users with a variety of sight characteristics:

50 *The audience for audio description*

> I want to try and get as close as I can to what a sighted person would experience when they go to the theatre, so I want to be able to experience [the actors'] actions and the movements and the looks and all the things that, as a blind person, I don't get. The best way of putting it is listening to other people laugh and not knowing why they're laughing. Because . . . it's quite an isolating experience to kind of hear other people laughing and to be thinking what's going on, why are you laughing? It might be that if I knew, I might not find it funny but it's just knowing that something is happening that's having an effect on everybody else but I'm out of that experience.
>
> (Male, aged 30, blind from 5 years old)

> I am a firm believer that blind people suffer from visual illiteracy – that is, when sighted people gather and discuss a movie, TV programme, or even a media image, they share the knowledge of what the thing looks like, with all the data points that image knowledge contains. I, as a blind man, lack this essential data, so I am at a disadvantage in this discussion.
>
> (Male, aged 60, who lost his sight in later life)

How important is it that the image built from a description matches what sighted people see? This is one partially sighted person's opinion:

> Most educated people around the world I suppose, or certainly the western world, would have an instant picture in their minds if you said 'Big Ben' to them. So I would like an accurate picture in my mind – everybody knows what it looks like, or at least there's probably a common perception of how it looks . . . maybe in reality close up it's grubby or smaller than perceived, or bigger, or crumbling or something? So I want to share in the common perception.

In addition to social inclusion, AD also aids comprehension, which in turn leads to increased independence:

> The AD added so much more and let me know that previously I hadn't really been understanding what was happening.

> The AD saves having to ask questions about what is happening.

> It is so good to be able to understand the programme and have a laugh at the right time and not to have to wait for someone to explain the joke or ask what everyone else is laughing at.

As John Hull expresses it, 'Cognition is beautiful, it is beautiful to know'.

4.8 Conclusion

This chapter shows another paradox at the heart of AD – that even though the audience is heterogeneous, describers are expected to create a 'one-size fits all' description. Unlike other areas of translation, there is rarely an opportunity for multiple versions in AVT. The challenge for the describer is to create a target text that satisfies most of the audience, most of the time. This will inevitably involve compromise whereby some information must be sacrificed. The coming chapters offer strategies to minimise this as much as possible.

4.9 Exercises and points for discussion

1. Find some examples from AV media where the auditory and visual information streams are incongruent, for example a person who says they are happy to see someone when their facial expression or body posture suggests the opposite, or an inside location accompanied by an external soundscape. How would that affect what and where you might describe?
2. Why do you think AD is important?
3. What have you learnt about blindness that you didn't know before?
4. What can audio describers use as cues?

4.10 Suggested reading

If you would like to know more about the lived experience of blindness, the following are recommended:

J. M. Hull, *On sight and insight: a journey into the world of blindness*. Oxford: Oneworld, 1997.
S. Kuusisto, *Planet of the blind*. New York: Delta, 2013.
G. Kleege, *Sight unseen*. Newhaven, CT: Yale University Press, 1999.
B. Magee and M. Milligan, *On blindness: letters between Bryan Magee and Martin Milligan*. Oxford: Oxford University Press, 1995.

References

Bertelsen, P. and B. de Gelder (2004). The psychology of multimodal perception'. In Charles Spence and Jon Driver (eds) *Crossmodal space and crossmodal action*. Oxford and New York: Oxford University Press, pp. 141–117.
Biocca, F. (1997). 'The cyborg's dilemma: embodiment in virtual environments'. *Journal of Computer-Mediated Communication* 3, no. 2. Retrieved from http://onlinelibrary.wiley.com/doi/10.1111/j.1083–6101.1997.tb00070.x/full#ss6 [accessed 11.08.15].
Bistricky, S. L., R. E. Ingram and R. A. Atchley (2011). 'Facial affect processing and depression susceptibility: cognitive biases and cognitive neuroscience'. *Psychological Bulletin* 137, no. 6: 998.
Cattaneo, Z. and T. Vecchi (2011). *Blind vision*. Cambridge, MA: MIT Press.
Crossman, A. R. and D. Neary (2014). *Neuroanatomy: an illustrated colour text*. London: Elsevier Health Sciences.
Fryer, L. (2010). 'Audio description as audio drama: a practitioner's point of view'. *Perspectives: Studies in Translatology* 18, no. 3: 205–213.
Gibson, James J. (1979). *The ecological approach to visual perception* (3rd edn, 1986). Boston: Houghton Mifflin

Gysbers, A., C. Klimmt, T. Hartmann, A. Nosper and P. Vorderer (2004). 'Exploring the book problem: text design, mental representations of space, and spatial presence in readers'. Presented at *PRESENCE 2004 – 7th Annual International Workshop on Presence 13–15 October, Valencia, Spain.* Available from http://astro.temple.edu/~lombard/ISPR/Proceedings/2004/Gysbers,%20Klimmt,%20Hartmann,%20 Nosper,%20Vorderer.pdf.

HSCIC (Health and Social Care Information Centre) (2014). 'Registered Blind and Partially Sighted People Year Ending 31st March 2014, England'. Report retrieved from www.hscic.gov.uk/catalogue/PUB14798/regi-blin-part-sigh-eng-14-rep.pdf [accessed 25.08.15].

Kleege, G. (1999). *Sight unseen*. New Haven, CT: Yale University Press.

Minshull, D. (producer) (2011, 28 February). Tracy Chevalier (writer/presenter), 'Listener, they wore it'. BBC Radio 3, *The Essay*. London: BBC. Retrieved from www.bbc.co.uk/programmes/b00xnbjw [accessed 23.08.15].

Ofcom (2015). Code on Provision of Access Services. Retrieved from http://stakeholders.ofcom.org.uk/binaries/broadcast/other-codes/tv-access-services-2015.pdf [accessed 29.07.15].

Orero, P. and Vilaró, A. (2014). *Secondary elements in audio description*. Amsterdam: John Benjamins.

Palmer, Keith T., Robin A. F. Cox and Ian Brown (2007). *Fitness for work: the medical aspects*. Oxford: Oxford University Press.

Petrilli, Susan and Augusto Ponzio (2013). 'Modelling, dialogism and the functional cycle: biosemiotic and philosophical insights'. *Sign Systems Studies* 41, no. 1: 93–115.

Piety, P. (2004). 'The language system of audio description: an investigation as a discursive process'. *Journal of Visual Impairment and Blindness* 98, no. 8: 453–469.

Pinchbeck, Daniel M. and Brett Stevens (2005). 'Presence, narrative and schemata'. In *Proceedings of the 8th Annual International Workshop on Presence, London, 21–23 September*. London: University College London, pp. 221–226.

RNIB (online) https://help.rnib.org.uk/help/newly-diagnosed-registration/registering-sight-loss/statistics.

Romero-Fresco, Pablo (2013). 'Accessible filmmaking: joining the dots between audio-visual translation, accessibility and filmmaking'. *Jostrans – The Journal of Specialised Translation* 20: 201–223.

Schank, R. C. and R. Abelson (1977). *Scripts, goals, plans, and understanding*. Hillsdale, NJ: Psychology Press.

Slater, M. (2002). 'Presence and the sixth sense'. *Presence: Teleoperators and Virtual Environments* 11, no. 4: 435–439.

Snyder, J. (2014). *The visual made verbal: a comprehensive training manual and guide to the history and applications of audio description*. Arlington, VA: American Council for the Blind.

Sutcliffe, T. (2000). *Watching*. London: Faber & Faber.

Whitehead, J. (2005). 'TV Trends'. RNIB internal report (August).

Film references

Millions, D. Boyle (2004).
Notes on Blindness, P. Middleton and J. Spinney (2014).

Psycho, A. Hitchcock (1960).
Schindler's List, S. Spielberg (1993).

Reference to live event

Translations, dir. J. Grieve (2014). Arts Theatre Cambridge. AD by VocalEyes (describer, Ruth James).

5 Audio description skills
Writing

5.1 Introduction

Arma cites Lehmann (1998), pointing out that 'AD texts are not spoken or written, they stand in between spoken-spoken texts (spontaneous, non-planned conversation) and written-written texts (formal, planned written texts)' (Arma, 2012: 42). This chapter discusses the language of description, concentrating on its oral nature, using as examples the scripts for the AD to *Notes on Blindness* and an AD created for *The First Action Movie* (Byrnes, 2014), describing an early black and white movie, *A Daring Daylight Burglary* (Mottershaw, 1903). As mentioned in Chapter 1, although radio descriptions have more in common with the AD of visual art than with dynamic AD, the AD for *A Daring Daylight Burglary* was timed to synchronise with the changing shots of the film as well as to capture the camera POV, to give the radio audience an impression of the visual style as well as the narrative of this early silent movie. The current chapter also draws on the description of the dance piece *Like Rabbits* (see Appendix 2), performed at London's Almeida Theatre (Duke and Kirkwood, 2013). It discusses the linguistic style that has become the AD norm and focuses on word choice as well as what to describe and how much detail to include.

It may seem self-evident but, unlike subtitling, the look and layout of the text in AD is less important than the way it sounds and flows. As with an AI (see Chapter 8), the language used by the describer 'should suit the language and tone of the [ST] and be appropriate for its intended target audience, i.e. [an AD] for a Shakespeare production could be more complex than the [AD] for a children's cartoon' (adapted from Fryer and Romero-Fresco, 2014: 24). Otherwise, blind people say, the atmosphere of a production can be lost. Canadian researchers John Patrick Udo and Deborah Fels (2009) took this idea to an extreme by writing the AD for a production of *Hamlet* in iambic pentameter and having the describer take on the character of Hamlet's friend Horatio. This was an example of what Agnieszka Szarkowska and Anna Jankowska (n.d.) call 'auteur description', which is discussed in Chapter 10. Most AD uses colloquial speech as its standard means of communication, with all the contractions that implies. Not only does saying 'there's' rather than 'there is' sound less stilted, replicating the informal type of AD that BPS people are used to from a friend or family member, but it is also more economical, taking less time.

One of the first and still perhaps the most useful analyses of language use in AD is 'The language system of audio description: an investigation as a discursive process', by Philip Piety (2004), based on his analysis of a corpus of American-described films. The article by Julian Bourne and Catalina Jiménez Hurtado (2007) comparing English and Spanish ADs for the same film, *The Hours* (Daldry, 2003), is also illuminating, revealing not only linguistic differences between English and Spanish description but also a difference in approach to the AD itself, with the English AD offering a much more detailed description. Saveria Arma (2012) has attempted to do the same for Italian in her article, '"Why can't you wear black shoes like the other mothers?" Preliminary investigation on the Italian language of audio description'.

Piety (2004: 11) observes that the language used in audio description 'can be seen as having four distinctive structural components – insertions, utterances, representations, and words'. In common with everyday speech, AD does not always use complete sentences. For example, when announcing a change of location, a describer might simply say 'The pub', using particular emphasis in the voice, or 'In the pub', rather than spelling out 'The action moves to the pub'. The reason for this, apart from accepted practice and the describer's maxim 'less is more', is usually timing constraints. Piety defines an insertion as 'a contiguous stretch of description that is uninterrupted by other significant audio content, such as dialogue'. An insertion can be very short, lasting only a few seconds, or much longer, lasting several minutes. The mean length of insertions in his corpus was 11.09 seconds, with several insertions in one film (*Gladiator*, Scott, 2000) lasting over four minutes. According to AD norms, four minutes seems unusually long, perhaps because Piety uses 'insertion' to cover longer sequences of description punctuated by sound effects such as a fight or a battle sequence. For the purposes of the software used for scripting and recording screen AD, such lengthy insertions are usually split to make multiple shorter utterances, with the SFX audible in between. The reasons for this are explained in more detail in Chapter 6. These divisions would be evident only from the written script; they would be inaudible to the ear.

5.2 The *What* of AD

Insertion is distinct from utterance, which, according to Piety, 'is the unit of language that is actually spoken', which may also be of varying lengths. Utterance is a useful term as it creates a way to distinguish between the complete description and a small constituent part. Its use has been adopted in this book. Piety's use of the term 'representation' 'was inspired by a definition coined by Halliday (1985) to describe functional grammar that includes processes, participants, and circumstances. Representations in this study were categorized into a taxonomy that includes seven types of information' (2004: 11). These information types can be defined as the *What* of AD. Piety (2004: 11–12) lists them as:

56 *Audio description skills: writing*

1 Appearance: the external appearance of a person, place, or thing.
2 Action: something in motion or changing.
3 Position: the location of description or of characters.
4 Reading: written or understood information that is literally read, summarised, or paraphrased.
5 Indexical: an indication of who is speaking or what is making some sound.
6 Viewpoint: relating to text-level information and the viewer as viewer.
7 State: not always visible information, but known to the describer and conveyed in response to visual information.

This last point (7) is in contravention of most current guidelines that require the describer not to add information drawn from their personal knowledge and not to interpret the visual information, but to restrict themselves to what is shown on screen. Piety's exact meaning is unclear, however, and (7) might refer to motivational or emotional state. This is also discouraged in AD guidelines, but will be returned to in a discussion of describing facial expression in Chapter 13. It has been contravened in *Like Rabbits* with the phrase 'itching to touch'. One strategy is to preface such a phrase with 'as if', to make clear that this is an inference and not a literal observation.

Some, notably the American, guidelines suggest that when it comes to the *What* of AD you simply say what you see, for which they have coined the acronym What You See Is What You Say (WYSIWYS). This is too simplistic. Gibson noted that 'however skilled an explicator one may become one will always, I believe, see more than one can say' (Gibson, 1979: 261). Gibson distinguished between visually apprehended *qualities*, such as colour, texture, size, shape, rigidity and mass and *affordances*, i.e. what an object allows us to do with it. Just as the meaning of a text may be unstable, so too might be what an object affords. A stiletto might be a glamorous shoe that affords height and elegance to its wearer, but held in the hand, it might become a weapon affording the opportunity to strike at an assailant. If the heel breaks, it may become a liability, hindering a victim's escape. Given limited time for your descriptive utterance, the aspect of the stiletto emphasised in your description should depend on what it affords. In a fashion show or when modelled by a glamorous heroine, importance might be given to the colour of the shoe. If the heroine is to become 'prey' you might emphasise her vulnerability by describing the height of the heel. In a murder scenario, it may be more important to describe the sharpness of the spike.

Point 6 of Piety's list (Viewpoint: relating to text-level information and the viewer as viewer) is also discouraged in theory, but, as his corpus shows, viewpoint is described in practice. This is discussed as an element of camerawork explored in Chapter 10.

There are other restrictions to Piety's point 7 (State: not always visible information, but known to the describer and conveyed in response to visual information). The make of a car or the identity of a famous building or type of weapon would be known, noticed and mentioned by some describers but not by others. You could argue that the utterance 'James Bond climbs into an Aston Martin' relies on specialist knowledge but is acceptable because it is visually presented information and obvious to any sighted viewer who is familiar with the appearance of the car or who can read the small font on the winged logo on the bonnet. It may also be deemed relevant or necessary, as it explains the speed of Bond's getaway and adds to our understanding of Bond's character as an English gentleman, as well as specifying what is in vision. José Dávila-Montes and Pilar Orero (2014) discuss at length the significance of mentioning brand names, arguing that naming the brand liberates the describer from having to characterise the precise appearance of an object, as the brand name brings with it the user's own knowledge of it, or experience of using it. They explain that 'the object has managed to inject into a common, shared (and not necessarily visual) iconography' (Dávila-Montes and Orero, 2014: 101). For example, naming the stolen painting in the Shanghai scene in another Bond film, *Skyfall* (Mendes, 2012) as a Modigliani is relevant more in the sense that it implies an artwork of high value rather than because the name of the artist will help blind people to 'visualise' the image in their mind's eye. In fact there is little evidence to suggest that that is how BPS people use AD. A sample of sixteen BPS people (Fryer, 2013) were asked whether, when listening to AD, they built up an image in their mind 'always', 'sometimes' or 'never'. The results are shown in Table 5.1. On a practical note, for describers who are not car enthusiasts, the website ICMDB.org (Internet Movie Cars Database) is extraordinarily useful.

Two of the sixteen participants in the study were congenitally blind (CB) both of whom, unsurprisingly, reported never building up an image. Perhaps more surprising is the fact that the seven Late Blind or adventitiously blind participants (AB) were more or less evenly divided in their responses ('always' 2/7, 'sometimes' 2/7 or 'never' 3/7), despite all having had sight at some stage. Less surprisingly, perhaps, partially sighted (PS) participants showed a greater tendency towards building an image: 'always' (3/7), 'sometimes' (3/7) or 'never' (1/7). One AB man said:

> When I go to an audio described [performance] . . . do I imagine it as a visual thing? No I don't think I do, but then I don't imagine a visual world that much anyway except when somebody asks me to do it . . . by which I mean that I can see you sitting there but what I'm seeing is your voice . . . my seeing, in that sense, is making inferences from the sense data I've got, it's not making visual images in my head . . . So if I don't visualise it, what do I think is happening? I'm imagining action . . . I make inferences from the dialogue, from the sound of the actors.
>
> (Fryer, 2013: 85–86)

Table 5.1 Number of respondents by sight status in response to the question: 'Do you build up an image in your mind?'

Sight status	Never	Sometimes	Always	Total
Congenitally blind	2	0	0	2
Adventitiously blind	3	2	2	7
Partially sighted	1	3	3	7
Total	6	5	5	16

58 *Audio description skills: writing*

Also addressing the *What* of AD, Marzà Ibañez (2010: 147) lists the following:

1   What to describe:

   a   Images

      i   Where: setting, spatial relations between characters, movement of characters
      ii When: film time
      iii What: action
      iv Who: physical description, facial and corporal expressions, clothing, occupation and roles
      v   How: lighting, decor, attitudes.

   b   Sounds: difficultly identifiable sounds, song lyrics, languages other than the source language.
   c   On-screen text: logos, opening titles and credits, cast lists, text on signs, subtitles.

As there are complex issues worthy of elaboration around all of these requirements, they will be encountered again as this book unfolds. However, the list is included here to be referred to as a tool when preparing one's description. While the elements on the list are perfectly acceptable, some concerns perhaps surround the order in which the items are presented. The visual nature of an AV text means that generally the spatio-temporal setting is noticed first (the *When/Where*) followed by *Who* is in the scene, *What* they are doing and *How* they are doing it. As the *When/Where* may be identified by a caption – possibly on-screen text – that comes last in Marzà Ibañez's list, this may in fact need to be the first that is mentioned.

5.3 Word choice

5.3.1 Need to know versus nice to know: narration and description

Dávila-Montes and Orero (2014) distinguish between two modes of AD: narration and description. The narration sets the scene in terms of characters and location (the *Who*, *What*, *Where*, *When* or preferably the *When*, *Where*, *Who*, *What*); the description fills in visual detail (essentially, the *How*). While the narrative elements are essential to allow blind people 'to keep up with the action' (RNIB, 2011: 5) it is these narrative elements that the UK ADA identifies as 'need to know', whereas the descriptive elements are more likely to come under the heading of 'nice to know'.

The question arises: how detailed does a description need to be? This question lies at the heart of AD. In Chapter 4, it is argued that a more general description might lead to an increased sense of presence. However, finding the precise word that encapsulates all the aspects of the object or action described is critical to economy of expression, for which AD strives. It is why Snyder (2014) believes AD is an art that is akin to poetry. The British academic and travel writer, Robert Macfarlane (2015), warns against being:

blasé, in the sense [of] meaning 'indifferent to the distinction between things.' To quote the American farmer and essayist Wendell Berry . . . 'people exploit what they have merely concluded to be of value, but they defend what they love, and to defend what we love we need a particularising language, for we love what we particularly know.'

In case this sounds a bit pretentious in relation to AD, here is a less-than-cerebral example. In the first few minutes of the first episode of the American TV series *Breaking Bad* (2008), the main character, Walt, is encountered driving a recreational vehicle (RV) wearing nothing except what can only be described as his underpants. Let us consider some other possible nouns. Pants is accurate and shorter but would be ambiguous in the American context, where it means trousers. An American is more likely to call them 'briefs' or 'tighty whities'. Briefs is too feminine in UK English usage. Tighty whities captures the humour but not the baggy appearance of this particular pair. Underwear is too vague, as it might also include a vest. Boxers is simply inaccurate. Y-fronts is a possibility, but the archaic connotation of underpants captures the nature of Walt's undergarment, which is intended to be unprepossessing and indicative of Walt's 'less-than-cool' middle-aged character. These nuances might present challenges for the translation of the AD as a strategy for creating AD scripts, as advocated by Jankowska (2015) and implemented by some AD companies. The noun, once chosen, could be supplemented by an adjective (white, grubby, baggy and saggy all spring to mind), but you need to ask yourself how much this adds to the image or to our understanding. There is always a balance to be maintained between giving enough information and overloading the user. Economy is the aim. Novice describers often try to describe too much. Arma points out that in 'Italian AD the idea of RAI [Italy's national broadcaster] is that audio description should use "essential, simple and clear terminology, so as to leave suitable room for personal interpretation and emotional involvement"' (Arma, 2012: 39). It should be assumed that by this she means personal interpretation and emotional involvement on the part of the user, *not* the describer.

Lack of specificity might at times be a positive strategy; for example, when a character or object is seen in long-shot and their identity (especially gender) is deliberately hidden, a term such as 'figure' allows a character to stay gender neutral, until such time as they are fully revealed to the sighted audience.

In another example from *Breaking Bad*, there are frequent shots in Series 2 of what appears to be an eyeball, or possibly a lychee, floating in a swimming pool. It is eventually revealed to be the eyeball of a pink teddy bear, part of the detritus from a plane crash that Walt has inadvertently caused. It is an example of what Dávila-Montes and Orero (2014: 98) describe as 'visual links between consecutive scenes or as anaphoric/cataphoric references in the relation of scenes that are chronologically distant within movies'. Given that the object's exact nature is not revealed until several episodes later, it is challenging for the describer to come up with appropriate terminology. AD users need to be able to 'recognise' the eyeball from episode to episode without its portent being weakened from knowing for sure that it is not human. By stating that it is a glass (or more likely plastic) eye, or even, more specifically, a teddy bear's eyeball, some of the power of the image is lost. It is probably best to acknowledge the ambiguity of the image by explicitly describing it as 'a mysterious eyeball' or by leaving it more ambiguously as 'a gleaming white orb' (this especially leaves its size open to question). Omission is always an option, but would appear to defeat the object of description. As the blind translator Frederic Grellier (2015) put it, 'translation and blindness are both about loss'. Although Jakobsen reminds us that 'the richer the context of a message, the smaller the loss of information' (Jakobsen, 2012: 116).

In the interest of brevity and economy, the use of adverbs is generally discouraged. The idea behind this is that it is better to choose a verb that captures the manner of the action in a single word, rather than choose a less vivid verb which then needs to be qualified. As always, there are exceptions: in *The Mottershaw Burglary* the describer says, '[in] an angle of rooftop – by the chimney – the Burglar steps *nimbly* across uneven tiles'. Although it may be possible to find a synonym for the verb *steps* that simultaneously implies nimbleness, somehow the adverb *nimbly* implies a certain degree of affectation, suggesting that the burglar is deliberately showing off his sure-footed agility. The intention is to contrast humorously with the leaden-footed progress of the policeman. We are aware that the burglar is leading the policeman a merry dance. Choosing the right verb is important. Snyder (2014) urges describers to develop their powers of observation. I would instead advocate that describers should reflect the casual observation of the average member of the sighted audience but develop their writing skills and grasp of language so as to be able to convey that visual information effectively.

The search for the perfect word can be taken too far. In an episode of the American sitcom *Friends*, one character, Phoebe, collapses with exhaustion onto a sofa; again, there is a studied deliberateness to her action. A new describer thought for a long time before coming up with the phrase 'Phoebe suspires onto the sofa'. There was no question that the verb correctly captured the melodramatic nature of Phoebe's action, however the word 'suspires' is so rarely used that its meaning is not immediately obvious. This risks the AD user taking a few moments to process it and missing the next bit of the programme while doing so. It is also out of keeping with the informal and contemporary language of the series.

Adjectives similarly should be used with caution, in particular a long string of them, as this means the listener is constantly forced to revise the image they may (or may not) be building in their mind's eye. The description for *Notes on Blindness* comes close to saturation point with the description of John's appearance at 09: 18: 'In his 40s, bearded, wearing glasses, John opens the door.' Here the guidelines were nearly broken because it was the first opportunity to include any description of John's appearance, although we have already spent nine minutes in his company. Cámara and Espasa (2011: 419) point out that the Spanish guidelines (AENOR, 2005: 8) advocate 'the use of concrete versus vague adjectives and of specific terminology'. Salway (2007), in his corpus-based study of ninety-one audio described films, observed this in practice, as concrete nouns appeared with surprising frequency, compared with in everyday speech. However, specific terminology may require explicitation. To return to the opening of *Breaking Bad*, Walt drives the RV through the desert of New Mexico, past impressive, 'flat-topped' rock formations. The correct term for this type of formation is 'mesa'. Spanish-speaking audiences are less likely to need any further explanation, as mesa means table and the rock-formation is indeed table shaped. For an English-speaking audience, apart from those familiar with the area, this compound adjective is probably more helpful than the technically 'correct' term.

Bourne points out that a useful feature of the English language is that it allows compound adjectives to be invented freely, allowing more condensed information to be inserted than may be possible in a language other than English. He gives the examples 'sun-dappled', 'snub-nosed' and 'gold-edged' (Bourne and Jiménez Hurtado, 2007: 180). The AD for *Like Rabbits* includes 'skin-tight' and even coins a compound verb 'hand-walks' for a style of locomotion the mechanics of which have been described in detail: 'He steps over her, raises her onto her knees and vaults, his feet hook on her shoulders; his weight on his hands. She steps forwards on her knees, he – hand-walking with her – a curious single beast.'

5.3.2 Cultural references

The previous examples fall into the category of 'describing and naming', which is one of the strategies proposed by Maszerowska and Mangiron (2014: 164) for dealing with cultural references. Describing and naming is a form of 'amplification' that may also be used to provide a fuller description of those movements for which we have no vocabulary. Agnieszka Szarkowska and Anna Jankowska (n.d.) call this strategy 'naming plus explicitation', but also offer 'omission' and 'explicitation without naming' as alternative strategies in their discussion of ways of dealing with 'extra-linguistic cultural references' in relation to describing foreign films. Within the field of AVT, specifically subtitling, Pedersen (2005: 2) defines a culture-bound reference as one 'which is assumed to have a discourse referent that is identifiable to a relevant audience as this referent is within the encyclopaedic knowledge of this audience'. In the James Bond example given above, 'Aston Martin' would count as such a reference, carrying with it an assumption that any British audience member would be aware of it as an expensive type of sports car. Describing it simply as a sports car would come under Pedersen's strategy of generalisation. Naming with explicitation is a common norm in UK AD.

Although their article discusses the AD of foreign films, Szarkowska and Jankowska argue that it may equally apply to any kind of linguistic reference with which the AD audience may be thought to be unfamiliar. Such references occur in *Joining the Dots* (Romero-Fresco, 2013) when Trevor refers to going to 'Charing Cross' and 'Moorfields', which are London hospitals, the latter specifically an eye hospital. The description for this film does not attempt to assist the AD user, as the information is purely verbal and is as accessible (or otherwise) to someone with a visual impairment as to any other member of the audience. *Like Rabbits* uses the expression 'jazz hands' to express hands held palms up, fingers splayed and possibly shaking, but adds an explanatory 'spread in a clownish greeting', in case the jazz move is unfamiliar. This offers a fifth possibility of naming and simultaneous generalisation, the explicitation achieved by means of a synonymous but more general reference. It has the advantage of providing multiple viewpoints that allow the users to make up their own minds, and the disadvantage of requiring more time to think.

Szarkowska and Pedersen both acknowledge the possibility of the explicitation strategy's being considered patronising, which is something describers should be keen to avoid. As Jan-Louis Kruger expresses it, 'Creating AD . . . is like walking a tightrope. On the one hand we would like the blind audience to share in the enjoyment of decoding a narrative – not patronising them by interpreting the scene for them. On the other hand (also in the context of the severe time constraints forced upon the mode), we have to provide sufficient information or enough relevant cues for the audience not to be left confused or unable to make sense of what they hear' (Kruger, 2012: 71). For Taylor (2014), whether or not to add explanation hinges on the likely knowledge of the rest of the audience (as in the mesa example above). In the case of *Like Rabbits* there is an assumption that the audience for a dance piece is more likely to be familiar with standard dance moves than is the audience for a straight play.

5.3.3 Ambiguity

Equally to be avoided, or at least used with care, are homonyms – words that have different meanings but sound the same. For example, a character picking up a file may be about to produce a document, manicure their nails or smooth a piece of metal or wood. The meaning is usually apparent from the context – for example, whether we are in an office, a beauty parlour or a workshop. But it can be easy to cause confusion. The term for a small glass bottle used to contain medicine is a 'vial', but this could be misheard as file or vile – a *file* of poison would sound distinctly odd, although, by providing context, the addition of the words 'of poison' might clarify the word as 'vial' for the listener. The transition from written script to oral delivery makes it easy for a describer to fall into the trap posed by homonyms. In a production of *Bakkhai* at London's Almeida Theatre (2015), the followers of the god wore what they described as 'fawn-skins', as did the god himself. Unfortunately, the word can easily be misheard. The descriptive phrase 'He plucks at his fawn-skin' was substituted by 'He plucks at his deer-skin', to avoid inappropriate sniggering. Ambiguous descriptions should also be avoided. A young girl could be aged anywhere between four and twenty-four. It is better to specify an age: 'a seven-year-old girl' 'a young woman in her twenties', rather than leave your audience wondering. Better still to give some corroborating visual evidence where appropriate: 'a seven-year-old girl missing her two front teeth'. Access to this type of information can be an advantage of working closely with the creative team, discussed further in Chapter 10.

In addition to individual word choice, phrases also need to be carefully selected if ambiguity is to be avoided. For example 'X helps her out' – might mean the character provides assistance, or ushers her from the room. One of the pitfalls for a student when creating an AD is that images tend to be described in isolation, without regard to the overall flow, sequence and juxtaposition of words. An unfortunate example of juxtaposition comes from the AD of *The History Boys* at Great Britain's National Theatre (Hytner, 2004). Hector, a flamboyant, inspirational but wayward teacher, is coaching a group of boys in French by encouraging them to act out a scene that they choose to set in a brothel. A door in the back wall of the classroom setting is open, giving the audience a view down the corridor along which the headmaster is approaching. Hector has his back to the door and is unaware of the head's imminent arrival. One of the pupils, Posner, who has recently come out as gay, is acting the part of a prostitute. The describer accurately said: 'Posner drops his trousers. [brief pause]. The head enters from behind.' Given the context and juxtaposition, the describer conveyed a more compromising image than he intended. However, this was spotted at the dry run and excised before the AD performance. The review process is outlined in Chapter 6. Although it varies from one provider to another, in general it takes the form of peer review, ideally with some input from BPS users.

5.3.4 Pronouns

Pronouns are another potential source of ambiguity. Although the AD script is intended to interact with the soundtrack (Braun describes it as 'non-autonomous' (2007: 359), it should also have enough internal coherence to stand alone (Taylor, 2014). It can be a good test when you write your own description to read through your AD script aloud to see if it reads like a story, with a smooth, coherent flow. The use of pronouns illustrates this. For example, unless there is only one male character, 'he' will be deemed by the user to refer to the last person mentioned in the AD, rather than, as new describers often assume, the last person heard to speak in the dialogue. A description should avoid raising more questions than it answers.

Pronouns, while useful in English, being monosyllabic and therefore short, can be safely used, without risking confusion, only when a single person or just one of that gender features in the action. Proper nouns tend to be used with greater frequency in AD than in other discourses. The AD for *Like Rabbits* benefits from the piece's having only two dancers – one of each gender. Although the man is named by the woman during the piece, the describer continues to use pronouns. This helps to blur the distinction between human dancer and rabbit character, just as the physicality and costumes of the dancers resulted in a visual ambiguity.

5.3.5 Tense

You may have noticed, from the clips you have watched or the scripts you have read so far, that description uses the present tense and generally avoids time-related constructs such as 'first' 'afterwards' and 'subsequently'. Piety points out (2004: 26):

64   *Audio description skills: writing*

> While most language use deals with information that is not present at the time of speaking, including past and future events and possible conditions (Chafe, 1994), the language used in audio description relates only to what is actually occurring on the screen at the time or close to the time . . . So, unless they are part of something that is included in a representation of reading [by which he means reading aloud on-screen text; see Chapter 8], there should be no words indicating conditions, past or future states, or any number of other valid language constructs that do not reflect the immediate reporting required for audio description.

The word 'now' is generally unnecessary, given that the aim of description is to keep the user apprised of what is happening. Novelty can be implied through the stress and intonation of delivery, which is addressed in Chapter 7. The ITC Guidance (ITC, 2000: 3.2) states: '"Now . . . " can indicate a change of scene: "Now on the stairs . . . ", "Now outside . . . ", but it should not be overused.' I would suggest it is rarely if ever necessary.

In this example, from *Notes on Blindness*, each change of scene is implied, rather than explicitly indicated by the word 'now'.

> 00.34 John, blurred, in an ultrasound clinic, a foetus pictured on the monitor

Here is the same script extract again. This time 'now' has been inserted, but the meaning is left unchanged:

> when did you get blind?
>
> 00.34 John, **now** blurred, in an ultrasound clinic, a foetus pictured on the monitor

The only contrary instance I can think of is if a character suddenly changes their appearance. For example, in *Oresteia* (Icke, 2015) Agamemnon undresses in the bathroom, visible through a glass wall, while action is happening simultaneously in the dining room in front of it. When the focus returned to the bathroom, it was appropriate to say 'Agamemnon, now naked, climbs into the bath', implying that his ongoing action was completed and bringing the AD users up to date with his current state of undress.

According to the training manual of the UK Audio Description Association, AD should resemble a football commentary, rather than a post-match report. We have already acknowledged the importance of keeping the AD user in the moment. Using the past tense is thought to remind people of not only of what they have missed, but also of the fact that they have missed it. Even in the case of a flashback, once this effect has been established, usually by explicitly saying 'In flashback' or similar, use of the present tense continues. In English AD, the simple present and the continuous present are both frequently employed. The simple present is used for one-off actions (e.g. 'John's fingers find the buttons on a cassette recorder and press record'); the continuous present is often used in the form of a modifier or participle to convey actions that are ongoing (e.g. 'John, cradling an infant'). This usage is clearly more economical than 'John is cradling an infant and he . . . '. Commonly, AD adopts a third-person perspective. Arma notes that 'Audio description makes consistent use of the third person but usually opts for active instead of passive forms' (Arma, 2012: 42). The examples used in this book often describe from the perspective of the first person plural (e.g. 'He turns to face us', rather than 'He turns to face the audience'). Although this is rarely encountered in screen AD, it is a style that has evolved to become the norm in theatre description in the UK. It is considered more immersive and inclusive, such that the users are more likely to feel themselves to be members of the same audience as their sighted peers, thereby increasing their sense of social inclusion. This assumption has yet to be tested.

As Piety noticed, at times verbs are not used at all. The mention of a character's name is enough to imply he is in vision, e.g.: '00.34 John, blurred, in an ultrasound clinic, a foetus pictured on the monitor'. The verb has been omitted for reasons of timing, but also because his movement is non-specific. He is simply there. John 'sits' would be an accurate and acceptable alternative, if time allowed. However, it feels a bit prosaic and, like 'now', can be omitted without loss of meaning.

5.3.6 Articles

While some aspects of grammar in English may be unnecessary, correct observance of others is crucial for clarity of meaning. In particular, the use of definite or indefinite articles is important. According to one congenitally blind AD user:

> There are several faults that audio describers have and they're entirely to do with them having sight. They will say, for instance, 'the man gives her the watch'; now I might be entirely ignorant of the fact that a watch is part of the scenery. They should say the man gives her *a* watch, unless the watch has been mentioned before. What this means to me is that they've seen the watch before and so they are treating it as though it were not a new object, whereas to me it is. If someone says to me a man gives her *the* watch it implies some significance in the watch, which it may or may not have in the plot. I think where an audio describer uses the definite article, the piece of equipment should have been mentioned previously and that's a common fault.

You may notice that a definite article was used before 'monitor' in the previous example. The justification here is that an ultrasound clinic would necessarily contain a monitor. Simply by introducing the location with its associated schema, the describer can be excused from having to itemise all the concomitant paraphernalia the location evokes. This leads us back to the Assumption of Normality, as discussed in Chapter 3. In addition to continuity, it can be used as a rule of thumb for what to describe. For example, we assume that someone would wear a tie around their neck. Only if the tie were worn somewhere unexpected – for example, being used as a belt – would it be worth specifying the location of the tie. The assumption of normality can help make AD more economical. As noted by Orero (2008), describers are expected to observe the four Gricean maxims of quality (say the truth); relation (be relevant); manner (be clear) and quantity (make your contribution as informative as is required, but not more, or less, than is required).

5.4 Sound symbolism

Jespersen (1954: 396) defines sound symbolism as 'a natural correspondence between sound and sense'. Such words are also referred to as iconic, reflecting instances of a visual correspondence rather than an aural one. Although not all sounds are naturally symbolic, the idea has long attracted the interest of psychologists. As Fryer, Freeman and Pring (2014) point out, since the 1920s researchers studying sighted populations have demonstrated a correspondence between words and shapes. Fryer, Freeman and Pring (2014: 164) explain:

> In experiments by Köhler (1929, 1947) English-speaking adults consistently matched the nonsense words 'Maluma' and 'Takete' with outline images of a rounded shape and a jagged, star-like shape respectively ... Ramachandran and Hubbard (2001), using 'Bouba' and 'Kiki', found a 95% correspondence rate between image-shape and word-choice.

Surprisingly Fryer, Freeman and Pring's research using 2-D cut-outs and 3-D shapes instead of line drawings to represent 'Bouba' and 'Kiki' found that 'People with a visual impairment who had residual vision or had had some visual experience also associated sharp/jagged shapes with Kiki and rounded/smooth shapes with Bouba at a level higher than chance, although the effect was significantly less strong than in their fully sighted peers.' This would suggest that onomatopoeia might not be as useful a strategy as describers might expect, although this needs to be tested further, as in a smaller study (Crowley and Fryer, 2015), onomatopoeia was found to be effective for describing comedy. The phrase 'Wobbling, she wibbles to the sofa' was used to capture one character's style of movement in the farcical *The Play that Goes Wrong* (Mischief Theatre, 2014).

5.4.1 Rhythm and rhyme

The way in which AD utterances are constructed should echo the rhythm of the existing soundtrack, otherwise the AD will sound incongruous, potentially breaking any sense of presence. For instance, the choice of word order in this utterance 'John stands with his son by the ship's rail – the little boy's hand clasped in his' could equally be rendered 'John stands with his son by the ship's rail – clasping the little boy's hand'. The describer's choice perhaps reflects the fact that we do not see the action of clasping, only that the hand is already clasped. If you read both examples out loud – and, incidentally, all description should be prepared in this way – you may find that the noun 'hand' retains a residual rhyme with the verb 'stand', which feels inappropriate and, by drawing the ear's attention, is potentially distracting. By contrast, sound symbolism can be used positively to enhance the AD; for example, in *Notes on Blindness* the action of the rain is echoed in the rhythm of the phrases used to describe it: 'Blurry droplets bounce from every surface as he holds his cup of tea.' The alliteration of the repeated 'b' sound makes the lips spring and bounce in the manner of the rain. The sequence of monosyllables that follows conveys the impression of the final, stuttering bounces as the drops complete their fall. Similarly with 'waves swell and ebb as night falls', the outbreath necessitated by the word 'falls' means that the words peter out along with the light.

This similarity between AD and poetry is likely to reach its peak in AD of dance and the visual arts (Fryer, 2009), reflecting the abstract mode of the information source, which I would term kinaesthetic rather than purely visual. In the AD of the dance piece *Like Rabbits* (2013) the describer uses the device of a transferred epithet – 'Cups his neck in his hand rolling a lazy shoulder, elbow lifted' – to convey the easy, relaxed nature of a dancer's movement. Using the adjective *lazy* as opposed to the adverb *lazily* is quicker and is also easier to say than 'rolling his shoulder lazily'. Care should be taken to avoid writing tongue twisters. It is easy for the tongue to stumble over the syllables of *lazily*, especially after the liquid phonemes in *rolling* and *shoulder*. The dance piece was based on 'Lappin and Lapinova', a short story by Virginia Woolf (1938), in which a new bride takes refuge from the social expectations arising from her marriage by imagining herself and her new husband to be rabbits, living wild. In order to immerse the AD user in that world, the describer uses verbs of animal movement for the human dancers who lope, bound, leap and nestle. Much of the movement was explicitly sexual. The AD uses language more commonly associated with animal mating, rather than human sexual intercourse: 'her hind legs clamped around him in a tight ball; she nuzzles down his chest, to his crotch . . . he scrabbles down her back . . . nibbles her neck . . . a tangle of urgent limbs, haunch against flank, forepaws scrabbling, teeth biting . . . he noses at her soft underside, pulls her up onto his chest, her rump level with his shoulder, his face buried between her hind legs'. In this way, as advocated by Taylor (2014), the AD is both intertextually cohesive and cohesive with the visual content it describes. One blind attendee reported: 'I very much liked the Audio Describer's word choice. It felt like a good fit for the piece.'

Rhyming was successfully used in the description of *A Taste of Honey* at the National Theatre of Great Britain (Sheibani, 2014). The lead character, Helen, is a feisty minx of a single mother, determined to catch a new man. At one point she rushes into the bedroom, hips wiggling seductively, as she knows the man she fancies is watching her, prompting the sighted audience to laugh. The describer, Andrew Holland, captured this moment with the following phrase: 'she makes a feline beeline for the bedroom.' The words, as delightful and fun as the action on stage, were designed to prompt a similar response from AD users as from the sighted audience.

5.5 Sight-specific references

5.5.1 Verbs of vision

You will notice that there is no need to begin each new utterance with words such as 'we see': as with 'now', such words and phrases are redundant. It is evident that we see something, otherwise the describer would not bother to mention it. Similarly, the use of the phrase 'X *appears*' on stage is not only unnecessary but also brings with it the possibility of a sudden, magical appearance, as of a ghost or a pantomime fairy. The manner in which they enter (strides in, marches in, scuttles in, etc.) is almost certainly more indicative of the character's role in the action, relationship with the other characters or state of mind. Certainly in live performance, clarifying the spot from which a character makes their entrance 'bursts through the door', 'skips down the stairs', 'clambers over the windowsill' can help an AD user with some degree of residual vision work out which part of the stage picture to focus on. Verbs referring to vision need not be avoided out of sensitivity. Indeed Andrew Salway's (2007) analysis of a corpus of British English AD products showed that verbs such as look, gaze and peer, denoting a character's focus of attention, occurred with significantly greater frequency than in general language. This is probably related to close-ups on looks and reaction shots in screen drama and may say more about the nature of film discourse than about AD. It could be argued that the use of visual references in AD is akin to the more general translation challenge referred to under the umbrella of cultural references, mentioned above. Other visual references of which congenitally blind people have no direct experience will include light and colour, but lack of experience does not necessarily mean they will not want to hear about it. As one congenitally blind man expressed it, 'I'm entirely fascinated by light and I love to hear talk of what light looks like and colours of fireworks and I love it all. But it doesn't bother me because I can't see it, I just love hearing about it.'

Anna Maszerowska (2013) identifies three functions of light in film: first, light can indicate the passing of time; second, it shapes our perceptions of people, objects and spaces; and third, it can focus our attention on particular parts of the screen or stage in an automatic processing manner known as 'bottom up', as opposed to a voluntarily directed 'top down' manner, where we seek out what to look at based on our own interests. Citing Brown (1996: 12), Maszerowska (2013: para. 8) says 'luminance is even credited with psychological values. Its colour can trigger emotional responses in the audience, so that, for instance, orange surfaces are associated with heat while blue spaces evoke a sensation of cold. Put differently, "[t]he filmmaker can present a story in such a way that it provides affectively charged reactions, and these affectively charged sensations are suggestive of, and may elicit, human moods."'

5.5.2 Colour

Whether to mention colour is a question often raised by new students of AD. There is a simple answer: yes, mention of colour is encouraged (certainly by the UK guidelines), as it has not only visual qualities but also cultural/emotional connotations, referred to above, of which most BPS people will be aware, having previously had sight. Even the minority who have never seen are, as Piety puts it 'members of the same speech communities as are sighted persons' (Piety, 2004: 29). In some senses they are more so, as explication plays a larger part in blind people's everyday lives than for sighted people, as discussed in Chapter 3. This means that they will share knowledge of the cultural implications of colour. In the UK, red, for example, tends to imply passion, danger and heat; green suggests youth and freshness or that something or someone is environmentally friendly. However, the French Charter on AD proposes that colours only be mentioned when they can be qualified or amplified by an adjective, ideally one that alludes to another sense. A shade may be a cool blue or petrol blue or sea blue or midnight blue. The choice should be dictated by context as much as by shade. However, it is worth remembering that cultural associations of colour change across space and time; for example, black in contemporary Western societies is associated with mourning, but Aslam reminds us, 'the social dress code of Renaissance considered black, purple and scarlet as mourning colours and the modern distinction of purple and red was alien in those times' (Aslam, 2005: 1). Arma points out that one distinction between Italian and English ADs for the same film (*Chocolat*, Hallstrom, 2000) is that the Italian AD does not mention the colour of the roses Serge brings, while the English version tells us they are pink and red. In fact, she notes, 'The Italian script seems less concerned with colour details and their semantic frequency and importance throughout the text' (Arma, 2012: 50).

Other aspects of appearance likewise need to stay true to the cultural environment of the fictional world of which they are a part. In the AD for *Wig Out!* (Tarell Alvin and McCraney, 2008), one character, Loki, was initially described as being dressed as a Goth, so, in order to establish coherence and continuity his top in the Cinderella Ball in the second act could better have been described as resembling cobweb rather than lace; although the character in Norse mythology for which Loki was named is often shown with a fishing net, so *net* could also have been appropriate for the description. Metaphors were used to capture spatial relationships between characters such as 'a planet to her sun', and Lucien was described as 'the meat in the men's sandwich'. Metaphors can help to convey a vivid image or humorous juxtaposition. In *Like Rabbits* we have 'an Odalisque in a pink rabbit suit'. As we have seen, AD favours the concrete over the abstract. Salway (2007) found that many of the top 100 words in his frequency analysis of AD films were 'concrete nouns and verbs that refer to material processes'. This is not surprising, as abstractions are difficult to observe, largely falling into Piety's point 7. Metaphors can be used to bridge the gap. Feng and O'Halloran suggest that the function of a metaphor 'is to construe abstract concepts in terms of concrete ones' (Feng and O'Halloran, 2012: 2069). Metaphors are more powerful, being more direct than similes, and usually require less time to say. In the above example a simile would require extra words: 'she's like an Odalisque in a pink rabbit suit'. Arguably, a simile flags up the description as an interpretation, suggesting room for doubt; a metaphor brooks no discussion. This may or may not be considered a good thing, with speed of delivery set against potential for confusion and objectivity set against subjectivity.

5.6 Creative use of language

5.6.1 Repetition

While novelty and creativity are to be encouraged in an AD script, as we have noted, unusual words or images are harder to process and potentially more distracting. Repetition can be an irritating source of redundancy, or part of the creative writer's armoury and deliberately employed. In *Like Rabbits* 'He pulls her into a *squat*. He *squats*, facing her', the use of squat as both a noun and a verb captures their mirrored movement. In particular, a repeated action sequence or a location revisited can be conjured by repeating much of the original description, perhaps précised the second time. In *Like Rabbits* change of word order provided variation on a theme: 'she dives over him, and ducks under, as he ducks then dives'. However, repeated use of the same word can also become wearisome. In one AD unit in London, the scripting software (see Chapter 6) has been configured to reject the word 'walk' in order to avoid repetition and to force the describer to be more imaginative in their selection of a verb of locomotion. As Kemmerer and his colleagues (2013) note, there are approximately 125 verbs of locomotion in English, so there are plenty to choose from.

5.6.2 Structure, word order, literary constructions

In the interests of brevity and clarity, complex literary constructs such as 'former' and 'latter', subclauses and long, looping sentences using parentheses are best avoided. Another observation from Arma (2012: 45) is that while there are 'few secondary clauses in the English script, the Italian one is characterised by many embedded secondary clauses, mostly noun phrases or temporal/causal clauses, typical of the Italian written language. In written language, the adjectival position before the noun stands for a more creative and free use of the language.'

Short conjunctions such as 'as' and 'while' are useful for conveying simultaneous actions, for example, 'As she rolls herself a cigarette, a young man spots her from the back of the space'. The positioning of 'As' is deliberate. To render that sentence 'She rolls herself a cigarette, as a young man spots her from the back of the space' could imply that she rolled the cigarette *because* he spotted her. The 'As' also implies that he spots her while she is in the act of rolling, such that the rolling and the spotting are happening at the same time, with the further implication that he is watching her.

5.6.3 Punctuation

Just as with grammar, in the written AD script liberties are often taken with punctuation. This is mostly to assist vocal delivery and will be discussed in more detail in Chapters 6 and 7.

5.7 Cues and notes

Cues have been included in parentheses throughout the text for *Like Rabbits*. Some of these are auditory (verbal/musical), others are visual; this being a dance piece, there is minimal dialogue. The describer has also included notes to herself, adding question marks either where elements vary from one performance to another or where she may be unsure of what is happening. It is a reminder to watch closely at those points, rather than to keep one's head buried in the script. One of the skills of live description is the ability to shift one's gaze constantly between the stage and the script, and for this reason the layout of the script is more important in live AD than for recorded media, where the software is designed to keep the relevant part of the script always in the centre of your visual field. Ellipses have been used to suggest places to pause, to ensure that the AD keeps in synchrony with the action. Ellipses also suggest points where the music should take precedence. Notes may also be helpful to remind the describer or inform the voice talent of any unusual pronunciations.

5.8 Conclusion

AD has its own mode of discourse that interacts with and is influenced by the language of the script in the ST, but otherwise diverges from most modes of narrative discourse, using the present tense and short sentences. Word choice and word order are critical to create AD that is economical yet vivid. When writing a script the describer must always bear in mind the oral nature of its delivery, with its inherent dangers of juxtaposition, ambiguity and tongue twisters.

5.9 Exercises and points for discussion

1. Flesh out the skeleton script you created in Chapter 3 by writing the AD. If you feel you do not have sufficient command of English, you may prefer to write the AD in your mother tongue and translate it into English, if required, ensuring that it still fits in the 'gaps'. Alternatively, transcribe any AD that is commercially available and translate that script into your preferred language. Start by describing in detail and then trim the words so that they will fit the available gap. This can be done in two ways, either by removing the elements that are 'nice to know' or by finding more economical ways to express what you have written, keeping the content unchanged. For example, 'He sits with his head in his hands' can more economically be expressed 'He sits – head in hands'.
2. Critically assess the AD as you transcribe it. Is there anything in terms of describer choices, including word choice, that you would change? If so, why? How effectively does the language of the AD convey the source programme?
3. What are the challenges of translating an AD script from your mother tongue into English? How does the translation of an AV text differ from that of any other text?
4. Should AD be restricted to native speakers? Is there any evidence that the native language of a describer has an impact on the quality of the description? Try this exercise in pairs, such that one person argues for a restriction, the other opposes it. To inform your debate, you may wish to refer to the following book: Nike K. Pokorn, *Challenging the traditional axioms: translation into a non-mother tongue*. Benjamins Translation Library, vol. 62. Amsterdam: John Benjamins, 2005.

References

Arma, Saveria (2012). '"Why can't you wear black shoes like the other mothers?" Preliminary investigation on the Italian language of audio description'. In Elisa Perego (ed.) *Emerging topics in translation: audio description*. Trieste: Edizioni Università di Trieste, pp. 37–55.

Aslam, Mubeen M. (2005). 'Are you selling the right colour? A cross-cultural review of colour as a marketing cue'. *Journal of Marketing Communications* 12, no. 1: 15–30.

Bourne, J. and C. Jiménez Hurtado (2007). 'From the visual to the verbal in two languages: a contrastive analysis of the audio description of *The Hours* in English and Spanish'. In Díaz Cintas Jorge, Orero Pilar and Aline Remael (eds) *Media for all: approaches to translation studies*. Amsterdam: Rodopi, pp. 175–188.

Braun, Sabine (2007). 'Audio description from a discourse perspective: a socially relevant framework for research and training'. *Linguistica Antverpiensia, New Series – Themes in Translation Studies* 6: 357–369.

Brown, Blain (1996). *Motion picture and video lighting*. Revised and updated edn. Boston: Focal Press.

Byrnes, Frances (producer) (2004). *The First Action Movie*. BBC Radio 4. Rockethouse Productions. Retrieved from www.bbc.co.uk/programmes/b041vvw0 [accessed 22.07.15].

Cámara, Lidia and Eva Espasa (2011). 'The audio description of scientific multimedia'. *The Translator* 17, no. 2: 415–437.

Crowley, Bridget and Louise Fryer (2015). 'The Laughter Lines Project Report'. Retrieved from http://audiodescription.co.uk/uploads/general/Laughter_Lines_Project_Report 29.pdf [accessed 23.09.15].

Dávila-Montes, J. and P. Orero (2014). 'Strategies for the audio description of brand names'. *Cultus* 7: 96–108.

Feng, Dezheng and Kay L. O'Halloran (2012). 'Representing emotive meaning in visual images: a social semiotic approach'. *Journal of Pragmatics* 44, no. 14: 2067–2084.

Fryer, L. (2009). *Talking dance: the audio describer's guide to dance in theatre*. Apt Description Series, 3. Place: Audio Description Association, ISBN 978-0-9560306-2-7.

Fryer, L. (2013). 'Putting it into words: the impact of visual impairment on perception, experience and presence'. Doctoral thesis, Goldsmiths, University of London: Goldsmiths Research Online.

Fryer, Louise and Pablo Romero-Fresco (2014). 'Audiointroductions'. In Anna Maszerowska, Anna Matamala and Pilar Orero (eds) *Audio description: new perspectives illustrated*. Amsterdam: John Benjamins, pp. 9–28.

Fryer, Louise, Jonathan Freeman and Linda Pring (2014). 'Touching words is not enough: how visual experience influences haptic–auditory associations in the "Bouba–Kiki" effect'. *Cognition* 132, no. 2: 164–173.

Gibson, James J. (1979). *The ecological approach to visual perception* (3rd edn, 1986). Boston: Houghton Mifflin.

Grellier, F. (2015). Talk given as part of the creative writers round table, at *Blind Creations Conference*, Royal Holloway, London, 29 June.

Halliday, M.A.K. (1985). *Introduction to functional grammar*. London: Arnold.

ITC (2000). ITC Guidance. Retrieved from www.ofcom.org.uk/static/archive/itc/itc_publications/codes_guidance/audio_descripion/index.asp.html [accessed 4.04.15].

Jakobsen, Roman (2012). 'On linguistic aspects of translation'. In Lawrence Venuti (ed.) *The translation studies reader*. London: Routledge, pp. 113–117.

Jankowska, Anna (2015). 'Translating audio description scripts: translation as a new strategy of creating audio description'. In Anna Mrzyglodzka and Anna Chociej (eds) *Text – meaning – context: Cracow studies in English language, literature and culture* vol. 12. New York: Peter Lang.

Jespersen, O. (1954). *A modern English grammar on historical principles, Part VII*. London: George Allen & Unwin.

Kemmerer, David, Luke Miller, Megan K. MacPherson, Jessica Huber and Daniel Tranel (2013). 'An investigation of semantic similarity judgments about action and non-action verbs in Parkinson's disease: implications for the embodied cognition framework'. *Frontiers in Human Neuroscience*, doi: 10.3389/fnhum.2013.00146

Kruger, Jan-Louis (2012). 'Making meaning in AVT: eye tracking and viewer construction of narrative'. *Perspectives* 20, no. 1: 67–86.

Lehmann, C. (1988). 'Towards a typology of clause linkage'. In J. Haiman and S. Thompson (eds) *Clause combining in grammar and discourse*. Amsterdam and Philadelphia: Benjamins.

Macfarlane, Robert (2015). 'The word hoard'. *Guardian*. Retrieved from www.theguardian.com/books/2015/feb/27/robert-macfarlane-word-hoard-rewilding-landscape [accessed 1.03.2015].

Marzà Ibañez, A. (2010). 'Evaluation criteria and film narrative: a frame to teaching relevance in audio description'. *Perspectives: Studies in Translatology* 18, no. 3: 143–153.

Maszerowska, Anna (2013). 'Language without words: light and contrast in audio description'. *Journal of Specialised Translation* 20: 165–180.

Maszerowska, Anna and Carme Mangiron (2014). 'Strategies for dealing with cultural references in audio description'. In Anna Maszerowska, Anna Matamala and Pilar Orero (eds) *Audio description: new perspectives illustrated*. Amsterdam: John Benjamins, pp. 159–178.

Orero, Pilar (2008). 'Three different receptions of the same film: "The Pear Stories Project" applied to audio description 1'. *European Journal of English Studies* 12, no. 2: 179–193.

Pedersen, Jan (2005). 'How is culture rendered in subtitles?' In *MuTra 2005 – Challenges of Multidimensional Translation: Conference Proceedings*. Retrieved from www.euroconferences.info/proceedings/ 2005_Proceedings/2005_Pedersen_Jan.pdf [accessed 24.12.15].

Piety, P. (2004). 'The language system of audio description: an investigation as a discursive process'. *Journal of Visual Impairment and Blindness* 98, no. 8: 453–469.

RNIB (2011). 'International AD exchange study: observations from a focus group study'. Retrieved from http://audiodescription.co.uk/uploads/general/RNIB._International_AD_Exchange_Report4.pdf [accessed 27.08.15].

Salway, Andrew (2007). 'A corpus-based analysis of audio description'. In Pilar Orero and Aline Remael (eds) *Media for all: subtitling for the deaf, audio description, and sign language*. Approaches to Translation Studies, vol. 30. Amsterdam: Rodopi, pp. 151–174.

Snyder, J. (2014). *The visual made verbal: a comprehensive training manual and guide to the history and applications of audio description*. Arlington, VA: American Council for the Blind.

Szarkowska, Agnieszka and Anna Jankowska (n.d.). 'Audio describing foreign films'. *Journal of Specialised Translation*, 23. Retrieved from www.jostrans.org/issue23/art_szarkowska.php [accessed 29.08.15]

Taylor, Christopher (2014). 'Intertextuality'. In Anna Maszerowska, Anna Matamala and Pilar Orero (eds) *Audio description: new perspectives illustrated*. Amsterdam: John Benjamins, pp. 29–40.

Udo, J. P. and D. I. Fels (2009). '"Suit the action to the word, the word to the action": An unconventional approach to describing Shakespeare's Hamlet'. *Journal of Visual Impairment and Blindness* 103, no. 3: 178–183.

Woolf, Virginia (1939). 'Lappin and Lapinova'. *Harper's Bazaar*.

Film references

A Daring Daylight Burglary, F. Mottershaw (1908).
Chocolat, L. Hallstrom (2000).
Gladiator, R. Scott (2000).
Joining the Dots, P. Romero-Fresco (2013).
Skyfall, S. Mendes (2012).
The Hours, S. Daldry (2003).

References to live events

A Taste of Honey, dir. B. Sheibani (2014). National Theatre of Great Britain, London. AD by in-house team (describers Louise Fryer and Andrew Holland.)

Bakkhai, dir. J. MacDonald (2015). Almeida Theatre, London. AD by VocalEyes (describers Roz Chalmers and Louise Fryer).

Like Rabbits, dirs B. Duke and L. Kirkwood (Lost Dog Productions http://lostdogdance.co.uk/) (2013). Almeida Theatre, London (describer Louise Fryer).

The Play that Goes Wrong, dir. M. Bell (Mischief Theatre, www.mischieftheatre.co.uk/) (2014). The Duchess Theatre, London. AD by VocalEyes (describers Roz Chalmers and Ruth James).

Wig Out! dir. D. Cooke (2008). Royal Court, London. AD by VocalEyes (describers Jane Brambley and Roz Chalmers).

The History Boys, dir. N. Hytner (2004). National Theatre of Great Britain, London. AD by in-house team (describers Louise Fryer and Andrew Holland.)

Oresteia (a new version of Aeschylus' original, created by Robert Icke), dir. R. Icke (2013). Almeida Theatre, London. AD by VocalEyes (describers Louise Fryer and Veronika Hyks).

Reference to TV programme

Breaking Bad, V. Gilligan et al. (2008–13).

6 Audio description skills
Script preparation

6.1 Introduction

This chapter is more didactic as the book moves away from the theoretical and towards the practical. Having discussed what to say and the words with which you say it, the chapter looks at ways to create your script both for screen AD and for live settings such as theatre. In a commercial setting, recording is expensive. It is cheaper to spend time ensuring that the script is accurate, well presented and easy to read to than to risk necessitating retakes. In live scenarios where there is no possibility of retakes, a clear and easy-to-read script is arguably more important. Common scripting errors are listed in section 6.4, giving you a framework against which to check scripts. The process of script development is outlined for both live and recorded AD as is the process followed by an AD user who is attending a live performance.

6.2 Screen software

Commercial AD units create script templates using bespoke software, currently available from two main providers: Starfish Technologies and Softel (Swift Adept). Licences for both packages can be expensive, but there is also freely accessible software such as LiveDescribe and YouDescribe that can be downloaded from the internet (see 6.2.4).

6.2.1 How it works

The software programs may vary in specifics, but tend to work along similar lines. The scripting software has a dedicated window allowing you to view the source programme at the same time as the window in which you write your script. Using timecode, you create a new scripting 'box' within the scripting 'window' for each AD utterance that you are about to write. All the elements can be moved around your desktop and resized as you wish. It can be a good idea to full-screen the source programme the first time you watch, so that you do not overlook any fine details. Near the viewing window the timecode is prominently displayed in hours: minutes: seconds: frames. Hitting a specific function key as the video runs will automatically open a new scripting 'box' capturing the timecode at that instant, which will be displayed in the scripting window. This is your 'In time', i.e. when your new AD utterance begins. At this point, one technique is to type what you want to say, then speak it aloud while running the source programme beneath it, checking the accuracy and duration of what you have written. Then hit a specific function key that will capture the 'Out time'. The 'Out time' will also be displayed. Some people prefer to delay the writing part and simply create a skeleton of blank 'boxes', creating a new one at each 'gap' in the soundtrack ready for the AD script to be added later, once the whole ST has been watched. Precision is needed, although both In and Out times can be amended manually later on, by over-typing or by repeating the 'enter time In/Out process'. Another key will allow you to advance or rewind the source programme by one or two seconds, to save you having to run through again from the beginning. In the more sophisticated, commercial programs you can also configure the software to select which key to use for this. Hitting the 'Out time' will automatically create a new 'box' below the first one and in this way your AD script will develop. However, as the new 'box' will have an 'In time' that has been automatically generated it is unlikely to be in the right place and you will almost certainly need to change it. Pressing the 'In time' key again will overwrite the previous 'In time'. Beware: this is easily done by accident!

The software will also automatically calculate the duration of the 'window' or 'box' you have created and the duration between this and the previous utterance, and will flag up an error message if you are trying to create two utterances too close together. In the early days, when you are learning description, it is good to take note of the automatic warnings. You can rectify the problem by changing the timecode so as to alter the place where you have inserted your description. Later you may choose to disregard some of the warnings, although this can be dangerous if you are not in a position to understand why you are doing so. The minimum duration between descriptions can also be set in the preferences menu. Usually a minimum of at least one second is recommended, as the software can also fade down the volume level of the source programme, allowing the description to be heard more clearly over the top; two sudden dips close together have the consequence of the background soundtrack disappearing, then popping back up, only to be quickly reduced again, creating a stuttering effect, which is not a pleasant listening experience. The *level* of the fade dictates the extent to which the soundtrack is suppressed, while the *shape* of the fade determines whether it is gentle or abrupt, at the beginning and end. The more gentle the fade, the smoother the listening experience will be, but you may prefer an abrupt fade so as to allow a particular sound effect to be heard, especially if your description is 'tight', i.e. will only just fit into the time allocated. If necessary you can resolve this by editing your script to make the word use more economical. Where two descriptions are too close together you may want to merge them into a single 'box'. Usually a combination of keystrokes will achieve this, preserving the In time of the first 'box' and the Out time of the second. Alternatively, if you need to hear a bit of dialogue or SFX in the middle of your utterance, you may choose to split your utterance into two separate boxes (again, a function key may split a description into two at the position of your cursor).

6.2.2 Timecode

You will have gathered by now that timecode plays a critical role in tying your description to the source programme. Ultimately, timecode is used to lock your recorded description to the source programme, so that the AD will always be broadcast in the right place. Occasionally, a broadcaster will re-edit its programme – perhaps to remove a contentious scene or a rude word if a programme is rescheduled to be broadcast before the watershed. In the UK this is set at 9pm. Material deemed to be harmful to children may not be shown before this time, or after 5.30am. Ofcom deems such material to include violence, graphic or distressing imagery and swearing. AD of this content type will be discussed in Chapter 11. It is vital that the programme provider advises the describer of any programme edits, otherwise there will be a danger that all the recorded description that comes after the edit point will come in the wrong place.

The software will also calculate automatically the duration of your description, meaning both what you have written and the duration of your description 'box' (the gap between the 'In time' and the 'Out time'). It will alert you if there is a problem, for example if you have written more words than the software calculates will fit in between the two timecodes you have entered, or not enough. Obviously, how much you can fit in will depend on how fast you are speaking. In the preferences section of commercial software packages you can specify your reading speed in words per minute (WPM).

6.2.3 Speech rate

In the next chapter we will see how important it is to be able to vary your pace, so you may need to override the default settings for WPM. Emma Rodero (2012) has explored speech rates in radio news because 'radio is the art of communicating meaning at first hearing' (Rodero, 2012: 391). She cites Pimsleur et al. (1977), who recorded a delivery rate of between 160 and 190 WPM for English and French radio news broadcasters, although 'in Spanish radio news . . . a high speech rate, of around 200 wpm, is used on all national radio stations' (Rodero, 2012: 393). Studies show that word comprehension by the listener seriously declines only at speeds over 250 WPM (Foulke, 1968). More recently, Uglova and Shevchenko (2005) noted that televised speech in US news programmes is approximately 200 WPM, although, as we have seen, speech comprehension is enhanced by access to the visuals, so radio provides a better analogy. In 2007 Anja Moos and Jürgen Trouvain showed that blind people could comprehend synthesised speech at much faster levels than sighted people, with comprehension declining only above speeds of 17 syllables per second (s/s), as compared with 9 s/s for their sighted peers. Given that there are, on average, 1.5 syllables per word, this equates to 680 WPM for blind people, as compared with 360 WPM for their sighted peers, although the authors point out that 'It is unclear how temporally compressed natural speech can be understood by the two groups' (Moos and Trouvain, 2007: 667). Snyder (2005) advises that description should be delivered at 160 WPM. However, there is a danger of speaking too slowly. Rodero points out: 'A presentation that unfolds at a slow pace can lead to it being difficult to maintain attention effectively (Berlyne, 1960) and can result in weakened comprehension (Mastropieri et al., 1999), because an increase in the flow of information can raise attention and learning (LaBarbera and MacLachlan, 1979).' Rather than aiming for a specific speed, let your pace be dictated by the pace of the scene you are describing.

It should be obvious that writing too much is a problem: either your description risks being clipped or cut short by the automatic software because the microphone ceases to be live as soon as the 'Out time' is reached; or your speech rate will need to be so fast that it becomes incomprehensible. Less obviously, for screen AD it is also problematic to write too little for any given duration. This is because it leads to the volume of the soundtrack being unnecessarily suppressed beyond your descriptive utterance, leading to a frustrating listening experience. This can be corrected if necessary by reducing the 'Out time' after the recording. In live AD, you should avoid leaving the microphone 'open' when you are not speaking, as it adversely affects the sound in the user's headset and may pick up extraneous sounds such as coughing or paper rustling. A microphone opened too early is likely to pick up the describer's in-breath, although the change in ambient sound may have a positive effect of cuing the user to attend to the AD. The describer must speak as soon as the microphone is fully open, if the user is to have that expectation satisfied. A checklist for common recording errors is included below (see section 6.4).

To check whether or not your description will fit within the duration and position you have allocated, commercial software has a 'rehearse' mode. This will automatically restart the programme a certain number of seconds before the 'In time' and play only that portion of the programme until the entered 'Out time'. Again, the amount of cue programme you hear (pre-roll) before the 'In time' can be set in the preferences window, as can the length of time it continues beyond the 'Out time' (post-roll). It may be tempting to make the pre-roll very short, in order to save time. However, the person who will read your script will benefit from hearing a longer passage of cue programme so that they deliver the script with the appropriate pace and inflection. You may need to experiment, but five to ten seconds is probably enough. Rehearse mode also triggers a feature otherwise available only in record mode, namely a visible countdown to the 'In time'. It is usually both numerical and graphic, showing a green thermometer that shrinks, turning red as the seconds tick away, the 'In time' is reached and the microphone (in record mode only) automatically becomes live. The specific description 'box' will be highlighted and centred within the script window to help you quickly find the right place in your script. A description 'box' that contains a very long utterance is likely to hide some of the text, requiring you to scroll down within it. If this is the case, split the box into two or more as necessary, with either no fade or a continuous fade level from one box to the next.

6.2.4 Creating the script

You should type your script paying attention to punctuation and capitalisation so as to ensure that it will be easy to read because, as pointed out in Chapter 1, it may need to be read by someone other than yourself. Although you may create your own idiosyncratic punctuation using dashes and ellipses to indicate the length of a pause, these markings may not mean much to somebody else. As the voice talent may also be unfamiliar with the source programme it may be useful to include pronunciation advice, particularly for character names or locations. There may be an in-house phonetic system you can use, or you may need to develop your own showing where the stress falls and how certain phonemes are pronounced. It is important that, however you show it, the pronunciation is consistent with the way a name is pronounced in the film. The phonetically written name is best either inserted in square brackets next to the actual name or used throughout instead of the correct spelling of the name, so as to avoid breaking the flow of the delivery. It may be tempting to take typing shortcuts such as leaving out capitalisations or the full stops in an abbreviation such as US. This is not a problem if the context is clear. However, you need to ensure that the reader does not say 'us', i.e. the first person plural, by mistake. Although they would probably soon realise their error, it might cause them to hesitate or stumble and, as a result, their recording time might increase in order to retake the phrase or sentence. Recording fluency is also why verbal cues can be helpful in addition to relying on the timecode 'thermometer'. Often one of the function keys can be allocated to a cue font which will ensure that the text of the AD utterance is visually distinctive from the cue. It also prevents the cue being included in the word count, which might lead to your utterance apparently exceeding the WPM rate you have set in the preferences. As pointed out in Chapter 5, you are writing words to be spoken, so contractions that are common in conversation are encouraged – for example: 'he's' rather than 'he is' – and should be written that way, with an apostrophe. If necessary, you can write your script in any word-processing package and then copy and paste it into the relevant 'boxes'. Frequent use of the 'save' command is recommended. By the end of the process, your AD script will be available as an .esf file. This can be converted to an .rtf file and exported complete with timecode information, if desired.

6.2.5 Freely available software

In order to increase the amount of AD content available and accessible to users, the Inclusive Media and Design Centre at Canada's Ryerson University has developed a free software package, LiveDescribe. According to its website, LiveDescribe is a 'stand-alone application that allows amateur audio describers to edit audio descriptions for blind audiences'. It is a Windows-based application that can be downloaded for free. One word of caution: the software automatically identifies 'gaps' in the soundtrack where AD can be inserted. It is preferable to identify your own gaps, as the 'gap' may be inappropriate. Piety (2004) suggests that utterances 'are strung together to fill the space between dialogue' – but just because there is a 'gap' does not mean that you have to fill it.

Another free facility is called You Describe (youdescribe.org). It has been created by the Smith-Kettlewell Video Description Research and Development

Center (VDRDC) at the Smith-Kettlewell Eye Research Institute in San Francisco, California, with the aim of encouraging the general public to create audio-described content (or described video content, to use the American term) for YouTube. If you watch any of the videos described by this method you will notice that the image is simply paused for the duration of the description. This means that the description is not integrated with the soundtrack and the describer is always required to post-describe. Although this acceptable for the purpose for which it was designed, it is a major limitation if you wish to master the art of AD. This 'pause for description' method is similar to that used in the production of the early typhlofilms (films for the blind) which were produced for the blind by Andrzej Woch in Poland in the 1990s (Jankowska, 2015) before current AD norms were adopted. Apart from the danger of destroying any sense of presence and increasing the total duration of a film, this method also prevents blind and sighted audiences from being able to attend the same screening.

6.3 Live scripting strategies

6.3.1 By hand

In the UK, describers working in the theatre until recently would always be given a paper script to which they would add their description in pencil (so it could easily be amended if necessary). In order to accommodate this, ideally, scripts were printed double-spaced and on one side of the page only. Even so, in scenes with lots of action but little dialogue describers would need to add in large arrows pointing to the back of the facing page or wherever there was enough space to write a description, or include the AD on a separate sheet of paper. Care had to be taken not to create too much extraneous noise from rustling pieces of paper while delivering the AD. Although stage directions in the script may seem to supply the narrative part of the AD text, treat them with caution. It is rare that a director follows the stage directions to the letter, and very unlikely that the directions will fit the timing available for your utterance. The tenor of the words is unlikely to fit the vivid style of your AD script and they will contain bland, generic verbs such as 'enter' and 'exit'. Stage directions are unreliable as to the *What* and generally lacking as to the *How* of the visual information.

6.3.2 Electronic scripts

These days it is more common to be given an electronic script and to read the description from a laptop or a tablet. It is useful to write the AD in a contrasting font so as to make it stand out from the dialogue and the stage directions. It is advisable not to reduce the full script to a series of short cues, as this limits the opportunity to insert your description at a different point if a change in the actor's delivery necessitates this by altering the position of the 'gaps'. The way the script is punctuated can help you to anticipate the likely location of the next suitable pause. The disadvantage of reading a script from a tablet is that the glow from the screen may distract members of the audience or the actors, depending on the location of the description point; the advantage of generating an electronic AD script is that it is silent to use, more legible and can be easily shared with and read by another describer in the event of accident or illness. An added advantage for a touring or long-running production is that the script can be easily updated as the production evolves and, potentially, shared with other describers. In live events such as festivals there may be no script; however, it may be useful to make notes of, for example, performers' names or short descriptive phrases, or even just verbs that have come to you while watching a rehearsal, otherwise you will need to completely improvise your description. While this can heighten the immediacy of your delivery, it may in turn limit your ability to find appropriate places to insert AD. It also risks repetition and lack of succinctness as you struggle to find the right words to express what you want to say. Whereas the position and duration of 'gaps' in recorded material will not change, for live AD you must write your script with the awareness that they almost certainly will. This means that it is safer to begin an utterance with the most important information, leaving details of less important information such as physical appearance, for example, until the end. In this way, if the 'gap' shortens you will be able to stop speaking without depriving your audience of critical information. Rather than 'the King, resplendent in a blue gown, is carried in by his retinue' you might say 'the King's carried in by his retinue, resplendent in a blue gown'. In the worst-case scenario you might just have time to say 'the King'. This will be enough to indicate his arrival, although it may not explain the huffing and puffing sounds made by his servants.

The script for a live performance is generally prepared using a video of the production. This may be taken from the show-relay monitor, used by the performers to watch what is happening on stage. In some theatres in the UK, describers struggle to access a video recording of the production. In this situation you are urged to do all you can to encourage the company or the producer or theatre manager to provide you with one or, at the very least, allow you to record your own. The relationship between describers and theatres in the UK tends to be very informal. However, the ADA can supply a model contract which specifies the right of access to a video. Frequently, the video is of poor quality, shot in lighting levels that are either too low to be able to see the action clearly or so high that they bleach out the picture, making it hard to decipher fine details such as facial expression. In any case, you are encouraged to prepare a draft script and then set up a 'dry run'.

6.4 Common scripting faults

Ana Marzà Ibañez (2010: 150) sensibly notes that in the absence of a clear, unequivocal standard for AD, students of AD need help in evaluating their work. She argues that 'By self-evaluating their descriptions from the very first moment, the students learn to systematize their choices ... '. Table 6.1 is Marzà Ibañez's checklist, which has been augmented with other scripting faults commonly encountered.

Table 6.1 Marking checklist

Abbreviation	Meaning	Definition	Description no.
AMB	Ambiguity	Lack of clarity, often stemming from use of pronouns, poor word order or simple typographical errors.	
GR	Grammar	Syntax and morphology errors.	
NMS	Not making sense	This may result from poor lexical choice, poor descriptive choice, poor grammar or a combination of the above.	
PAT	Patronising	Over-explicitation of extralinguistic or intertextual references that can be deduced from the soundtrack.	
REG	Register	Inconsistencies in field, mode or tenor with respect to the original, for example using contemporary slang when describing a period drama.	
SEM	Semiotics	Unsolved extralinguistic references or cultural implications, unsolved intertextual references.	
TEX	Textual	Lack of coherence, lack of logic, poor use of conjunctions.	
VAG	Vagueness	The use of non-specific vocabulary; inadequacy of the vocabulary for the text being described.	
VOC	Vocabulary	Barbarisms, inappropriate lexical choices.	
Sty	Style	Cacophonies (ugly-sounding, as opposed to euphonious), pleonasms (redundancies), unnecessary repetitions, uneconomic use of words, poor style.	
Sty AD	Style (AD)	Not complying with stylistic norms of AD.	
PRA	Pragmatic and intersemiotic transfer	Inability or omission to convey the intentionality, irony, inferences, presuppositions, implications, illocutionary acts of the text to be described. (N.B. Illocution refers to the implied meaning of a person's words. E.g., if a telephone caller asks "Is John there?" the illocutionary meaning is "Can you fetch John so I can speak to him?" (see Sbisà, 2007).)	

Audio description skills: script preparation 83

SUP	Suppression	Suppression of visual, acoustic or textual information needed to understand the ST, especially setting the scene (plot, time and space) and the characters in the scene. Suppression of relevant thematic connections.
EX	Excess	Diluting the mood of the scene with too much description, covering too much musical information or significant SFX.
TIM	Timing	Descriptions that are over-long for the 'gap' allocated, meaning that they will obscure the dialogue, or descriptions that are too short for the allocated description 'window', meaning that the soundtrack will be suppressed for longer than the duration of the descriptive utterance; or starting one description window too close to the end of the previous one. Descriptions that should have been split or merged.
INC	Inconsistency	Inconsistency in naming and/or pronunciation of characters and places.
STB	Spilling the beans	Giving away plot-sensitive information too early.
AoN	Assumption of Normality	Overlooking the AoN rule by stating the obvious.
CEN	Censorship	Providing a bowdlerised version of explicit sexual or violent action.
TT	Tongue twister	Phrases that are hard to say.
OM	Omission	Failure to answer the narrative questions Who? What? Where? When?

6.5 Exercises

6.5.1 Exercises using software

1. Find out about speech-rate comprehension either in your native language or the native language of your target audience.
2. If you have access to AD software, use it to complete the skeleton script you prepared at the end of Chapter 3. Alternatively, script a short clip of another film of your choice, paying attention to accurate 'In' and 'Out' times and offering

pronunciation advice where necessary. Swap scripts with a partner or colleague and offer a critical review, pointing out any places that caused you confusion and discussing any contentious points pertaining to the description's content. You may wish to refer to the list of common scripting faults in Table 6.1.

6.5.2 Exercises by hand

If you have no access to software, do exercise 2 above using pencil and paper or a normal word-processing package. Develop your own cuing system, to compensate for lack of timecode. If you still feel unready to write your own script in English, transcribe an existing AD. Be prepared to alter it if necessary, and to argue your case for doing so.

6.6 Discussion points

1. What are the pros and cons of working with software?
2. What are the pros and cons of using a paper script versus reading it from a laptop or tablet?
3. What are the pros and cons of LiveDescribe versus YouDescribe versus commercial AD software?

6.7 The process

The way in which a script is developed may vary from one organisation to another. However, the following lists will help you recognise the processes that need to happen, even if the order/personnel changes.

6.7.1 Screen AD

1. Watch the ST.
2. Write the script.
3. Write Check – have your script checked by another describer.
4. Record the script (or have it recorded by another voice).
5. Rec. Check – check the recording (see Chapter 7 and Table 7.1).

6.7.2 Live AD

1. Watch the play and take notes on costumes, characters, sets and visual style.
2. Write the AI (see Chapter 12).
3. Write the script.
4. Dry run, with feedback from at least one other describer, plus ideally an AD user.
5. Adjust the script/AI as necessary.
6. Deliver the AD at the live performance.
7. Gather audience feedback, either directly or via front-of-house staff. Make a note for future performances.

6.7.3 The process for the AD user at live events

1. Book tickets. In the UK, theatres often offer price concessions to people with disabilities: generally tickets are half price or, if you are visually impaired, a free ticket may be provided for a sighted companion. It is important to state that you will be listening to the AD, so that the theatre applies the concession and sends you the AI in advance. You should also ask whether or not there will be a touch tour (see Chapter 3) and book to attend it, if required. This is also the time to state any other requirements you may have, such as seat preference and, if you are intending to bring a guide dog, whether or not you would like the dog to be looked after during the performance. Some theatres are happy for the dog to accompany you into the auditorium, although some performances may not be suitable because, for example, they feature gun shots and smoke effects.
2. Arrive in good time for the touch tour.
3. Collect your headset (some theatres require you to leave a deposit) if these are not distributed at the end of the touch tour. Headset designs can vary, so ask for a short lesson in how it works, if necessary. Most headsets have two channels – one that receives the AD and one that enhances the volume to the show relay. The best headsets allow you to vary the volume of each channel independently. There may be an opportunity to test out your headset to ensure that it is working properly. Ask if there is a system to attract an usher's attention if your headset stops working.
4. Take your seat in the auditorium in good time before the AI begins (usually 15 minutes before curtain up).
5. Enjoy the show!
6. Return the headset at the end of the performance, and pass on any feedback about the AD to the theatre ushers or the theatre's Head of Access. Find out if the theatre has an access mailing list that it can keep you informed of future described performances.

6.8 Conclusion

This chapter has shown that, in both screen and live AD, attention must be paid to the way a script is laid out. Consideration must be given to ease of reading, especially if the writer and reader of the AD are not the same person. Timecode facilitates script creation and synchrony in screen AD. In live AD, scripts must be prepared with some built-in flexibility. The process for creating a script was explained, and a checklist was provided to help spot common scripting errors. The standard sequence of events for those attending an AD performance was outlined.

References

Foulke, Emerson (1968). 'Listening comprehension as a function of word rate'. *Journal of Communication* 18, no. 3: 198–206.

Jankowska, Anna (2015). *Translating audio description scripts: translation as a new strategy of creating audio description*, trans. Anna Mrzyglodzka and Anna Chociej. Frankfurt am Main: Peter Lang.

LiveDescribe (n.d.). Retrieved from https://imdc.ca/ourprojects/livedescribe [accessed 23.09.15].

Marzà Ibañez, A, (2010). 'Evaluation criteria and film narrative: a frame to teaching relevance in audio description'. *Perspectives: Studies in Translatology* 18, no. 3: 143–153.

Moos, Anja, and Jürgen Trouvain (2007). 'Comprehension of ultra-fast speech – blind vs. "normally hearing" persons'. In *Proceedings of the 16th International Congress of Phonetic Sciences*, vol. 1, pp. 677–680. Retrieved from retrieved from: http://www.icphs2007.de/conference/ Papers/1186/1186.pdf.

Piety, P. (2004). 'The language system of audio description: an investigation as a discursive process'. *Journal of Visual Impairment and Blindness*, 98, no. 8: 453–469.

Pimsleur, P., Hancock, C. and Furey, P. (1977). 'Speech rate and listening comprehension'. In M. K. Burt, H. C. Dulay, and M. Finocchiaro (eds) *Viewpoints on English as a second language*, New York: Regents, pp. 27–34.

Rodero, Emma (2012). 'A comparative analysis of speech rate and perception in radio bulletins'. *Text & Talk* 32–3: 391–411.

Sbisà, Marina (2007). 'How to read Austin', *Pragmatics* 17, no. 3: 461.

Snyder, Joel (2005). 'Audio description: the visual made verbal'. *Vision 2005 – Proceedings of the International Congress, 4–7 April 2005, London.* International Congress Series, vol. 1282, pp. 935–939. Elsevier.

Uglova, Natalia, and Tatiana Shevchenko (2005). 'Not so fast please: temporal features in TV speech'. Paper presented at the meeting of the *Acoustical Society of America*, Vancouver, BC.

YouDescribe. http://youdescribe.org.

7 Audio description skills
Delivery

7.1 Introduction

In his book *The Man Who Mistook His Wife for a Hat* (1998), Dr Oliver Sacks uses case studies of people with neurological disorders to reveal how the human brain processes information. He states that 'speech – natural speech – does not consist of words alone . . . It consists of utterance – an uttering-forth of one's whole meaning with one's whole being – the understanding of which involves infinitely more than mere word-recognition . . . spoken language is normally suffused with "tone", embedded in an expressiveness which transcends the verbal' (Sacks, 1998: 85). Sacks reports how a group of people with aphasia sat laughing as they listened to the US President speaking on TV. Aphasics have a disorder of the left temporal lobe of the brain and lose the ability to understand specific words. What they can pick up on is the emotional intention. According to Sacks, blind aphasics in particular 'have an infallible ear for every vocal nuance, the tone, the rhythm, the cadences, the music, the subtlest modulations, inflections, intonations, which can give – or remove – verisimilitude to or from a man's voice' (ibid., 1998: 86–87). What caused them to laugh were the false tones and cadences of the President's voice. As Sacks puts it, it 'was to these . . . most glaring, even grotesque, incongruities and improprieties that my aphasic patients responded, undeceived and undeceivable by words' (ibid., 1998: 87).

7.2 Delivery and prosody

Although Salway (2007: 7) noted that one of the main concerns for best practice amongst describers is 'how to voice audio description appropriately', very little research time has been devoted to the delivery of AD. This is despite the fact that, as Silverman et al. (1992) argue, 'prosody . . . not only accounts for much of the variability in speech signals, but also conveys much of the information that is necessary for recovering the intended meaning of an utterance'. Snyder (2014: 47) agrees: 'we make meaning with our voices.' The supra-linguistic aspects of speech convey meaning through stress, pitch, tempo, dynamic range and, especially, the way the words are segmented, i.e. those momentary pauses and intakes of breath, often indicated by, but not restricted to, those indicated by punctuation. Silverman and her colleagues (1992) define prosody as the 'supra-segmental information in speech, such as phrasing and stress which can alter perceived sentence meaning without changing the segmental identity of the components'. Identifying word boundaries is crucial to understanding. Cutler et al. (1997) cite the example 'of hearing *how big is it? as how bigoted*' (their italics).

7.2.1 Accent, gender and emotion

The way in which words are stressed, inflected and segmented, as well as the sound and length of phonemes, determine accent. Traditionally, UK describers have been encouraged to use a particularly neutral way of speaking known as received pronunciation or RP. Rai et al. (2010: point 5) cite the ITC Guidance (ITC, 2000), which states:

> the delivery should be steady, unobtrusive and impersonal in style, so that the personality and views of the describer do not colour the programme. However it can be important to add emotion, excitement, lightness of touch at different points in different programmes to suit the mood and plot development – the style should be matched to the genre of the programme.

Despite this, a neutral delivery has come to be recognised as 'the norm', even though the Guidance also states 'where the background music is menacing, the voice should reflect the tension, without becoming melodramatic. In comedy, the narration should be steady but delivered with a slight smile in the voice' (ITC, 2000: para. 6.4). ADA UK uses the phrase *scene sympathy* and Snyder (2014: 47) suggests that 'overall, the voicer's delivery should be consonant with the nature of the material being described'. Udo and Fels (2010: 4) cite a study of their own testing a creative audio description for a fashion show 'that combines conventional audio description techniques with colour commentary techniques to allow emotion and excitement as well as description of the important visual elements'. In their evaluation with members of the audience who were either visually impaired or sighted, they found that 'most participants reported that the describer's commentary and emotional delivery positively affected their enjoyment of the fashion show'. The ITC Guidance (ITC 2000) also makes some recommendations for delivery style in relation to children's programmes. These are discussed in the context of genre in Chapter 7. One of the author's partially sighted research participants was more emphatic: 'I think a good AD is one that sounds interesting for a start, someone who has a bit of character in their voice, so that's important.' Geoff Cousins, who oversees audio-described content for the Australian Broadcasting Corporation, says: 'All programs require sympathetic treatment, such as the gender or accent of the voice over, to ensure the [AD] subtly complements the program rather than overwhelms the viewer' (Cousins, n.d.). The RNIB (Rai, 2011) organised a focus group to gauge blind people's responses to American descriptions of an American TV programme (an episode of *CSI*) and a very English programme (Agatha Christie's *Miss Marple*), with a view to encouraging exchange of audio-described material. On the whole, the response was positive, the AD users concluding that what was important was vocal quality, especially tone and clarity, rather than accent per se. They also noted differences in AD style, with the American AD providing more sign-posting of the chronology of the story, using words such as 'now' and 'later', which the English AD users found unnecessary. The use of accent is taken to an extreme in the description for the film *Borat* (Charles, 2006). The audio subtitles are read in a fake (and ludicrous) Kazakhstan accent. This is in sympathy with, rather than competing with, the main character, played by Sasha Baron Cohen, who himself speaks English with a strongly caricatured accent. The humour of the film is enhanced for the blind audience by the contrast between the dry delivery of the main part of the description and the flamboyant nature of the accented speech, not to mention the vocabulary. Audio subtitles are discussed in detail in Chapter 9.

The French Charter cautions: 'if a [describer] with too strong a personality is used he will be competing with the actor in the film' (Gonnant and Morisset, 2008; Rai et al., 2010: App. 3). Although most guidelines don't mention anything about the production or delivery of AD, there are a few references to gender. The ITC Guidance (ITC, 2000: 1.2) suggests: 'Where a documentary is being audio described which has its own narrator, it is helpful for the audio describer to be of the opposite gender to the narrator, to avoid confusion.' In a Polish experiment designed to test the suitability of electronic speech (Szarkowska, 2011), a female voice was chosen in order to break 'the hegemony of male voice talent'. It was thought that comprehension would be facilitated by having the AD delivered by a voice of a different gender from the standard male voice-over because the processing effort expended by visually impaired viewers when watching a film – where on top of a number of original actors' voices there will be the male voice-over artist's voice – was deemed challenging enough not to be compounded by another male voice (Szarkowska, 2011).

Creative possibilities in live AD are opened up by having more than one describer available to deliver it. For example, in the National Theatre of Great Britain's production of *Waves* (Mitchell, 2006) the actors on stage set up camera shots that were simultaneously projected and shown on screen. The describers opted to have one voice describing the on-stage action and another describing the on-screen projection to clarify for the audience what was taking place where. Similarly, for Kneehigh Theatre's production of *The Riot* (Darke, 1999) the frequent shifts in time and space between Newlyn in Cornwall in 1896 and the South African Transvaal of the Boer War were clarified by using a different voice for each. The creative use of gender and delivery is not limited to live AD. The AD of the animated children's film *The Incredibles* (Bird, 2004) is voiced at first by a man. It suddenly switches to a woman's voice and the gender of voice alternates throughout the film. It gradually becomes apparent that the male voice is used for the episodes in which the characters are shown in their superhero roles. The female voice is used for the episodes in which the characters are shown as their alter egos, i.e. their 'normal' selves. This switch is reinforced by the naming strategy. As 'supers', the man calls the main character Mr Incredible and his sidekick Elastigirl. In their alter egos, the woman calls the main character Bob and his wife Helen. No overt mention is made of the delivery strategy, leaving the blind and partially sighted audience to infer it for themselves. This would seem to be the politically correct approach even if the association between female and the domestic sphere and male and superhero is less so.

7.2.2 Stress and segmentation

Stress or emphasis is the basis of rhythmic structure in a language. It is an important tool for the describer. Stress is fundamental to meaning making. Inappropriate stress can alter the meaning of a sentence, even though the words remain unchanged. For example, the meaning of the phrase 'it's not *having* blue Smarties that makes me cross' can be completely reversed by changing only the stress while keeping the words and word order intact: 'it's *not* having blue Smarties that makes me cross'. Giving a word added emphasis directs our attention to it. It has long been observed that 'speakers use intonational emphasis to accent information that is novel in the context of prior discourse' (Fernald and Mazzie, 1991). In a paper concerning words emphasised by mothers telling stories to infants, Fernald and Mazzie state that 'acoustic studies of the prosodic attributes of linguistic focus have shown that "new" words are highlighted by means of increased duration and fundamental frequency relative to words conveying background information' (Fernald and Mazzie, 1991: 210). In a similar way, 'the prosodic structure of adult speech also influences speech perception and language convention for adult listeners . . . stressed words and sentences are processed more rapidly by subjects in a phoneme monitoring task' (ibid.). Stress therefore, gives the describer an opportunity to point up the arrival of a new character or a new location simply through vocal delivery. Conversely, it can be confusing for the listener if the name of the character is stressed even though they have been in the scene for some time. In the AD for *Girl with a Pearl Earring* (Webber, 2003) the main character's name, Griet, is stressed throughout the film, as if we have never encountered her before.

Meaning is also affected by segmentation. Cutler and colleagues (1986: 385) suggest that 'a major part of the listener's task of extracting meaning from speech is segmenting the continuous signal into portions which can be mapped onto . . . meaning units'. They add: 'speech segmentation procedures may differ in speakers of different languages . . . they form part of the processing repertoire of the listener and differ as a function of the listener's language experience.' The following example is taken from the opening sequence of the AD for *Girl with a Pearl Earring*, which is commercially available on DVD. The choice of words and word order in this extract will be discussed in the next chapter, which deals with strategies for describing text on screen, but I shall focus on its delivery here. The warm female voice is of a relatively low pitch and well enunciated, but her focus on clear articulation is such that she uses exaggerated segmentation. Segmenting every word is as confusing as segmenting none. The result is that we are left to work out the segmentation for ourselves. This is illustrated by the following utterance (stressed words are underlined): 'She <u>slices</u> <u>red</u> cabbage, <u>potatoes</u> and <u>onions</u> into <u>neat</u> <u>circles</u> in <u>association</u> with the <u>UK</u> <u>Film</u> <u>Council</u>.' Listening hard, it seems possible that 'in association with the UK Film Council' has been added in later. Occasionally on-screen text is added to the final cut of the film, after the AD has been recorded. So this indeed may be a later addition. This was the case for *Notes on Blindness*. If this was the situation here, then, although understandable, it is regrettable that it ends up sounding as though the heroine, Griet, is being helped in her kitchen duties by members of the Film Council. A few moments later any doubts we may have as to Griet's self-sufficiency are confirmed as '<u>Griet</u> goes <u>upstairs</u> with the <u>support</u> of <u>Film</u> <u>Fund</u> <u>Luxembourg</u>'. Then 'Griet packs a <u>bundle</u> in her room, <u>takes</u> a moment to look back, and <u>goes</u> to her <u>mother, Scarlett Johansson</u>'. This looks almost acceptable, and might be if the pause before the name Scarlett took the form of a colon, meaning it was considerably longer than other pauses within the utterance and if the actress's name had been further set apart using novel stress and intonation, to imply that the describer is reading on-screen text. In the absence of these delivery strategies it ends up sounding as though the mother is played by Scarlett Johannsson (she is not).

In summary, delivery is fundamental to comprehension. A blind man in Fryer and Freeman's study (2014) comparing BPS users' emotional response to film when the AD was delivered by a human or an electronic voice found that comprehension was an issue with the AD automatically verbalised using TTS software. He said: 'When you're listening to TTS it's harder to understand, so you have to concentrate more. Especially when there's a lot going on, it's harder to pick up the thread than with human AD. TTS is pulling you away from the scene.' A partially sighted woman felt that 'It's not as clear, which means you have to concentrate on the describer, which you don't want to do. And it sounds colder. We like human beings.' She added: 'it's got a tone so you can't put your interpretation on it. It's not neutral. You're trying to interpret. I definitely felt disconnected. It's a human voice gone wrong. It's fine for factual books but it ruins fiction.'

The argument that the style of delivery should suit the situation and take into account the expectations of the audience has already been made for interpreting. Ingrid Kurz (2001: 395) quotes Herbert (1952: 82f.), who says:

> it is quite clear that in a diplomatic conference the greatest attention should be paid to all the nuances of words, while in a gathering of scholars, technical accuracy will have greater importance; in a literary and artistic gathering, elegance of speech; and in a political assembly, forcefulness of expression. Similarly, the style and tone cannot be the same in a small group of three or four sitting around a table, in a committee room with a membership of twenty or fifty, and at a large public meeting where many thousands are gathered.

In her own research, Kurz found a discrepancy between the constituents of vocal quality considered necessary by interpreters and what constitutes quality for the users. She notes: 'Some of the criteria that members of the interpreting profession considered highly important, such as native accent, pleasant voice, and correct usage of grammar, were given much lower ratings by the users' (Kurz, 2014: 398). It is possible that this is also the case in AD.

A partially sighted person commented: 'It doesn't bother me. As long as I've got somebody describing it, it really doesn't bother me. It's just nice to have the description.' A similar attitude was found amongst visually impaired participants in Szarkowska's (2011) study in Poland, the majority of whom opted for an electronic voice if it meant that more source content could be described. Fryer and Freeman conclude that TTS may be better for documentaries and HVAD more useful for more emotive target texts such as films and dramas. This is currently being tested in the HBB4all project.

7.2.3 Tone

In spoken English, rising intonation at the end of an utterance is typical of questions but can also suggest that a statement has still to be completed. This type of suspension is common in live description when the describer is uncertain whether or not an actor will add in another piece of business and whether there is time to describe it before the dialogue resumes. It has the effect of leaving the listener hanging, waiting for the conclusion and sense of release that comes with the downward inflection that completes a cadence. It is often better to complete the sentence and lower the intonation rather than leave the description and the listener in a state of suspense. However, it can be used to advantage to capture continuous movement such as that of a dancer who leaps and sails through the air before landing. Shriberg et al. (1998: 443–450, 9–10) showed that 'hesitant-prosody could indicate an incomplete utterance (from the point of view of the speaker's intention), even if the utterance is potentially complete based on words alone'. In their review of the literature, Cutler et al. (1997) cite several studies (Buxton, 1983; Meltzer et al., 1976; Tyler and Warren, 1987) showing that 'disruption of prosodic structure via cross-splicing of utterances or insertion of standard intervals leads to longer latencies in word or phoneme target detection tasks'. They conclude that 'all these lines of research combine to show that processing of speech input is facilitated in several ways by coherent prosodic structure appropriate for sentences' (Cutler et al., 1997: 144). Given that words are not spoken or processed in isolation but that contextual information is important in decoding prosodic meaning, it seems likely that AD delivery that is incongruent or not in sympathy with the rest of the soundtrack would be harder to process than AD delivery that is congruent. For example, describing a funeral procession in a sombre tone would be easier to process than a description of a marriage ceremony in a fearful voice – unless it were a description of *Jane Eyre*, in which the audience is aware that the heroine's marriage to Rochester is doomed by the presence of his wife in the attic.

This would argue against the objective delivery advocated by some guidelines, especially during emotive scenes. Yet, just as for interpreters, some caution must be exercised against melodramatic performance by describers. As one participant in the RNIB focus group put it, 'I don't want the audio describer to win an

Oscar' (Rai, 2011: 15). Many describers instinctively echo the affective valence of the soundtrack, although the effect of congruent versus incongruent delivery on AD users has not been thoroughly tested. Fryer and Freeman (2014), in their study looking at the effects of TTS versus human delivery in emotion elicitation, concluded that 'AD elicited an emotional experience that was, at worst, equal to watching with no AD and, at best, significantly more emotive'. They found that the addition of verbally presented visual information does 'not detract from emotional engagement and can positively increase it *but only when delivered by a human voice*' (italics added). Furthermore, 'Comparing text-to-speech delivery with delivery by a human voice, only human voice AD positively enhanced presence and emotion elicitation. This suggests prosody is a critical element of AD content' (Fryer and Freeman, 2014: 99). Another implication is that, for BPS people, sound effects and emotive music may be redundant where sufficient information can be accessed from film dialogue. With regard to guiding AD practice, the findings suggest that delivering AD in a suitably emotive way is important because emotion is carried more effectively by the vocal tone of the describer than by the non-verbal element of film soundtracks (e.g., SFX and music). Just as with visually presented information, the perception of prosody, which Scherer et al. (2001) call 'the decoding process', is two-way, or interactive. Scherer et al. suggest that it consists of 'the inference of speaker attitudes and emotions based on internalised representations of emotional speech model modifications', and conclude that 'different types of emotion [are] actually characterised by unique patterns or configurations of acoustic cues'.

In 1980 Vivien C. Tartter reported that just as a smile is obvious visually, so it is also audible. Sighted people robustly identified straight-faced versus happy or sad delivery at a level greater than chance. She suggests that this is due to changes in the vocal tract through the action of smiling. Tartter also found that listening to 'smiled speech was associated with the pleasant emotions usually producing it'. Smiling was linked to delivery characterised by higher frequencies, amplitude and longer duration. This might explain the higher ratings of empathy found by Fryer and Freeman (2014) for scenes watched with HVAD, as compared with TTS. It also explains why a heightened delivery style is important in the AD of humour (Crowley and Fryer, 2015).

7.2.4 Pace, pitch, segmentation

As well as tone, the pace of delivery can also be varied to suit the scene – a fast-action sequence benefits from a quicker pace, while a slower delivery would be more appropriate for a lyrical love scene. Often pace is dictated by the speed of the action and the metre of the music that underscores a scene. As well as deliberately speeding up or slowing down, pace is more subtly affected by elements of prosody. Stress, for example, decreases the pace by increasing the duration of an utterance. So too does increased segmentation. For most of an ST, a measured pace will suffice. However, variety of delivery is as welcome as variety of word choice, in refreshing the ear of the listener.

7.2.5 Authenticity, the I-voice and delivery of live AD

The user necessarily has to rely on, and must therefore trust, the describer. The describer must sound authentic in order for the user to accept what they say. The French filmmaker and composer Michel Chion identifies the 'acousmêtre' or 'Acousmatic being' as a common feature in film – someone who is heard but not seen, the omniscient narrator, or the Great Oz in *The Wizard of Oz* (Fleming, 1939). Chion calls this voice the 'I-voice' and suggests what 'makes this an "I-voice" is not just the use of the 1st person singular, but its placement – a certain sound quality, a way of occupying space, a sense of proximity to the spectator's ear, and a particular manner of engaging the spectator's identification' (Chion, 1999: 49). As we saw in Chapter 5, describers are dissuaded from using the first person singular, but it can be argued that the describer is nonetheless an I-voice, with the same features of 'ubiquity, panopticism, omniscience and omnipotence' that Chion outlines (1999: 22). The describer knows what is coming up and tells you as it happens or just before it is about to happen. Describers effectively have the power to make something happen or not. With that power comes responsibility. Except in 'live' situations, at sporting occasions and open-air festivals, for example, or moments of improvisation in a stage performance, the describer has prior knowledge of their source material. Within given time constraints, they decide what to mention and what to leave out, which words to use and how to deliver them (for a discussion of AD and censorship, see Chapter 11). The AD user is in the describer's hands. But just as the Great Oz is revealed to be nothing more than a weakling hiding behind a curtain, a describer can easily lose his or her authority. Quite apart from an error such as misnaming a character or mispronouncing a word, simply the sound of a voice can change, depending on motivation and confidence. Tension raises the voice; a user soon loses faith in a nervous describer. Engagement with the material, commitment and energy all are transmitted vocally: with positive or negative effects on the recipient. Incidentally, as is the practice for radio announcers, there is no harm in acknowledging a fluff or delivery error with a very brief apology before trying the sentence again. This is more likely to be possible during an AI, as the dynamic AD is limited by tighter time constraints. That said, if you stumble over a character's name, it is better to correct it immediately, with no apology, to avoid confusing your audience.

Chion explains that film has codified the 'sound' of the I-voice, with criteria of tone colour, auditory space and timbre to which a voice must conform. The voice is not projected but close-miked, without reverb; the voice is neutral in terms of colour and timbre 'so that each spectator can make it his own' (Chion, 1999: 54). Chion describes these as 'full-fledged norms, rarely violated: dramatic norms of performance, technical norms of recording' (ibid., 50).

These are also the norms that govern the auditory characteristics of the AD and its position in the sonic field. As noted above, AD delivery is officially encouraged to be engaging but neutral – or, as the Ofcom Code on TV Access Services (2006) puts it, 'delivery should be steady, unobtrusive and impersonal in style'. For recorded media such as film and TV the describer's voice is placed in the foreground of the sound picture. This is not the case in theatre description, where the AD is delivered through tiny headphones which allow the stage sound to be heard 'naturally' or enhanced, if necessary; but here the 'proximity' Chion refers to is all the more pronounced – replicating what Chion identifies as the 'telephone voice' which 'brings to the acousmatic situation a vocal intimacy that is rarely encountered in social life, for ordinarily you do not permit just anybody to speak right in your ear' (Chion, 1999: 63). This trust can be broken by a voice that sounds untrustworthy. One key element of trust is built on pronunciation.

7.2.6 Pronunciation

In many dramas, a describer can be faced with proper nouns in a foreign language that they may find difficult to pronounce. Documentaries also often include place names or the names of speakers. These often appear as captions that will need to be voiced (see Chapter 8). Research may be necessary if the describer is not familiar with the pronunciation. It is particularly important that the chosen pronunciation matches the way the name is pronounced by the protagonists in the ST. In a stage performance it is not unknown for a character's name to be pronounced in different ways by different members of the cast. Describers should choose the one most commonly used and stick to it. In the UK there are often established anglicisations that are inaccurate. For example, Paris is pronounced PA-riss, sounding the final 's', and with the stress on the first syllable rather than ParEE as a Parisian might say. To say ParEE because it is more accurate would nonetheless sound affected and ridiculous to an English-speaking audience. In live AD, using two describers, where one person describes Act 1 and another person describes Act 2, consistency of pronunciation must be maintained across the two acts. This is generally achieved informally by verbal agreement. Discrepancies often become apparent at the dry run and should be settled then, if not before.

Before moving on to practicalities, let's take some advice from an AD user who used to be a radio producer for the BBC.

> When I used to train people to present at the microphone . . . I mostly worked in educational broadcasting with inexperienced people who've never been in front of a microphone before. First of all they were always far too quick; well, first of all they couldn't write scripts, got over that one, then they always read it far too quickly. We could slow them down on that one without feeling too awkward, and then they wanted to project too much because they were talking to a room of people. I mean. it's a cliché. So gradually you got them to write in a different way; then you got them to slow down presentation and, to their enormous surprise, when they'd stopped projecting and were just talking normally – in that old cliché, to one person sitting on the other side of the microphone or, you know, 'tell it to me', they suddenly found that they could talk slowly in a normal sort of way and it didn't feel odd, and they knew when they'd got it right. And as a producer, you always sort of knew – or I always knew – when my presenter suddenly felt comfortable with his or

her voice. And you could feel it. Similarly I think with [a describer's] voice what I want is somebody . . . not whispering in my ear, because there's nothing more irritating than whispering, particularly to the ageing – and that's most of your customers, they're ageing – talking quietly to me, almost intimately, sharing what they're seeing with me . . . they've got eyes, they can see, um I want them to pass on to me: things that they really think are important about what's happening on the stage or on the screen. Um, and to do it in a quiet, intimate sort of voice; and that on the whole they achieve, because you don't get describers sort of projecting or gabbling far too quickly. So it's that sort of quiet intimacy I want.

7.2.7 Fluency

Another factor influencing listener confidence is fluency. This is more important in an audio-only mode than in an AV mode. Engstrom (1994) found that when '80 subjects viewed or listened to either audiotaped or videotaped versions of a newscast in which the same announcer made varying numbers of speech errors, ratings of the speaker's competence decreased as the number of such errors increased in newscasts in which the announcer was only heard.' When the speaker was in vision, audiences were more tolerant of error. Addington (1971: 247) found that 'faulty articulation adversely affected ratings of a speaker's credibility'. This underlines the need for preparation prior to delivering or recording an AD. Clearly, those describing for a recorded medium such as TV or cinema have an advantage in that errors may be corrected. However, as previously mentioned, this adds to the cost through extra studio time, so a flawless delivery is to be encouraged, whatever the setting.

7.3 Preparing the voice

7.3.1 Warming up

The vocal muscles are like any others in the body and benefit from being warmed up. They also benefit from exercise and training. As there are many books specialising in vocal warm-ups and vocal technique, I will direct you to those rather than going into detail here. Suffice it to say that singing exercises, humming, tongue twisters and exercises to release tension in the jaw can all help to ensure that you do not go into the studio unprepared. Find a few that suit you and practise them. Cicely Berry and Patsy Rodenberg are well-respected voice coaches who have published a number of useful books (listed under Suggested Reading, below).

7.3.2 Microphone technique

The important thing about using a microphone is to position it correctly. It should not sit directly in front of your lips. Try it to one side or slightly above or below. If you place your fingers on the microphone, you should not be able to feel a jet of air on them as you speak, and particularly not as you make a plosive 'p' sound. If you do feel any breath, readjust the positioning. The other key thing to remember is that you do not need to project. The microphone does this for you. Try to speak as naturally as possible. Be clear, but avoid exaggerated segmentation. Think about the meaning of your words and not the individual words themselves, and all should come out well. If there are any words or phrases over which you are likely to stumble, rewrite the phrase or divide the words with a slash or a stroke as a visual reminder to segment them, i.e., you need to take them slowly. A newsreader for the BBC used to struggle to say United Arab Emirates, until they took to marking the script: United/Arab/Emirates. You may need to experiment with ways of marking up your script that work for you.

7.4 Recording

7.4.1 Recording strategies

If you have a studio set-up with a level meter, showing your volume, you should aim for the needle to be vertical, usually peaking between 4 and 5. If you stumble or make a mistake you may be able to over-record individual utterances or 'drop in' an individual word or short phrase, depending on your software. Should you do this, listen back to the preceding description or portion of dialogue or soundtrack for five to ten seconds to ensure that you use the right inflection. Some people prefer to correct as they go along; others prefer to complete the whole recording and then re-record any mistakes at the end. As your voice may change as it warms up during the recording session, it may sound different by the end as compared to how it sounded at the beginning. This means you may need to re-record more than you had hoped. Some software gives you the option to jump from one description window to the next without having to view the ST in between. Again, make sure that you give yourself enough pre-roll to get into the mood of the scene, especially if you have not written the script yourself. It is important to take an in-breath before the microphone is live and deliver all your AD utterance before the microphone is automatically cut at the 'Out time'. This is why it is helpful to divide longer utterances into shorter ones, as a shorter utterance is easier to time. You want to avoid any sound of panic if you find yourself racing to squeeze in the last few words.

7.4.2 Listening back

It is critical to listen back to your recording, listening out for stumbles, hesitations and errors and also for technical issues such as splats or explosive 'p' sounds (known as popping), as well as for the rattle of the microphone cable, the creaking of your chair or clothes, the jangle of earrings or the tap of your ring on the desk. (It is advisable to remove jewellery before you begin to record.) If you are using software that turns the microphone on and off automatically, you need to be especially vigilant that your utterance has not been truncated or cut off too soon (clipped) and that you have not jumped in too early, staring to speak before the

98 *Audio description skills: delivery*

microphone was live. Just as with proofreading, it is often easier to detect errors on another person's recording than on your own. You will tend to hear what you want to hear, as opposed to what you actually recorded. A checklist of common recording errors is given in Table 7.1.

7.5 Live delivery

In the theatre, it is stating the obvious to say you will not be able to go back and correct any mistakes at the end. Your voice needs to be warm before you begin. Reading the introductory notes can be helpful for this. Introductory notes or AIs are discussed in detail in Chapter 12. If there are two describers and you have chosen to share the delivery of the introductory notes between you (this can be useful, as a new voice can refresh the listener's ear), arrange it so that the describer for Act 1 delivers the last few paragraphs of the notes. This way they can link seamlessly from the AI into the description itself.

Table 7.1 Common recording faults

Abbreviation	Meaning	Definition	Description no.
ST	Stumble	Tripping over all or part of a word.	
Br	Breath	Audible breath in an inappropriate place.	
Cl	Clarity	Lack of clarity in delivery.	
Clip	Clipped	Missing start to a word because the mic. turning live was pre-empted.	
CO	Cut off	End of word cut off by turning off the mic. too soon.	
Emph	Emphasis	A word or syllable emphasised inappropriately.	
Hes	Hesitation	Pausing too long before a word, so it interrupts the flow and sounds under-confident.	
LIP	Lip-smacking	Audible sound of lips colliding from poor speech motor control.	
NO	Noises off	Micophone rattle, audible page turn, clanking jewellery, squeaky chair, rustling clothing etc.	
Pace	Pace	Pace is inappropriate, either too slow or too fast for the scene described.	
Pop	Popping	Distortion on plosive consonants.	
MisP	Mispronunciation	Name or word mispronounced.	

7.6 Conclusion

This chapter has further discussed the role of oral delivery in conveying meaning – an element of AD that is often limited to discussion of broad categories such as accent and gender. It has deconstructed the role of prosody, including stress and segmentation, pace, pitch and tone, fluency and pronunciation, all of which aid in establishing the describer and the description as trustworthy and authentic. Reference has been made to the work of Michel Chion and parallels drawn between the describer and the media norm of the *acousmêtre*. Finally, some practical advice has been given to aid fluent delivery.

7.7 Exercises and points for discussion

1 Assemble a small collection of vocal warm-up exercises with which you feel comfortable. Be prepared to demonstrate/present them to your colleagues/ family.
2 Find some examples of description using voices that you like or dislike. Identify what it is that you like or dislike about their delivery.
3 Take a short sequence of script and record it in different ways: more or less emotively; more or less conversationally. You may choose a description script or short piece of prose from a novel. Play around with pace and vocal colour. It can be good to try reading in an exaggerated way and then rein it in. Listen back and check it for errors, using the list in Table 7.1.
4 Take every opportunity to practise reading aloud. Reading out newspaper articles with friends and family, or children's stories, can all help you to familiarise yourself with your voice. This also helps with confidence, in that you know your voice will react in the way you want it to.

7.8 Suggested reading

C. Berry, *Voice and the actor*, New York: Random House, 2011.
P. Rodenberg, *The right to speak: working with the voice*, London: Routledge, 2012.

References

Addington, David W. (1971). 'The effect of vocal variations on ratings of source credibility'. *Speech Monographs* 38, no. 3: 242–247.
Buxton, H. (1983). 'Temporal predictability in the perception of English speech'. In A. Cutler and D. Robert Ladd (eds) *Prosody: models and measurements*. Berlin: Springer, pp. 111–121.
Chion, Michel (1999). *The voice in cinema*. New York: Columbia University Press.
Cousins, Geoff (n.d.). 'Clearly a success!' Retrieved from www.captioningandsubtitling. com.au/news/abc-audio-description-trial-%E2%80%93-clearly-a-success/ [accessed 18.09.15].
Crowley, Bridget and Louise Fryer (2015). 'The Laughter Lines Project Report'. Retrieved from http://audiodescription.co.uk/uploads/general/Laughter_Lines_Project_Report 29.pdf [accessed 23.09.15].

100 Audio description skills: delivery

Cutler, Anne, Delphine Dahan and Wilma Van Donselaar (1997). 'Prosody in the comprehension of spoken language: a literature review'. *Language and Speech* 40, no. 2: 141–201.

Cutler, Anne, Jacques Mehler, Dennis Norris and Juan Segui (1986). 'The syllable's differing role in the segmentation of French and English'. *Journal of Memory and Language* 25, no. 4: 385–400.

Engstrom, Erika (1994). 'Effects of nonfluencies on speaker's credibility in newscast settings'. *Perceptual and Motor Skills* 78, no. 3: 739–743. Retrieved from www.amsciepub.com/doi/abs/10.2466/pms.1994.78.3.739?journalCode=pms accessed [23.07.15].

Fernald, Anne and Claudia Mazzie (1991). 'Prosody and focus in speech to infants and adults'. *Developmental Psychology* 27, no. 2: 209.

Fryer, Louise and Jonathan Freeman (2014). 'Can you feel what I'm saying? The impact of verbal information on emotion elicitation and presence in people with a visual impairment'. In A. Felnhofer and O. D. Kothgassner (eds) *Challenging presence: proceedings of the 15th International Conference on Presence*. Vienna: facultas.wuv, pp. 99–107.

Gonant, F. and L. Morisset (2008). *La charte de l'audiodescription*. Paris: Ministère des Affaires Sociales et de la Santé. Available from www.social-sante.gouv.fr/IMG/pdf/Charte_de_l_audiodescription_300908.pdf [accessed 15.01.13].

Herbert, Jean (1952). *The interpreter's handbook: how to become a conference interpreter*. Genève: Librairie de l'Université.

ITC (2000). ITC Guidance. Retrieved from http://www.ofcom.org.uk/static/archive/itc/itc_publications/codes_guidance/audio_descripion/index.asp.html [accessed 4.04.15].

Kurz, Ingrid (2001). 'Conference interpreting: quality in the ears of the user'. *Meta: Journal des traducteurs/Meta: Translators' Journal* 46, no. 2: 394–409.

Meltzer, R.H., Martin, J.G., Mills, C.B., Imhoff, D.L. and Zohar, D. (1976). 'Reaction time to temporally-displaced phoneme targets in continuous speech'. *Journal of Experimental Psychology: Human Perception and Performance* 2, no. 2: 277.

Ofcom (2006). Code on TV Access Services. Retrieved from http://stakeholders.ofcom.org.uk/broadcasting/guidance/other-guidance/tv_access_serv/guidelines/ [accessed 23.09.15].

Rai, Sonali, Joan Greening and Leen Petré (2010). 'A comparative study of audio description guidelines prevalent in different countries'. London: RNIB, Media and Culture Department.

Rai, Sonali (2011). 'RNIB International AD exchange study: observations from a focus group study'. Retrieved from www.rnib.org.uk/sites/default/files/AD_pdf.pdf [accessed 18.09.15].

Sacks, Oliver (1998). *The man who mistook his wife for a hat: and other clinical tales*. New York: Simon and Schuster.

Salway, Andrew (2007). 'A corpus-based analysis of audio description'. In Pilar Orero and Aline Remael (eds) *Media for all: subtitling for the deaf, audio description, and sign language*. Approaches to Translation Studies, vol. 30. Amsterdam: Rodopi, pp. 151–174.

Scherer, Klaus R., Rainer Banse and Harald G. Wallbott (2001). 'Emotion inferences from vocal expression correlate across languages and cultures'. *Journal of Cross-cultural Psychology* 32, no. 1: 76–92.

Shriberg, Elizabeth, Andreas Stolcke, Daniel Jurafsky, Noah Coccaro, Marie Meteer, Rebecca Bates, Paul Taylor, Klaus Ries, Rachel Martin and Carol Van Ess-Dykema (1998). 'Can prosody aid the automatic classification of dialog acts in conversational speech?' *Language and Speech* 41, no. 3–4: 443–492.

Silverman, Kim E. A., Mary E. Beckman, John F. Pitrelli, Mari Ostendorf, Colin W. Wightman, Patti Price, Janet B. Pierrehumbert and Julia Hirschberg (1992). 'TOBI: a standard for labeling English prosody'. In *International Conference on Spoken Language Processing*, vol. 2, pp. 867–870.

Snyder, J. (2014). *The visual made verbal: a comprehensive training manual and guide to the history and applications of audio description.* Arlington, VA: American Council for the Blind.

Szarkowska, Agnieszka (2011). 'Text-to-speech audio description: towards wider availability of AD'. *Journal of Specialised Translation* 15: 142–163.

Tartter, Vivien C. (1980). 'Happy talk: perceptual and acoustic effects of smiling on speech'. *Perception & Psychophysics* 27, no. 1: 24–27.

Tyler, L.K. and Warren, P. (1987). 'Local and global structure in spoken language comprehension'. *Journal of Memory and Language* 26, no. 6: 638–657.

Udo, John Patrick and Deborah I. Fels (2010). 'Re-fashioning fashion: an exploratory study of a live audio-described fashion show'. *Universal Access in the Information Society* 9, no. 1: 63–75.

Film references

Borat, L. Charles (2006).
Girl with a Pearl Earring, P. Webber (2003).
The Incredibles, B. Bird (2004).
The Wizard of Oz, V. Fleming (1939).

References to live events

The Riot, dir. N. Darke (1999). Kneehigh Theatre, National Theatre of Great Britain, London. AD by in-house team (describers Louise Fryer and Andrew Holland).

Waves, dir. K. Mitchell (2006). National Theatre of Great Britain, London. AD by in-house team (describers Roz Chalmers and Bridget Crowley).

8 Beyond the basics

Audio description by genre

8.1 Introduction

This chapter looks at how the genre of a ST affects AD strategies in terms of writing and delivery. While the broad principles of AD apply to all categories and genres, there are some differences that are useful to note.

Genre is discussed at the level of the various subsets of film and TV programmes.

8.2 Genre and suitability of AD

Genre is important as regards audience expectation. This may help a describer to narrow down and select what are relevant visual features: certain features may be more relevant in one genre than in another. As Evans and Pearson note in their audience research for the RNIB (Evans and Pearson, 2009: 387), 'In certain genres, but not all, the image is the central site of meaning making'. Toms and Campbell (1999: 9) showed that the attributes of a printed document's genre determined the ease with which a person could interact with it, such that a

> user, even before reading the content, may recognize a document, for example, as a newspaper through the appearance of columns and headlines; an annual report features numerous tables, and a dictionary contains an alphabetic sequence of tabs. These features evolved as an efficient means of representing the semantic contents of particular types of information. As such, they trigger a user's recognition of socially-familiar discourses – in essence a user's mental model – to such a degree that if the words labelling the form were omitted, the documents' functions would remain perceptible and interpretable.

In the same way, the ability to recognise that an AVT ST lies within a particular genre should ease the cognitive load on the part of AD users.

In the UK, some genres and therefore channels are exempt from AD, such as the BBC's Parliament channel. Ofcom's Code on the Provision of Access Services (Ofcom, 2015: point A4.24) states: 'Although visually-impaired people like to watch the same sorts of programmes as everybody else, not all programmes lend themselves to audio description. Some programmes are too fast-moving, or offer

Beyond the basics: audio description by genre 103

little opportunity to insert audio description (e.g. news), or may not be significantly enhanced by the provision of audio description (e.g. quiz programmes).' The focus-group participants in Evans and Pearson's report into visually impaired audiences and TV (Evans and Pearson, 2009: 385), commented: 'There's a lot of programmes out there that should be described, and there's a lot of things described when they don't need to be, like [the quiz show] *University Challenge*.' Indeed, in the case of *University Challenge*, AD was felt to be detrimental to participants' enjoyment:

> *Cathy:* They used to audio describe *University Challenge*, which must be really easy to follow; it's a quiz programme – to my mind, that was a waste of very, very valuable resources. Put it more on films, more on dramas where there are silences, where we need it.
> *Michael:* They'd audio describe on *University Challenge* something like a picture round, but that's stupid – people should have been shot for that!

Audio description was felt to be inappropriate for programming which already relies heavily on aural cues, with current affairs programming particularly cited. Said Michael, 'You're not as excluded from news or current affairs, or a game show than [*sic*] you are from dramas or film.'

Participants in Fryer's research agreed. One man with partial sight said:

> There are a couple of quiz shows which are [audio described] which is a bit of a waste of time in my opinion, um *The Crystal Maze*, which anyone who knows the game show, knows it's impossible to describe. There might be one or two games on the whole show, on the whole programme, that might be describable but not really, so that person should be sitting describing something that's of more use, really. Um, and another one which is *Catchphrase*, another game show from the '90s, it's impossible, I've watched it and several times attempted to watch it but never got it, never understood it, so that's no use to me, so those people should definitely be describing something else.

A woman who is partially sighted said:

> *N:* They have [AD] on these game shows that are usually repeated ... yet they don't tell you when there's something visual in the quiz but they tell you, like, the person is a bit portly or they have just taken another step towards the target – and you think that wasn't really relevant. What matters is when the picture comes up on the quiz and you've got no idea what the picture is, they should tell you what that is. I've actually found they're doing *Catchphrase* at the moment, which is quite funny and it's good because you can play along with it and they're describing the picture and we can do it. If they don't describe it we can't. But I mean, *Blockbusters* was on the other day and they're like 'so and so's just pressed the button' and I'm like 'huh!' and there's this letter flashing and they're going to tell you that in a moment anyway so it's really irrelevant.

104 *Beyond the basics: audio description by genre*

    L: And would you rather they just said nothing at all at those moments?

    N: Yes, because it's irrelevant. . . . I don't think it's really important that a contestant's got a blue dress or, so with a quiz show, no I don't think you do. Some of the comedies, some of the sitcoms that are on, they don't always have [AD] and in some of that there are parts that are really visual and you don't know who's come in and it would be nice to have them [AD] on some of those.

A similar view was expressed by another participant in relation to cookery programmes: 'Like *Ready Steady Cook* or something like that. And they tell you oh he's just like beating the eggs together or he's just done this or done that, pointless.'

8.3 Movie genres

Rasheed and Shah (2002) developed a system of classifying movies into two major classes (action and non-action movies), with non-action movies further subdivided into romance, comedy, horror and drama/other. Their system automatically analyses the audiovisual features of previews and estimates the visual disturbance or motion content, sound profile and average shot length. As genre affects the audio and visual streams differentially, there are direct implications for AD. For 'action movies, the audio is always correlated with the scene. For example, [scenes of] fighting, explosions etc. are mostly accompanied with a sudden change in the audio level . . . Movies with more action contents exhibit smaller average shot length. On the other hand comedy/drama movies have low action content and larger shot length' (2002: 4). Reflecting the differences in shot length, description for action movies is best kept short and punchy – limited, for example to the scale of the explosion and the visual evidence of the damage caused. For romantic films, descriptive utterances will feature longer sentences, with a more lyrical turn of phrase. Describers may also have the challenge of describing the visual attractions of the protagonists, which can be controversial. For example, one partially sighted woman in the author's research said:

> It bothers me in films when [the describers] say something like, when they're introducing a character and they say 'Jenny an attractive blonde' or something . . . it bothers me in the sense that like they think she's attractive and I think are they saying that they think she's attractive or are they saying that it's pretty obvious that this woman fits the general stereotype of attractive blondiness in a certain type of film . . . and they're trying to get across this is the attractive blonde type to me, but because I haven't been able to see enough for ages, I'm not really aware of what people mean by that stereotype, but on the other hand there's not time in a film to say any more, so I can understand why they do it but it still bothers me a bit in films. But I've just generally found that description for theatre and art work seems to me to be of better quality, probably because there's more time and although . . . obviously the

describer's own perception comes into it, I feel like that most of the time they do their best to um, to describe it as accurately as they can, and quite often they'll say something like, I don't know, this image might make you feel like this, or like this, or like this and it sort of gives you an idea where they're coming from, but it's open enough to know that you might have a different interpretation yourself.

An AI might resolve this constraint on character description in films and will be discussed in Chapter 12.

There may also be scenes of a sexual nature that will need to be described. Vocabulary needs particular attention, especially in explicit scenes. (This is addressed in detail in Chapter 11.) Action movies often bring with them the issue of the corpse. Can we be sure that a character is dead? If we know, do we need to say so, or is it self-evident? One strategy is to follow the American guidelines and simply say what you see – that the body lies very still or that the eyes glaze over, and draw no further inference. This may be more convincingly portrayed on screen than is possible in a live performance. In a live show, the 'corpse' usually gets up to take a bow at the end.

8.3.1 Spectacle

In their article analysing visual scenes, Matamala and Remael (2015) discuss the phenomenon of the cinema of spectacle 'with its supposed focus on visual effects to the detriment of storytelling' (ibid., 2015: 63), arguing that 'effect-driven narratives require carefully timed and phrased ADs that devote much attention to the prosody of the AD script, its interaction with sounds and the use of metaphor'. This is because the point of the film is not to follow the logic of the narrative. Such a prosaic *raison d'être* is overridden by a desire to dazzle and amaze with effects designed only to 'bewilder the eye' (Paci, 2006: 313, cited in Matamala and Remael, 2015). In this situation the *What* is trumped by the *How*. A similar situation occurs in live events, especially in grand-scale musicals, where audiences who have paid high ticket prices expect dazzling effects from the set. One of the reasons why the musical *The Lion King* (Taymor, 1994) has been enduringly popular (as of June 2015, it had sold more than 80 million tickets around the world) is the way the creatures of the African plains, and even the plains themselves, are brought to life. As described by VocalEyes in the AI:

> [The Lion King] Mufasa and his family live on Pride rock – a stylized circular staircase that twists up out of the stage. When fully raised, with Mufasa standing on its summit, the rock towers some five metres over the grassy plains below. These plains are shown in a number of ways. At times they're a simple strip of tall grass which travels like a conveyer belt across the front of the stage. At other times they are more animated – literally – as dancers balance squares of pale, dry grass on their heads like hats – swaying and swishing them in different formations.

106 *Beyond the basics: audio description by genre*

One of the delights for the sighted audience is to be transported to the plains or Pride Rock while simultaneously being able to see how those locations are created. Simply to state the location, in the AD, would allow blind people to follow the story but deny them the same sense of awe and wonder experienced by the sighted audience at the spectacular stagecraft on display.

Lighting, as previously noted, is also often a distinguishing feature of genre, as is colour. According to Rasheed and Shah (2002: 3):

> High-key lighting means that the scene has an abundance of bright light. It usually has lesser contrast and the difference between the brightest light and the dimmest light is small. High-key scenes are usually happy or less dramatic. Many situation comedies also have high-key lighting whereas 'In horror movies shots are mostly low-key. On the other hand, comedy movies tend to have more high-key shots.

While it may seem obvious to mention long, looming shadows in a horror movie, it is easy to neglect to mention sunny scenes in a comic genre, as by default they seem less noticeable.

8.3.2 Horror

Irena Michalewicz (2015) points out that in horror movies the action usually takes place in a restricted space. The isolation of a location (carrying with it the implication of limited possibilities for escape) needs to be emphasised in the AD if sufficient tension is to be generated. For example, the Overlook Hotel in *The Shining* (Kubrick, 1980) is cut off not only by its location halfway up a mountain but also by the time of year (it is closed for the winter) and a fall of snow. The lack of people available to come to Danny's aid is underlined by a shot of only three lighted windows across the hotel's façade as dusk falls. An AD that failed to highlight this aspect of the spatiotemporal setting would be selling its audience short in the build-up of tension as events unfold. Tension is also increased in horror movies by the cinematic trope of metonym, whereby a part represents the whole. A shot of a hand pushing open a door allows us to speculate (fearfully) as to who the owner of the hand may be. This is often more successful in developing tension than a full reveal. Camerawork is also key. Filming over a character's shoulder as they walk away gives us the sensation that the character is being followed. Voyeuristic camerawork focusing on a character carrying out everyday activities such as cooking, filmed through an uncurtained window or an open doorway, especially at night, gives the sense that they are being watched. In *The Shining*, as Danny plays with his cars in an empty corridor of the hotel a tennis ball rolls up to him, seemingly from nowhere. This lack of agency is critical to generating an impending fear that Danny is not alone.

Michalewicz (2015) also notes an increase in cross-genre films – for example, overlaps between horror and other genres. The strapline for *Zombieland* (Fleischer,

2009), for example, was 'a comedy that kills'. The generic horror storyline of the hero/heroine as prey is also common to the wildlife documentary. Here, spatial distances between the animal 'characters' can be key to understanding how near our 'hero' is to escape. In a thriller, actual spatial relations may be suspended. The describer of any James Bond movie will quickly realise that truth is not allowed to get in the way of a good story (or at least, geographic fidelity is not allowed to get in the way of a good chase sequence). The description will need to reflect the narrative fiction by concentrating on the relative positions of the characters (who is gaining on whom) rather than on trying to create an accurate map in the mind of the user.

An awareness of genre is also important from a practical point of view. Films that come under the explosion/fire subdivision of Rasheed and Shah's action film category are likely to take longer to script by requiring more description and being more difficult to time than romantic films. In both types the soundtrack will be important, but for different reasons. Action movies will have a louder soundtrack and description will need to be threaded through bursts of gunfire, explosions, etc. One blind user who lost his sight in an accident when he was seven years old feels very strongly that it is 'important for the describer not to skirt round stuff like sex or blood' (interviewed by author). This excludes him not only from content but from the shared audience experience. As he puts it:

> A: Sometimes you get a glossing-over feeling.
> LF: What leads you to suspect they're glossing over?
> A: Because it's bound to be worse than it is.
> LF: Maybe your imagination makes it . . .
> A: . . . If your neighbour knows but you don't know – that's the difficulty.

A more detailed analysis of descriptions of sexual and violent content is given in Chapter 11.

8.3.3 Historical films and costume dramas

Exclusion can also stem from visual references that are oculo-culture-specific. For example, according to Claire Monk and Amy Sargeant, British historical cinema has been 'central to the popularity, commercial success and exportability of British cinema since its earliest decades. Indeed, British period films have often been closely equated in the eyes of the world – many would say too closely – with Britain's "national cinema" itself' (2002: 1). As examples they cite *Shakespeare in Love* (Madden, 1999) and *The Private Life of Henry VIII* (Korda, 1933), and they point to the 'strongly held belief that the central duty of films set in the past is to document historical fact – or at least the material world of the period depicted – as faithfully as known sources permit'. This creates a burden of research on the describer in terms of accuracy of terminology (see Chapter 5), and for the AD user in terms of culture-specific references relating to costumes and artefacts.

8.4 Intertextuality

Porter defines intertextuality as the principle 'that all signs arise from a single network: what Vygotsky called "the web of meaning" . . . Examining texts "intertextually" means looking for "traces," the bits and pieces of Text which writers or speakers borrow and sew together to create new discourse' (Vygotsky, 1986: 34). This places a burden on the describer to recognise those references and incorporate them into their AD so that their audience can enjoy the same warmth of recognition as the sighted audience.

8.4.1 Intertextuality and historical films

Intertextuality is particularly evident in historical films. For example, McKechnie (2002) points out that much of the visual template of Shekhar Kappur's film about England's sixteenth-century queen, *Elizabeth* (Kappur, 1998), is based on two contemporary portraits, in particular the Coronation portrait, painted in 1559 (displayed in the National Gallery, London), and the Ditchley portrait of 1592 by Marcus Gheeraerts (displayed in the National Portrait Gallery, London). Although the describer would not necessarily make overt reference to these portraits, the AD should give sufficient detail of Elizabeth's appearance that such an inference may be drawn by anyone familiar with the portraits. As the *mise en scène* is a major part of any historical film's appeal, given that anyone conversant with British history will generally already know the plot, what constitute the essential visual elements will be different from what might be deemed essential in another genre. Similar observations might be applied to TV costume drama such as adaptations of Dickens, Jane Austen, or Hilary Mantell's *Wolf Hall* (Kosminsky, 2015), or to stage productions such as that of Sondheim's musical, *Sunday in the Park with George* (Pimlott, 1990), in which Seurat's famous pointilliste painting *Un dimanche après-midi a l'Ile de la Grande Jatte* was recreated and brought to life on stage. In *Girl with a Pearl Earring*, when Griet first enters Vermeer's workshop, a reflection of her profile is captured in a mirror with a gold frame, foreshadowing the painting of the title. This anaphoric reference is not mentioned in the description, either implicitly or explicitly, and yet it is a visual reference that will have passed few sighted viewers by. Taylor (2014: 31) argues that, given such intertextuality, 'the describer must decide whether the audience needs any assistance', i.e., a describer must decide how much explanation to include. In the example cited above it may be enough simply to say 'as she passes the mirror, Griet's image is caught in its gilt frame', without having to spell out the reference any further. In *Sunday in the Park with George*, describing the arrangement of the characters on stage should be enough to make the reference clear, without explicitly naming the painting they recreate.

Concerning intertextuality in general, a describer must be able to recognise the reference, and for this they may need to recognise their own shortcomings, research widely and seek help if necessary. In live AD settings, access to the show's designer or director, stage or company manager are possible routes.

In recorded AD, useful information may be contained in the screenplay, which may be available online. This is another reason for the describer to work in house with the creative team, as advocated in the approach known as accessible film-making (Romero-Fresco, 2013). This will be discussed further in Chapter 10, under the topic of auteur description.

As discussions on historical films by the sighted audience often centre on authenticity, it is critical that the describer reflects the *mise en scène* as shown. Monk and Sargeant (2002) also point out that a history film tells us more about the time in which the film was made than about the time in which it is set. Obviously this is not exclusive to film. It may also be true of historical operas and other stage productions. For example, Benjamin Britten's *Gloriana* (Jones, 2013), designed by Ultz at London's Royal Opera house, presented an Elizabethan England that was closer to the 1950s, on the accession of Queen Elizabeth II, when the opera was written, as opposed to that of the first Queen Elizabeth, in the sixteenth century. The opera was presented as a 'play within a play', the curtains lifting to reveal a view of a village-hall stage and beyond, into the wings, where a first-aider sat next to the prompter on one side; the director paced about on the other side; the stage hands were waiting and, between scenes, changed the set in front of us as the action alternated between public occasions – a joust, a pageant, a masked ball – and more intimate scenes between Elizabeth and her favourite courtier, Essex, Elizabeth and her advisors, or Essex and his confederates – his wife, his sister and his sister's lover, Lord Mountjoy. During the Prelude, director Richard Jones gave us a quick canter back through history as one British monarch after another ascended a wooden throne, in reverse chronological order, the visual style reminiscent of the drawings in the spoof history book *1066 and All That* (Sellar and Yeatman, 1931). The source needed to be made clear in the AD if the laughter of the sighted audience was to be understood by those who could not see.

8.5 Factual programmes

8.5.1 Sport, news and current affairs

Annette Hill (2007) points to the increasing hybridity between factual programmes and fictional genres and acknowledges news as the most recognisable factual genre. It may seem surprising to a sighted person that a blind person should choose to watch the news on TV rather than listen to the radio. Evans and Pearson explained in reference to one member of their focus group that 'turning on the television instead of the radio seemed more natural; his habitual allegiance to television has prevented radio from taking a significant role in his life since he became blind' (Evans and Pearson, 2009: 379)

Both the live nature and the high speech content of news mean that it is rarely audio described, yet there is still plenty of visual content that remains inaccessible. Research has shown that 'rapid judgements about the personality traits of political candidates based solely on their appearance, can predict their electoral success' (Olivola and Todorov, 2010: 83). A Polish project for talking newspapers for the blind (e-kiosk), recognising the importance of the visual dimension of news, recruited young people to audio describe the photographs that accompany the news stories (Sadowska, 2015). In the UK, TV news channels are exempt from AD, on the grounds of practicality – that there is little time to fit in any AD and it is hard to avoid treading on the audio content, given the live and therefore unpredictable nature of the genre. In the USA, Fox News used the objectivity/subjectivity argument to seek exemption. Bridge Multimedia (2011) reported:

> The Fox News Channel and The National Association of Broadcasters have petitioned the Federal Communications Commission (FCC) requesting that news organizations be given exemption from video description requirements mandated in the *21st Century Communications and Video Accessibility Act of 2010*, which became law last October. According to the National Association of Broadcasters, 'Unlike closed captioning, which is intended to repeat words spoken as precisely as possible, video description inherently carries a subjective element, and accordingly should not be required to add a non-journalist describer's words into the editorial product.'

8.5.2 Documentaries

Documentaries offer a very different genre in AVT, although they often pose similar challenges, such as requiring a degree of technical knowledge and specialist terminology with which the audience may or may not be familiar. As suggested in Chapter 5, suitable strategies include omission, explicitation and, probably the best, naming with explication. Methods of comparison to more familiar objects via analogies, similes and metaphors are likely to be required, with attention being paid to qualities that go beyond the purely visual, to involve other senses, e.g. haptic and tactile, such as weight and texture. Lidia Cámara and Eva Espasa (2011: 417) argue that in the literature 'AD has been addressed in non-fiction documents only as an exceptional case'. They point out the paucity of guidelines for documentaries, explaining that 'The Spanish Standard on audio description, UNE 153020, mentions that it is generally applicable for documentaries (AENOR 2005: 4), although, unlike the ITC Guidelines, there are no specific sections for each programme type.' By contrast, 'The ITC Guidelines provide two further specific instructions: the recommendation to use specialist vocabulary with precision (ibid.: 9) and the relative importance of providing details in the script (ibid.: 22).'

8.5.3 Nature documentaries

Cámara and Espasa point out that, as the camerawork is often particularly important in a nature documentary, the first Spanish documentary to be described (*Los ritmos de la vida/The Rhythms of Life*) was fifteen minutes longer in the described version than in the original, due to the insertion of an AI explaining techniques such as slow motion and animated 'infographics'. The AD also used rhetorical language with plenty of metaphors and similes, and the authors note 'that this is consistent with current AD guidelines' and also 'a distinctive feature of popular scientific discourse, which helps to convey very specialised knowledge to general audiences, as is shown by the start of National Geographic documentaries' (Cámara and Espasa, 2011: 420–421).

This poetic type of discourse is very much a feature of the AD of the National Geographic film *March of the Penguins* (Jacquet, 2005), which describes the penguins as a 'superfluity of nuns' and 'like a slow chugging train', as well as providing a detailed description of their appearance:

> [they] have smallish black heads adorned with white and yellow ear patches, short thick necks, a streamlined shape short wedge-shaped tails and tiny flipper-like wings . . . the Penguins' apron-like bellies are white but with their upper breasts showing a pale yellow. Viewed from the front they appear like a group of waiters heading with due diligence to their posts.

It seems ironic that for a scientific genre that may be thought to require the most objective language, the AD for this documentary employs more vivid, and potentially more subjective, language than for most dramas. One reason for this is the large amount of space available in the soundtrack. Narration for wildlife documentaries is typically sparse. Another reason is that the nature documentary long ago left behind the travel-and-safari style in favour of Walt Disney-style drama, so that, in an anthropomorphised way, animals play out human themes such as survival against the odds, territorial conflict and love stories. In order to achieve this, the camerawork is less than objective and so, too, is the narrative form with which the AD will interact. The complexity of filming is such that recent David Attenborough documentaries come packaged with a 'making of' mini documentary showing the shenanigans the camera team had to go through in order to achieve particular shots. Michael Gunton, the executive producer of the BBC Natural History Unit's series *Life Story* (2015), emphasised that a unique aspect of the filming was having cameras at the animals' eye level. The effect was to give the viewer a 'tiger's eye' view of a chase or to put viewers in the tree canopy with the bonobos. This extra sense of spatial presence was, he felt, one reason for the series' huge popularity. This was reinforced by focalisation techniques that sharply picked out an individual, while consigning the rest of the pack, group or herd to a more blurred image. Following the experience of a single animal made it easier to identify and empathise with the individual. In addition to describing the camerawork, the describer may be called upon to do much extra research, especially in terms of the ecology of the environment in which the encounter takes place. Again, naming and explication is the way to go. Largely freed from time constraints, the describer is able to create a vivid script limited only by their literary abilities and imagination. Again, heightened observation is not necessary. The ITC Guidance (ITC, 2000: 22) points out: 'In a nature film, there may be wildlife in the distance, but if they are too far away to identify, there is little point in examining them through a telescope. If they were more than incidental to the sequence, they would have been filmed in close-up.' As with films, the description will, to some extent, mask the emotive music in the soundtrack, but the ambient sounds of the creature's habitat, along with any characteristic cries, should be left unobliterated if the sense of otherness and elsewhere is to be effectively conveyed to the AD user.

As with all description, as well as relying on the soundtrack, it is good to be able to draw on sensory information other than vision in order to get across the characteristics of the creature being described. For example, a chameleon not only comes in a variety of colours, but its skin has the texture of a beaded purse. As locomotion or gait is often an identifying characteristic, the speed, direction and effort involved should all be described. Scale is often hard to judge or may be cheated for effect. A giraffe might look particularly tall if filmed amongst young saplings. Comparisons with human metrics or everyday objects are often preferable to actual measurements using centimetres or inches. For example, a spider might fit on the tip of your finger or be the size of a dinner plate. Other measurements such as the weight of a creature will often be provided in the narration, but can be inferred, either from the soundtrack or, for example, from the depth of a footprint in soft ground.

Documentaries were traditionally made for the purposes of instruction or to document reality. They both show and tell. This suggests that accuracy of description is paramount, although the describer must take care to avoid redundancy. In one of the earliest reception studies of AD (and Kirchner and Schmeidler, 2001) participants reported that some description repeats information people could have figured out themselves. This can happen as a function of filmmaking because the editing of speech requires a cut-away – an image to distract the viewer from the non-consecutive mouth movements of a speaker. In general, a shot is chosen that illustrates the topic being discussed and the image may add limited extra detail. As the information is often conveyed by real people (as opposed to dramatic characters), their physical appearance is likely to have little bearing on our understanding of the subject matter; instead, the interviewees or speakers may be identified by a caption stating their name and perhaps job title or area of expertise. Ways to deal with text on screen are discussed in Chapter 9. This is also relevant to documentaries in which interviewees from a different country, if not dubbed, may well have their speech captioned.

8.6 Soaps and serials

Adopting of the same terminology as the ST is a way to establish coherence, characterised by Braun (2007: 365) as 'connectivity in discourse'. Braun furthermore distinguishes between local and global coherence, with 'local coherence being created within individual scenes and global coherence reaching out across scenes'. The longer the duration of the AVT product, the potentially more difficult global coherence becomes. For example, it is common practice in the UK for the description of a stage play to be split between two describers, each taking one act. Once each has prepared their part of the AD script (usually this work is carried out independently, although they may have brief discussions following their initial viewing of the production) they must work together to ensure consistency of terminology. The same might happen when describing a film with a tight turn-around before broadcast, as different reels of the film may be allocated to different describers in order to speed up the scripting process. The potential problems become heightened with other genres such as series and serials, whether for TV or for films that elapse over a longer time span or a larger number of episodes. Point A.34 of the Ofcom Code advises: 'Ideally, the same people should be used to describe a series of programmes, both to ensure a consistent style (e.g. in terms of level of detail) and because the description forms a part of the programme for users' (Ofcom, 2015). For example, the Harry Potter films were all described by the same describer, Di Langford, to ensure consistency over the ten years of their release (2001–2011).

For soaps and long-running series it can be helpful for an AD unit to maintain an up-to-date database of names used for characters and locations. Standard descriptions for opening titles may also be shared so as to provide consistency and to avoid having to reinvent the wheel. Titles are discussed further in Chapter 9. The Code on Provision of Access Services (Ofcom, 2015: 4.3) suggests using the opening sequence to provide a brief summary of the previous episode. Although many series do this as a matter of course, editing together a montage of short snippets from the previous episode, in practice these usually contain little space for description and the BPS audience may have to rely on dialogue alone, or their own memories. Some series make this montage explicit; the words 'previously on Ally McBeal' spring to mind, as these prefaced the opening of every programme in the series before a quick montage recapped events in the previous episode(s). This type of montage has become an industry standard for TV series (see Michlin, 2011). Where this is not the case, the describer may choose to provide a similar introduction to prepare the AD user for what is about to follow.

Matamala and Remael (2015) discuss working on the Flemish soap opera *Thuis*. They point out that in a soap the storyline generally revolves around intrigue and emotion, carried through the dialogue, and each episode follows a predictable format consisting of a recap, the credits, then the episode itself, ending with a preview of what to expect next time. A limited number of settings are frequently revisited, and most scenes involve only two or three characters, who are strongly connected to particular places. Most soaps also have an accompanying website where descriptions of characters could be made available, as there is rarely time within the dialogue-heavy episodes and descriptions of regular characters could quickly become tiresomely repetitive for a dedicated fan. Remael also suggests that such descriptions could include the character's biography, e.g.: 'Simonne is Yvette's daughter. She and Frank have one son, Franky. A few years ago she met her father Stan, who was one of Yvette's puppy loves. Simonne has always had a very good relationship with Frank's mother, Florke, who has meanwhile passed away and with Florke's husband Rogerke. When she needs someone to talk to, she can rely on her best friend Julia.' This may be helpful not only to AD users but also to sighted audiences watching for the first time.

8.7 Children's programmes

The RNIB (2009) has produced some specific guidelines on describing for children, based on 'feedback from parents, children and teachers and in consultation with the speech and language therapists'. Benecke warns that blind children 'have normally a smaller memory of images, because they were born blind or simply had a shorter period in which they could see – compared to grown-ups this at times had the [sic] whole youth to fill their memory of images. The describer therefore has to be very careful not to rely on too much presupposed knowledge and has to describe in more detail – if the gaps between the dialogues allow that' (Benecke, 2007: 5). Over-complex AD for children is best avoided. The RNIB points out that a significant proportion of visually impaired children may also have learning disabilities or hearing problems if their sight impairment is part of a spectrum of other disabilities, often stemming from being born prematurely. Blind children are also likely to have delayed language development and may display other speech problems such as pronoun reversals and formulaic speech (Hobson and Bishop, 2003; Pring, 2004). However, Pring (2004) suggests that the majority later 'catch up'. The RNIB guidelines point out that AD can help facilitate this because the AD 'signposts objects and events, and reinforces the meaning of words'. When audio describing for children, repetition can be beneficial rather than dull. Leaving space for sound effects is all the more important to help blind children make cross-modal associations. Below is an example featuring plenty of repetition from the AD of a stage adaptation of the children's book *The Elephantom* by Ross Collins, directed by Finn Caldwell and Toby Olié at the National Theatre of Great Britain (2013). The production was mimed by actors, whose movement was choreographed to a soundtrack, and used an inflatable puppet as the mysterious Elephantom, which apparently appears from nowhere and behaves like a naughty and oversized poltergeist.

> Slowly, slowly, an enormous blue balloon starts to blow up on her bed, Bigger and bigger. The girl stares. Clutches the duvet. Bigger and bigger. Bluer and bluer. Suddenly, little balloon legs dangle. The girl dives out of bed. Bigger and bigger – the size of an elephant. An elephant's head floats on and joins its body. Elephantom glides off the bed, blue and blowing. He sails round in the air to face the little girl.

Playing with rhythm is also recommended, as is verbal economy. In an attempt to describe the American cartoon *The Powerpuff Girls* in the early days of TV description in the UK, the describers at ITFC adopted a particularly playful style, abandoning a narrative form, such that when one of the protagonists was about to come to a sticky end, the describer might simply say 'she aims a punch at the window, [pause] . . . Oh dear! [SFX: shattering glass]'. This approach allowed the sound effect to convey that the action resulted in the glass breaking.

AD for children is not specifically mentioned in the Spanish guidelines, whereas the ITC Guidance (ITC, 2000: 3.2) advocates using a more intimate tone, such as describing in the first person plural, e.g. 'Now he's coming towards us. His mouth hangs open. His arms are outstretched and he's breathing heavily . . . '.

Orero (2011) discusses the film *Monsters Inc.* (Docter, Unkrich and Silverman, 2002), in which the opening sequence is given over to description of the characters rather than a description of the action. It is important to remember that a programme described for children is likely to be watched by the child on their own, but also possibly by sighted parents watching with their blind child. Or by a sighted child watching with their blind parent(s) or by a blind child watching with their sighted sibling(s). The aim should be to create a description that a family can enjoy together. In terms of delivery, the Spanish standard advises: 'When AD is for children the voice-talent (male or female) should have a tone which is more adequate for children and which can be more expressive' (AENOR, 2005: 12). Ofcom (2015: A4.35) suggests: 'Language and pace of delivery for children's TV need particular care, having regard to the age and background of the target audience, as well as feedback from children and their parents. A more intimate style may be appropriate than would be the case for programmes aimed at adults.'

A Polish study (Krejtz et al., 2012) using eye-tracking data showed another useful application of AD for children: that of helping to guide the attention of sighted children. This is one of the many educational functions of AD, along with aiding foreign language learning.

8.8 Genre and live performance

The importance of recognising variation between genres is not limited to screen AD. In the theatre, the production genre carries similar implications for the AD. Description of comedy may benefit from breaking the rule of never letting the description override the dialogue (Crowley and Fryer, 2015). In some genres, such as pantomime and popular musicals, it may be necessary to describe the antics of the audience (e.g. dancing in the aisles in *Mamma Mia!* or joining in the actions during the community song in a pantomime). Occasionally plays are deemed to need only an AI rather than a full AD. One example is the production of *Under Milk Wood* at the National Theatre of Great Britain (1995, dir. Michell), the justification being that *Under Milk Wood* was conceived by its author, Dylan Thomas, as a radio play or 'a play for voices'. It was therefore possible to follow the play with no AD, as the settings, characters and actions are identified in the dialogue, which left extremely limited space for any AD. Yet, it was beautifully brought to life and the costumes and stage design added to its charm.

As with screen series and serials, it is important to have continuity of voices and set/character descriptions for two- or three-part plays – for example, the two plays adapted by Nicholas Wright from Philip Pullman's trilogy of novels known collectively as *His Dark Materials*, staged at the National Theatre of Great Britain in 2003. Or more recently, *The James Plays*, a trio of history plays by Rona Munro (2014) that were all staged on the same set in a co-production between the National Theatres of Scotland and Great Britain and the Edinburgh International Festival. A single description of the set sufficed for all three; it would have been ridiculous and confusing to have it described three times by different describers.

8.9 Conclusion

In this chapter we have explored how the need for AD and the style of AD can change according to programme genre. We have discussed the importance of consistency and continuity in series and serials. It is acknowledged that not every genre benefits from AD. Where resources are limited, they should be concentrated on describing genres that are the most popular or can most benefit from the addition of AD.

8.10 Exercises and points for discussion

1. Watch two short, described films or programmes of your choice – of contrasting genres. Under the categories of *Who*, *What*, *Where*, *When*, note any differences between genres. Look for differences in the language and delivery style of the description as well as the content.
2. Practise your verbal skills by describing some still images of animals. Try again using moving footage. How does your descriptive focus change?

References

AENOR (2005). Standard UNE 153020: 2005. Retrieved from www.en.aenor.es/aenor/normas/normas/fichanorma.asp?tipo=N&codigo=N0032787#.VoPaufGTRxU [accessed 30.12.15].

Benecke, Bernd. (2007). 'Audio description: phenomena of information sequencing'. In *EU-High-Level Scientific Conference Series MuTra 2007 LSP Translation Scenarios: Conference Proceedings*. Retrieved from http://www.euroconferences.info/proceedings/2007_Proceedings/2007_Benecke_Bernd.pdf [accessed 31.12.15].

Braun, Sabine (2007). 'Audio description from a discourse perspective: a socially relevant framework for research and training'. *Linguistica Antverpiensia, New Series – Themes in Translation Studies* 6. Peter Lang. Available from: http://epubs.surrey.ac.uk/303024/1/fulltext.pdf.

Bridge Multimedia (2011). Retrieved from www.bridgemultimedia.com/audiodescription/ad_news.php#fox [accessed 2.07.15.]

Cámara, Lidia and Eva Espasa (2011). 'The audio description of scientific multimedia'. *The Translator* 17, no. 2: 415–437.

Crowley, Bridget and Louise Fryer (2015). 'The Laughter Lines Project Report'. Retrieved from http://audiodescription.co.uk/uploads/general/Laughter_Lines_Project_Report 29.pdf [accessed 23.09.15].

Evans, Elizabeth Jane and Roberta Pearson (2009). 'Boxed out: visually impaired audiences, audio description and the cultural value of the television image'. *Participations: Journal of Audience and Reception Studies* 6, no. 2: 373–402.

Fryer, Louise (2013). 'Putting it into words: the impact of visual impairment on perception, experience and presence'. Doctoral thesis, Goldsmiths, University of London. Goldsmiths Research Online. Available at: http://research.gold.ac.uk/10152.

Hill, Annette (2007). *Restyling factual TV: audiences and news, documentary and reality genres*. London: Routledge.

Hobson, P. R. and M. Bishop (2003). 'The pathogenesis of autism: insights from congenital blindness'. *Philosophical Transactions of the Royal Society of London. Series B: Biological Sciences* 358, no. 1430: 335–344.

ITC (2000). ITC Guidance. Retrieved from www.ofcom.org.uk/static/archive/itc_publications/codes_guidance/audio_descripion/index.asp.html [accessed 4.04.15].

Kirchner, Corinne and Emilie Schmeidler (2001). 'Adding audio description: does it make a difference?' *Journal of Visual Impairment and Blindness* 95, no. 4: 197–212.

Krejtz, Izabela, Agnieszka Szarkowska, Krzysztof Krejtz, Agnieszka Walczak and Andrew Duchowski (2012). 'Audio description as an aural guide of children's visual attention: evidence from an eye-tracking study'. In *ETRA '12: Proceedings of the Symposium on Eye Tracking Research and Applications*. New York: ACM, pp. 99–106.

Matamala, Anna and Aline Remael (2015). 'Audio-description reloaded: an analysis of visual scenes in 2012 and Hero'. *Translation Studies* 8: 63–81.

McKechnie, Kara (2002). 'Taking liberties with the monarch: the royal bio-pic in the 1990s'. In Claire Monk and Amy Sargeant (eds) *British historical cinema: the history, heritage and costume film*. London: Psychology Press, pp. 217–236.

Michalewicz, Irena (2015).'Is it a monster? Audio describing horror film'. Paper presented at *Advanced Research Seminar on Audio Description (ARSAD) 2015*, Barcelona (March).

Michlin, M. (2011). 'More, more, more. Contemporary American TV series and the attractions and challenges of serialization as ongoing narrative'. *Mise au point. Cahiers de l'association française des enseignants et chercheurs en cinéma et audiovisuel* 3.

Monk, Claire and Amy Sargeant (eds) (2002). *British historical cinema: the history, heritage and costume film*. London: Psychology Press.

Ofcom (2015). Code on Provision of Access Services. Retrieved from http://stakeholders.ofcom.org.uk/binaries/broadcast/other-codes/tv-access-services-2015.pdf [accessed 29.07.15].

Olivola, Christopher Y. and Alexander Todorov (2010). 'Elected in 100 milliseconds: appearance-based trait inferences and voting'. *Journal of Nonverbal Behavior* 34, no. 2: 83–110.

Orero, Pilar (2011). 'Audio description for children: once upon a time there was a different audio description for characters'. *Entre texto y receptor: accesibilidad, doblaje y traducción*. Frankfurt: Peter Lang, pp. 169–184.

Paci, V. (2006). 'The attraction of the intelligent eye: obsessions with the vision machine in early film theories'. In Wanda Strauven (ed.) *The cinema of attractions reloaded*. Chicago: University of Chicago Press, pp. 121–137.

Porter, James E. (1986). 'Intertextuality and the discourse community'. *Rhetoric Review* 5, no. 1: 34–47.

Pring, L. (2004). *Autism and blindness: research and reflections*. London: Wiley.

Rasheed, Z. and M. Shah M. (2002). 'Movie genre classification by exploiting audio-visual features of previews'. In *Proceedings of the 16th International Conference on Pattern Recognition, 2002*, vol. 2. IEEE, pp. 1086–1089. Retrieved from http://vision.eecs.ucf.edu/projects/movieClassification/icpr02_old.pdf [accessed 6.01.2016].

RNIB (2009). 'Audio description for children'. Retrieved from http://www.docin.com/p-650002545.html [accessed 7.01.2016].

Romero-Fresco, Pablo (2013). 'Accessible filmmaking: joining the dots between audiovisual translation, accessibility and filmmaking'. *The Journal of Specialised Translation* 20: 201–223.

Sadowska, Anna (2015). 'Kid's stuff'. Presentation at *Advanced Research Seminar on Audio Description (ARSAD) 2015*, Barcelona (March).

Sellar, Walter Carruthers, Robert Julian Yeatman and John Reynolds (1931). *1066 and all that: a memorable history of England*. London: Methuen.

Taylor, Christopher (2014). 'Intertexuality'. In Anna Maszerowska, Anna Matamala and Pilar Orero (eds) *Audio description: new perspectives illustrated*. Amsterdam: John Benjamins, pp. 29–40.
Toms, Elaine G. and D. Grant Campbell (1999). 'Genre as interface metaphor: exploiting form and function in digital environments'. In *Proceedings of the 32nd Annual Hawaii International Conference on Systems Sciences, 1999. HICSS-32.* IEEE. Available from https://www.computer.org/csdl/proceedings/hicss/1999/0001/02/00012008.pdf [accessed 30.12.15].
Vygotsky, Lev S. (1986). *Thought and language*, trans. A. Kozulin. Cambridge, MA: MIT Press.

Film references

Elizabeth, S. Kappur (1998).
March of the Penguins, L. Jacquet (2005).
Monsters Inc., P. Docter, L. Unkrich and D. Silverman (2002).
The Private Life of Henry VIII, A. Korda (1933).
Shakespeare in Love, J. Madden, (1999).
Girl with a Pearl Earring, P. Webber (2003).
The Shining, S. Kubrick (1980).
Zombieland, R. Fleischer (2009).

References to live events

Gloriana, dir. R. Jones (2013). Royal Opera House, London.
Sunday in the Park with George, dir. S. Pimlott (1990). National Theatre of Great Britain, London (pre-dates UK description).
The Elephantom, dir. F. Caldwell and T. Olié (2013). National Theatre of Great Britain, London. AD by in-house team (describers Bridget Crowley and Louise Fryer).
The James Plays, dir. R. Munro (2014). National Theatre of Great Britain, London. AD by in-house team.
The Lion King, dir. J. Taymor (1994–ongoing). Lyceum Theatre, London. AD by VocalEyes (original describers Louise Fryer and Andrew Holland).
Under Milk Wood, dir. R. Michell (1995). Royal National Theatre of Great Britain, London. AD by in-house team (describers Louise Fryer and Andrew Holland).

References to TV programmes

Life Story, Sophie Lanfear (2015).
Wolf Hall, P. Kosminsky (2015).

9 Beyond the basics
Text on screen

9.1 Introduction

So far we have been considering visual information translated into verbal information; however, there is also another mode that needs to be considered in the context of access for those with a sight impairment: verbal information presented visually. Text is commonly present at the start and end of each programme or film in the form of opening titles and end credits, and this information is unavailable to BPS people unless it is read aloud. Verbalising text can present problems, as text rarely appears on its own or remains on screen for as long as it takes to read it out loud. This chapter reviews types of text on screen and discusses options for making text accessible to a visually impaired audience. Interestingly, in the days of the silent movie, intertitles would be read out by the so-called film explainer for an illiterate audience. The explainer was also there to interpret the cinematic language for those unfamiliar with the language of cinema. In Japan such people were called Benshi (Nornes, 2007). For a sight-impaired audience some of their skills are still needed.

9.2 Tops and tails

9.2.1 Title sequences

According to Edward Said (1997: 5), the 'beginning ... is the first step in the intentional production of meaning'. The Vimeo video school (OnlineVideo.net, 2012) states that: 'Title sequences are some of the most memorable elements of classic films and TV shows ... They entrance us from the first frame with animated title sequences that perfectly set the mood for the stories that follow'. This concept of framing is one we have met before. It allows audiences to select an appropriate mental script and therefore interpret incoming information more effectively. For example, the opening titles of the US TV series *Breaking Bad* (Gilligan, 2008–13) starts with a teasing snippet of action, then lexically presents not only functional information such as series and episode title, names of the main actors and production crew (creator, producer and co-producers etc.) but also images of a periodic table and the chemical formula for methamphetamine. The typeface is plain white, except that letter combinations in the names that symbolise chemical elements are picked out in green, so Br and Ba appear in green before

120 *Beyond the basics: text on screen*

the remaining letters are added in white to complete the title *Br*eaking *Ba*d. The words are wreathed in an acid-green smoke on a green-black background reminiscent of a school chalk board. This all contributes to establishing the atmosphere and underlining the premise of the series about a chemistry teacher who decides to raise cash by cooking crystal meth. This illustrates that it is not just what the words say but the manner in which the text is presented that carries meaning. As Georgina Kleege puts it, talking about fine art, 'Paint is paint. But the paint is also the point' (Kleege, 1999: 94).

The importance of title sequences is shown by the fact that they are usually contracted out to specialists and have their own Emmy award.

Dan Gregoras is the creative director of the agency Imaginary Forces that produced the opening sequence for the film *The Manhattan Project* (Brickman, 1996). In a discussion of TV titles on the blog site Art of the Title (Art of the Title, 2015) he says: 'The good ones are iconic and hard to forget. Show fans may not remember every scene from every episode, but they'll have a lasting memory of a good title sequence. It creates a sense of permanence.'

Another memorable opening sequence comes from the feature film *Valkyrie* (Singer, 2008). After the roaring lion logo of Metro-Goldwyn-Mayer and the UA of United Artists, words in German 'Das folgende bruht auf wahren begebenheiten' appear briefly before they transmute into their English translation ('the following is based on a true story'). This visual device of swapping one language for another is echoed audibly when the spoken German of the main character, von Stauffenberg, in the opening frames is replaced by Tom Cruise's American voice-over. The same happens with the film's title, shown first in German (Walküre) before the letters change places and alter to spell out *Valkyrie*. The black font that is used for the title is called Fraktur script, which was common in all German-speaking countries in the early twentieth century. It was the style used in medieval manuscripts and is still in use in the masthead of many newspapers such as the *Frankfurter Allgemeine Zeitung* and even the *New York Times*. Ironically, although there is a strong association between Fraktur and the Nazi regime, the script was banned by Joseph Bohrmann in 1941 for being a 'Jewish' hand. In the film the text is written in black on a red background and this background billows and waves. We gradually realise that it is the fabric of a Nazi flag as the shot widens and a white disc bearing a black swastika is slowly revealed. The audio track is of male voices chanting, and the English translation of their words (an oath to the Führer) is superimposed in text on the flag. As hearing an English voice over German speech is entirely in keeping with the soundtrack in other parts of the film, there is no difficulty here for the describer in talking over the soundtrack. All the describer needs to do is voice the translation, making its origin clear (e.g. prefacing the translation with 'white letters read', or similar). If such a preface is not given, it risks sounding as though the audio describer is a fully paid-up member of the Nazi party. The on-screen text continues as a black screen gives way to a caption announcing the setting of the next scene: 'The German 10th Panzer division, Tunisia, North Africa'. The next form of on-screen text is the entry von Stauffenberg is writing in his diary. The image is too small for us to see the text clearly on the page, meaning that the describer is under no obligation to read it out. In any case it is unnecessary, as von Stauffenberg himself repeats the content as though in his head. The juxtaposition of voice-over and text, in addition to the echoing quality of his voice and the fact that he is alone, is enough for us to infer that he is voicing what he is writing. He shuts the diary quickly when he is disturbed, and briefly we see the cover, showing the logo and name of his regiment. As this is information that has already been given in the opening caption, and given the time constraints that prevent the describer's reading it verbatim, a brief summary, 'official diary', is enough. Such incidental text is often a useful source of information. Later in the film, the title of the music, from which the codename of the operation to assassinate Hitler and the film's title come, is shown on the centre label of an LP that von Stauffenberg plays over and over at home. The piece (Wagner's *Ride of the Valkyries*) is so familiar as to not need naming, and in any case need not be identified, as AD users can hear it and either be able to name it or not, just as members of the sighted audience. Yet, the director has deliberately chosen to include a close-up of the label, leaving the name of the piece in no doubt. As the label spins one way, the camera spins the other, the dizzying visual effect further focusing the attention of the sighted audience. In addition to the title, the label shows the name of the performers, 'the Philharmonischer Orchester, Berlin', reinforcing the patriotism of the piece and the main setting of the film in Berlin, Germany. Although to voice this information necessitates speaking over the music, as previously mentioned, Fryer and Freeman (2014) have shown that when describing over emotive music 'the addition of verbal information did not lead to a reduction in presence or levels of elicited emotion, despite AD partially masking the soundtrack', suggesting either that the content of the verbal information is more important or that blind people are especially good at tasks requiring divided auditory attention. This has been shown in other studies, e.g. Röder et al. (1999).

9.2.2 Logos

Valkyrie, like most films, begins with the film company's logo – in this case the roaring lion of Metro-Goldwyn-Mayer. Although the roar is audible, the lexical information and the way it is presented must also be described. A logo is more than a collection of words and images. A logo is a representation of a brand, defined by Celia Lury (2004: 1) as 'a set of relations between products and services'. In a film it is often a stamp of quality. It helps frame a movie in terms of our expectations. We expect a Disney film to have a certain style and type of content. Most logos are subject to slight changes over time. Paul Grainge (2004: 346), for example, points out how the torch-holder of Columbia Pictures has become thinner to suit the modern aesthetic. Grainge discusses logos in terms of nostalgia. Logos are also altered to reference the world of a particular film; for example, 'owls and bats flew from the corners' of the Warner Brothers shield in *Harry Potter and the Sorcerer's Stone* (Columbus, 2001). The halo appearing on the Pathé cockerel was mentioned in Chapter 3, so it is evident that a description of the logo is necessary for a host of reasons: recognition, contextualisation and as a

122 *Beyond the basics: text on screen*

time-stamp. That said, unless the logo has been transformed, most AD providers have established an in-house description for its describers to use. This ensures consistency, aiding recognition and saving cognitive load on the AD users as well as saving describer's time.

9.3 Text on screen and delivery

In *Valkyrie*, the describer should not be tempted to provide their own German translation but, rather, read it as shown. There is no obligation to correct a poor translation, only to make the AV product, watched by sighted viewers, accessible to people who cannot perceive it themselves. There is a question here as to accent. When reading out translations of foreign speech, there is the possibility of the describer reinforcing its 'otherness' by adopting an accent. As discussed in Chapter 7, this is done to a humorous degree in the AD of *Borat* (Charles, 2006). Given the serious content of *Valkyrie*, it would be inappropriate here. In general, a director, by choosing to subtitle rather than dub speech, has done so with the intention of preserving the sound of the original actor. A curious mixed approach is taken in the English AD for *Coco Before Chanel* (Fontaine, 2009). This a French film with English subtitles. In the audio-described version, the words of Coco are spoken by a female with a strong French accent. However, the rest of the characters are voiced with English accents. This mix-and-match approach is simply confusing, so that we wonder why Coco's sister sounds English, and so different from Coco herself. The pair scrape a living performing music-hall songs. Unfortunately, there is no translation of the song lyrics, even though they are subtitled. However, the title is translated, as *Coco Before Chanel*, even though it is shown only in French – *Coco Avant Chanel*. Such translation is questionable practice. As the ITC Guidance (ITC, 2000) is silent on the subject of translating lyrics, research is needed to discover ways in which lyric content of foreign songs can be conveyed without masking the music. This is all the more problematic when a song is used as background music with competing dialogue over the top. Often the words offer a wry comment on the action. Currently AD offers no solution to enable AD users to benefit from sung content in a foreign language when the lyrics are subtitled. In live contexts a similar situation may occur in a pantomime, when the audience is invited to 'sing along'. The technique here is for the describer to speak the forthcoming words in the short interval between the lines of a song. To the author's knowledge this technique has not been tried for screen AD.

9.3.1 Audio subtitles

An extended sequence of subtitled speech occurs in *Kill Bill 2* (Tarantino, 2004) when the Bride is sent to learn martial arts skills with the Chinese Master Pai Mei. The audio describer for this film handles it deftly, timing his speaking of the subtitles such that the voice of Pai Mei is established for a few seconds before being dipped under the AD, as is common practice in audio translations, such as radio news. Furthermore, although the describer begins by prefacing the first few phrases of the speech with 'he/she says', reinforcing his source of information by stating 'yellow subtitles appear', this prefacing is soon rendered unnecessary owing to the content, the way the AD is phrased and delivered and there being only two characters in the scene (of opposite gender). By including descriptive information about one character's actions before voicing their speech, it is obvious which of them is speaking.

> AD: She looks disheartened, 'I speak Japanese very well'; 'I didn't ask if you speak Japanese, I asked if you speak Cantonese.'

Although this is voiced with no accent, the describer puts plenty of expression into his voice. While not actually acting, he manages to convey prosodic information through a tone of irritation for Pai Mei alternating with one of humility or resignation for the Bride. Braun and Orero (2010) report on more experiments in the Netherlands and Sweden, trialling TTS. In this instance subtitles were read out automatically by a synthesised voice triggered by the subtitle file, while the AD was written and delivered by a describer, the idea being that it would be cheaper if the subtitles were voiced automatically and it would be clearer if the describer's voice were different from the voice used for the subtitles. However, the authors cite Ofcom's conclusion that 'the expressionless quality of a synthesised voice is not suitable for an entire drama or a film, and it is not feasible to recognise a variety of different speakers within the programme' (Ofcom, 2006: 2). As Braun and Orero (2010: 5) point out: 'One particular challenge for AST [audio subtitles] is that subtitles often greatly reduce the ST message, relying on the recipients' ability to use visual input to compensate for condensations and omissions in the subtitles. This creates problems for an audience who has no access to the visual mode.' The importance of this interaction between sound and vision is reinforced by the stage director, Julie Taymor, when discussing her film version of Shakespeare's *A Midsummer Night's Dream* (2015), who said: 'My big belief about Shakespeare on film is that, if you can show close-ups of mouths moving and reaction shots of other actors in the scene, you have double the understanding' (Taymor, 2015). By weaving his description around the spoken (audio) subtitles, the describer for *Kill Bill 2* managed to fully convey the information from both visual and auditory modes. By giving the describer control over voicing the subtitles, there is a better opportunity to weave them into the AD more effectively by condensing or summarising the subtitled words and integrating them into the description, rather than simply reading them out verbatim. In practice a few words often have to be added to make a caption suitable to be voiced. For example, in the opening sequence of *Coco Before Chanel* the caption 'Obazine Orphanage 1893' is rendered '*a caption reads* Orphanage *at* Obazine 1893', clarifying the source and making it easier on the ear. The describer has made room to voice the on-screen text by using a range of strategies: starting the AD early; beginning the description over a black screen that shows only the production credits; grouping the actor credits; and omitting the production information altogether.

124 *Beyond the basics: text on screen*

Although it is often called 'opening titles', a particular difficulty arises when a title sequence begins ten or fifteen minutes into the film, interrupting the narrative flow. An audible indication of the credits comes from the music. This is easier to recognise in a series than in a film, when the opening titles, including text on screen, come out of the blue, or in the first episode of a series, before the audience has become familiar with the signature tune. The text is presented at the same time as a lot of visual information, introducing characters and locations that will go on to be significant as the story unfolds. In this case, Orero and Braun (2010, cited in Matamala, 2014) suggest various options: omission, condensation and verbatim reproduction either in synchrony with the text's arrival on screen or asynchronously. In Chapter 6 we noted the awkward juxtapositions that may arise from attempting a synchronous rendition. This is particularly difficult in *Girl with a Pearl Earring* (Webber, 2003), as the credits for the actors' names continue to pop up for several minutes after the story has got underway. Even adding information about the source of the text does not really clarify the clash between the narrative mode of the AD and the voicing of the text on screen, as the following shows:

> AD: White letters: Delft 1665. Tom Wilkinson. The massive Oude Kirk dominates the cobbled market place which is surrounded by high stone buildings with red shutters. Griet carries her bundle across the marketplace laden with vegetables. The square is busy with shoppers in black or grey. Geese wander around the large open space.

Although the confusing appearance of Tom Wilkinson may be avoided by using a different (a second) voice or by highlighting the derivation of the words with a more explicit phrase such as 'more credits appear', another technique is to abandon any attempt at synchrony and read out all the cast names earlier, at a more suitable point – this is the strategy adopted in *Coco Before Chanel*. Condensation is a technique familiar to subtitlers that may also be necessary for AST, i.e. reading out an abbreviated summary of the subtitled foreign language when it appears. However, condensation of credits inevitably results in omission, as it would be ludicrous to condense, for example, by reading out only the surnames rather than the actors' full names. The describer, therefore, needs criteria for selection, such as importance of role or perhaps familiarity; for example, a famous actor's voice should be easier to recognise than that of a newcomer. As in the above example, actors' names sometimes appear in isolation, without being tied to the character name. The describer may choose to offer extra help by adding in this information, although it may not be possible, due to time constraints; or they may choose to relocate the information, such that the actor's name is given just before the actor speaks. This allows links to be made between the character, the actor playing that role and the sound of the character's voice.

9.4 AD and voice-over

Szarkowska (2011) reported on an experiment in Poland where foreign AV products are the norm. She reasons that the popularity of voice-over, whereby the dialogue is given a spoken translation by a single voice, should be advantageous to people with a visual impairment, compared with subtitled speech, in that foreign-language dialogue is already translated. However, in the Polish experiment it became obvious that without the visuals it was hard to tell who was speaking, especially in scenes with multiple characters of the same gender. This was resolved by incorporating names more frequently into the AD script, a practice that, as we have seen, should in any case be encouraged.

9.5 Text and live events

Although the problem of subtitles may seem to relate only to screen (not live) AD, opera surtitling is a major exception, although not the only one. On rare occasions, an artificial voice has been used to voice on-screen text, to capture the non-human nature of the source. In the National Theatre of Great Britain's 1997 production of Patrick Marber's play *Closer* (dir. Marber), one scene featured two men contacting each other via the internet. On stage the actors sat with their backs to the audience, facing a large screen, on which their typed messages were displayed to the sighted audience. The AD needed to convey the text but one of the men was pretending to be a woman, which raised an issue of which gender should voice the words: it was obvious to the sighted audience that both correspondents were male. Compounding the problem was the fact that the comments were sexually explicit and some of the 'words' were merely a collection of abstract symbols, not easily pronounced. A 'virtual' orgasmic climax was indicated by a random series of punctuation marks on screen. The solution was to use an electronically generated 'synthesised voice' – of neutral gender – which helped to capture the artificiality of the typed conversation and saved the describers from having to whisper obscenities direct into the ears of their audience. In a less extreme example, a new adaptation of the *Oresteia* at London's Almeida Theatre (Aristophanes, adapted/dir. Icke, 2015) included LED displays of text spelling out key lines of dialogue as well as giving the real time in hours, minutes and seconds. This was mentioned in the AI as well as in the dynamic AD. The stage adaptation of *The Curious Incident of the Dog in the Night-Time* (dir. Elliott, 2012–) included graphically presented words and symbols and was performed within

> [a] stage . . . like a large box, open at the front. The inside of the box looks like graph paper – but black with a white grid. At each intersection on the grid is a small white dot. On the stage floor, Zero marks the centre line which runs from the steps at the front to the back wall. To the right, the squares of the grid are numbered up to 7. To the left, down to minus 7. The grid on the walls is lettered from F at the front to letter Q at the back.
>
> As [the actors] move around the space, the dots at each intersection of the graph paper light up in various colours – creating pathways, lines and patterns across the stage. Words or sentences are projected onto the walls, gliding up and down, spinning, shrinking and growing, merging into each other.

126 *Beyond the basics: text on screen*

The above extract comes from the AI for the show, allowing the describers to convey the production's visual style. The words that appeared did not always need to be voiced by the describer, as often they were visually amplifying words spoken by the cast. At the end of the show, the lines formed diagrams that helped to explain how Christopher solved an equation in his maths A-level. The need to provide access to such diagrams is not limited to theatre (e.g. Horstmann et al., 2004). As Gambier (2006) reminds us, most texts, not just AV products, are actually multimodal.

9.6 Multilingualism

According to Remael (2012), AV products are also increasingly multilingual. In the UK there is limited multilingualism, although some plays and live events have multilingual elements – for example, the stage version of Michael Morpurgo's children's book *War Horse* (dir. Elliott, 2007–2016). The production has evolved since it was first staged so that it is now monolingual. However, in its earliest incarnation the play featured German spoken by the soldiers at the front, and French spoken by the little peasant girl Emilie and her mother, Paulette. Emilie befriends Joey, the horse of the title, when he is briefly billeted at their French farm. Even in a production aimed at English children, who were unlikely to have even a basic knowledge of French or German, this was not a problem, as the actions of the actors made the meaning clear. For example, the meaning of a senior officer shouting 'Mütze ab' was clarified by the soldiers taking their caps off. The describer simply needed the space to insert the description of their action for the dialogue to make sense.

9.7 Simultaneity and asynchrony

Just as in subtitling the simultaneity of verbal translation presents problems – such as when speech is heard over the image of somebody reading a newspaper – so in AD there can be a clash between an action needing description and visually presented text. An example of this comes in the opening minutes of the film of the musical *Chicago* (Marshall, 2002). One of the stars of the show, Velma Kelly, totters up an alley to the theatre, pausing to rip a strip off a poster. Multiple copies of the same poster line the wall of the alley. The words on the poster are critical:

> Kelly Sisters
> back by
> popular demand
> Velma and Veronica
> as themselves

It appears that Velma tears away words at random, because the lower portion of the poster is not well fixed down. However, later it becomes clear that she was deliberately ripping off her sister's name, as she has murdered her. As Velma later sings, 'All that remains is the remains of a perfect double act'. This moment presents two problems. In the commercial DVD there is no description at this point because we do not yet know Velma's identity. The describer also felt that the poster reference is not understood on first viewing by the sighted audience (Hyks, personal communication) and would be lost on the blind. However, as we have already noted, such anaphoric references should be given, as they might be appreciated on a second viewing, if not on the first, and can never be appreciated by the BPS audience if the AD does not include them. The other problem is the lack of time to describe Velma without being able to use the shorthand of her name (as this is the first time we have met her and she has yet to be identified in the dialogue), her action and the wording of the poster. The problem of simultaneity becomes even more acute moments later, as, in order to capture the subtle timing of the choreography of the song 'All That Jazz', the AD would need to express that Velma blinks slowly and deliberately on the two accented beats before the lyrics of the title, and in doing so would mask that moment in the score. As we have seen in the section on translating music, the recommendation is that AD is limited to repeats or bars between the lyrics, which obviously severely constrains the AD of dance. In the AD of live musicals, a further problem is the volume of the music, which often makes the AD hard to hear, quite apart from competing for attention. One devotee of musicals who is blind says she will often go more than once, first to hear the description and then a second time to enjoy the music. One advantage of a DVD is that it is relatively simple to listen to more than once, with and without the descriptive track.

9.8 End credits

Many of the same problems of the opening titles recur at the end of a film or TV programme, with the end credits. It can be a contractual obligation for the description company to include all the credits, even the publishing details of the music if commercial tracks have been played. Often any attempt at synchrony is abandoned, as, in a film, the AD track can run on if necessary. This is not the case in broadcast TV, when the announcer might fade the closing music without warning in order to keep their broadcast schedule to time. Access to this type of textual information that may be of interest to a minority of viewers could potentially be provided via an AI hosted online.

In live events the equivalent of the end credits is the curtain call. Although there is no on-stage text showing the performers' names, a sighted audience member is able to refer to their programme if they want a reminder of who played whom. For an AD user this is not so simple. Also it is good to know the order in which the actors appear, so that you know who is being applauded. One technical difficulty is being able to hear the AD over the volume of the applause, but there is little a describer can do to affect this, as omission is not a very satisfactory option. Again, audience response might need describing at this point. For example, an AD user might wish to know if a particular actor is receiving a standing ovation, so they can decide whether or not to join in.

9.9 Conclusion

In this chapter we have reviewed common instances of text on screen and looked at ways of making visually presented text audible by weaving it into the AD. Omission is rarely an option, as the written information has been deliberately included and is often critical to the plot and our understanding of the narrative.

Options include reading it verbatim, or summarising the verbal information. It is important to include visual information such as the actions and facial expression of the characters as well as the font and format of the text, if we are to understand its full meaning. Most screen products have opening title sequences that form an important reference frame for what is to follow, and a long list of end credits that a describing company may be contractually obliged to voice, although the exact specifications will vary from one film/TV company to another.

9.10 Exercises and points for discussion

1. Create the AD for a title sequence of your choice. The film *To Die For* (1995, Van Sant) is especially challenging. You may like to reflect on the difficulties you encountered and justify your choices. You may create your script by hand or using AD software (see Chapter 6).
2. On the accompanying website, using the script for *Joining the Dots*, create an AD for the subtitled version, incorporating audio subtitles. How much of the original description must you sacrifice? How much can you retain?

References

Art of the Title (2015). Retrieved from www.artofthetitle.com/news/2015-emmy-nominations-for-main-title-design/ [accessed 30.07.15].

Braun, Sabine and P. Orero (2010). 'Audio description with audio subtitling – an emergent modality of audiovisual localisation'. *Perspectives: Studies in Translatology* 18, no. 3: 173–188.

Fryer, Louise and Jonathan Freeman (2014). 'Can you feel what I'm saying? The impact of verbal information on emotion elicitation and presence in people with a visual impairment'. In A. Felnhofer and O. D. Kothgassner (eds) *Challenging presence: Proceedings of the 15th International Conference on Presence*. Vienna: facultas.wuv, pp. 99–107.

Gambier, Yves (2006). 'Multimodality and audiovisual translation'. In *MuTra Conference Audio Visual Translation Scenarios, Copenhagen (May 1–5, 2006)*, pp. 1–8. Retrieved from www. euroconferences. info/2006_abstracts. php# Gambier [accessed 24.08.15].

Grainge, P. (2004). 'Branding Hollywood: studio logos and the aesthetics of memory and hype'. *Screen* 45, no. 4: 344–362.

Horstmann, Mirko, Martin Lorenz, A. Watkowski, G. Ioannidis, Otthein Herzog, Alasdair King, David Gareth Evans et al. (2004). 'Automated interpretation and accessible presentation of technical diagrams for blind people'. *New Review of Hypermedia and Multimedia* 10, no. 2: 141–163.

ITC (2000). ITC Guidance. Retrieved from www.ofcom.org.uk/static/archive/itc/itc_publications/codes_guidance/audio_descripion/index.asp.html [accessed 4.04.15].

Kleege, Georgina (1999). *Sight unseen*. New Haven, CT: Yale University Press.

Lury, Celia (2004). *Brands: the logos of the global economy*. London: Routledge.

Matamala, Anna (2014). 'Audio describing text on screen'. In Anna Maszerowska, Anna Matamala and Pilar Orero (eds) *Audio description: new perspectives illustrated*. Amsterdam: John Benjamins, pp. 103–120.

Nornes, Markus (2007). *Cinema babel: translating global cinema*. Minneapolis: University of Minnesota Press.

Ofcom (2006). [Revised version]. Guidelines on the provision of television access services. Available from www.ofcom.org.uk/tv/ifi/guidance/tv_access_serv/guidelines/guidelines.pdf.

OnlineVideo.net (2012). 'How to Make an animated title sequence: video 101'. Retrieved from www.onlinevideo.net/2012/12/how-to-make-an-animated-title-sequence-video-101/#ixzz3ceQPguQ3 [accessed 29.07.15].

Orero, P. and Braun, S. (2010). 'Audio description with audio subtitling – an emergent modality of audiovisual localisation'. *Perspectives: Studies in Translatology* 18, no. 3: 173–188.

Remael, Aline (2012). 'From audiovisual translation to media accessibility: live-subtitling, audio-description and audio-subtitling'. In *AUSIT 2012: Proceedings of the 'Jubilation 25' Biennial Conference of the Australian Institute of Interpreters and Translators*. Newcastle-upon-Tyne: Cambridge Scholars Publishing, p. 134.

Röder, B., W. Teder-Sälejärvi, A. Sterr, F. Rösler, S. A. Hillyard and H. J. Neville (1999). 'Improved auditory spatial tuning in blind humans'. *Nature* 400, no. 6740: 162–166.

Said, Edward W. (1997). *Beginnings: intention and method*. London: Granta Books.

Szarkowska, Agnieszka (2011). 'Text-to-speech audio description: towards wider availability of AD'. *Journal of Specialised Translation* 15: 142–163.

Taymor, Julie (2015). 'When women fail, they don't get another opportunity'. *Guardian*. Retrieved from www.theguardian.com/stage/2015/jun/19/lion-king-director-julie-taymor-women-opportunity [accessed 21.06.15].

Film references

A Midsummer Night's Dream, J. Taymor (2015).
Borat, L. Charles (2006).
Chicago, R. Marshall (2002).
Coco Before Chanel, A. Fontaine (2009).
Harry Potter and the Sorcerer's Stone, C. Columbus (2001).
Kill Bill 2, Q. Tarantino (2004).
Girl with a Pearl Earring, P. Webber (2003).
The Manhattan Project, M. Brickman (1996).
To Die For, G. Van Sant (1995).
Valkyrie, B. Singer (2008).

References to live events

Closer, dir. P. Marber (1997). National Theatre of Great Britain, London. AD by in-house team (describers Louise Fryer and Andrew Holland).
Oresteia, dir. R. Icke (2015). Almeida Theatre, London. AD by VocalEyes (describers Louise Fryer and Veronika Hyks).
The Curious Incident of the Dog in the Night-Time, dir. M. Elliott (2012–ongoing). National Theatre of Great Britain, London. AD by in-house team (describers Roz Chalmers and Andrew Holland).
Warhorse, dir. M. Elliott (2007–2016). National Theatre of Great Britain, London. AD by in-house team (describers Louise Fryer and Andrew Holland).

Reference to TV programme

Breaking Bad, V. Gilligan et al. (2008–13).

10 Beyond the basics
Accessible filmmaking and describing camerawork

10.1 Introduction

This chapter discusses the AD of camerawork. Although this might seem to be mainly relevant to those working in screen translation, live events increasingly incorporate mixed media, with on-stage projection of film, either pre-recorded or shot live as part of the action as, for example, in plays directed by Katie Mitchell, including *Waves* (2008) and . . . *Some Trace of Her* (2006) at the National Theatre of Great Britain, Theatre de Complicité's adaptation of Bulgakov's *The Master and Margarita* (McBurney, Barbican Theatre, 2012) and Robert Icke's new version of Aristophanes' *Oresteia* (Icke, 2015) at London's Almeida Theatre.

It has been suggested that AD should seek to be 'a verbal camera lens' (Snyder, 2014: 1105) in the sense that it should be objective, yet a camera is only as objective as its operator. There is always somebody framing the shot, deciding on the angle and distance and, in a moving picture or film, choosing the sequence of shots. In film, as with any 'text', this is all carefully constructed in accordance with the language of the medium, such that there is little objective about it. Directors make conscious choices to manipulate their viewers (e.g. Branigan,1992). It seems curious that, given describers' concern for the visual, they should not seek to communicate this.

10.2 The language of cinema

In the early days of AD, as indicated by the ITC Guidance on standards for AD (ITC, 2000) it was assumed that, because film relies on a visual code, to people with a visual impairment, 'expressions like *in close up*, *pan across*, *mid-shot*, *crane-shot*, etc. may not mean anything' (ibid., 1.2). The ITC Guidance also points out that 'the wide variety of backgrounds among the audience should be taken into account. Some will remember television and film quite clearly and may be familiar with cinematographic terminology.' Somehow, these comments were overlooked and it was the first part of the message that gained precedence. Over the years the attitude to describing camerawork hardened, such that in their review of guidance Rai et al. (2010: 3.4) assert, 'Use of technical terms (i.e. camera angles) is discouraged and should only be used sparingly.'

Yet, just as any translator needs to be familiar with the source language in order to fulfil their task successfully, so too must a describer understand the visual language of film. Chaume (2004: para. 14) put it this way:

> A film is composed of a series of codified signs, articulated in accordance with syntactic rules. Its typology, the way it is organised and the meaning of all its elements results in a semantic structure that the spectator deconstructs in order to understand the meaning of the text. What interests the translator is knowing the functioning of each of these codes, and the possible incidence of all signs, linguistic and non-linguistic, within a translation.

In an intriguing paper Kim et al. (2014) discuss the affective influence of particular combinations of shots and camerawork. For example, the combination of 'a whip-pan with a bouncy motion' and 'either full or medium frame' is associated with joy, whereas fear is induced by a canted angle and what they call an 'inventory point-of-view' such that 'whatever the character is carrying shows up in the frame and allows the audience to see what he is holding' (Austin Community College, n.d.). However, Kim and colleagues go on to promote a coded vibration system, as opposed to description, in order to convey this affective information to people with impaired vision.

The US 'guidelines' for description, set out by the ADC in their third edition (2009), do allow that although 'one should generally avoid filmmaking jargon and describing filmmaking techniques, sometimes the brevity and simplicity of something like, "The screen fades to black" is appropriate.' They also advise describing 'the point of view when appropriate – "from above," "from space," "moving away," "flying low over the sandy beach," etc.' (ADC, 2009: 17). Essentially, this is an argument about language and terminology. The German guidelines find 'slow motion' acceptable (Benecke and Dosch, 2004), cited in Perego as being 'an understandable concept for the blind' (Perego, 2014: 106). Is the phrase 'from above' easier for a blind person to 'visualise' or to understand than 'aerial shot'? This seems unlikely, given Piety's recognition that blind and sighted people are 'members of the same speech community' (ibid., 210). Difficulties in understanding filmic terms seem even less likely, given that photography is a popular hobby for BPS people. There are professional photographers who are blind, such as Kurt Weston, whose work was exhibited at the University of California (*Time* magazine online), and Pete Eckert (http://www.peteeckert.com/), who has blogged about his experience of taking up photography after being diagnosed with retinitis pigmentosa, which can lead to 'tunnel' vision and sometimes to total blindness.

One research participant talked with enthusiasm about a course at York University on photography for the visually impaired:

> *A:* And it was there that I learned about depth of field and I had no concept about depth of field before somebody explained it to me.

L: Why would you, in fact?

A: Exactly. And um, it's quite interesting, but you can and I found a way of actually being able to create depth of field in my photographs although it didn't make a great deal of difference to me.

L: So how did you do that?

A: OK I got a good camera and a good lens and what I did was, I brought the subject matter as close as I could to me, um . . . right down to about 28 er 28–70, that particular lens, so if I put it down to 28 and if you then, um, use the other ring to increase depth of field. So all it was for me, it was a bit like the old contrast of a black-and-white TV set where you had a blurred picture and then you mushed around with the contrast you could get a slightly sharper one. Now if I was looking at something like a tree on a white background, then with the old black-and-white TV set I could get the contrast quite good, and I used, I discovered that I used the same sort of technique with the camera and then once you've done that and were fairly satisfied with and you'd got a sharper picture you could then . . . umm . . . then you could extend the focus and take up to 35 or 50 or something like that so you got a better panoramic view with the subject in the middle. And you take a picture and you'd know that the field of vision, the depth of vision was right.

L: Right, and so knowing that you were achieving something that you couldn't perceive yourself . . . was that a more satisfying experience?

A: Oh yeah, well it improved my pictures a great deal. And if I then looked at them when they were processed then I could see, 'cos you would suddenly see, if you'd taken a picture of somebody standing on the lawn on an autumn day, you would suddenly see the leaves in front of them or something, rather than, how can I put it, rather than a sort of um, an indistinct carpet of leaves, you actually saw that right in the very front of the picture there was an individual leaf.

L: Yes.

A: And I had never understood the value of that before. But it had to be explained to me. Once it was explained to me, I understood it.

10.3 Cinematic audio description

Kruger (2010) argues that an AD user's lack of access to the visual code means that AD must not only describe the visual elements but also add in 'narrative markers', providing what he terms 'audio narration' (AN) for its audience to understand film. He suggests that there is a 'continuum with AD at one end and AN at the other. At the descriptive extreme the emphasis would therefore be on substituting the visual codes (what can be seen by a sighted audience), and at the narrative extreme the emphasis would be on creating a coherent narrative that corresponds more closely to the narrative effect of the visual codes than with the codes themselves' (ibid., 233). Kruger's aim is 'to provide blind and visually impaired audiences with access to the film as an integrated narrative text'.

Accessible filmmaking and describing camerawork 133

While Kruger's aim is laudable, the filmic code is not beyond the reach of AD users, especially given that, as pointed out in Chapter 4, most will have had sight at some stage. Responses to cinematic terminology were tested in Fryer and Freeman's empirical research (2013a; 2013b) comparing user responses to and immersion in the film *Brief Encounter* (Lean, 1946) described in two ways: using an abundance of cinematic terminology and with a standard description omitting cinematic terminology, prepared in accordance with the ITC Guidance. The film excerpt was also shown with no description (the main character, Laura, narrates much of the action in the form of a flashback as she describes her 'affair' to her husband). Technical terms were deliberately included to test the tolerance of the blind participants. The filmic language was functional and blunt, as in the following:

Dolly:	It's almost 20 to 6.
Standard AD:	Hope fades from her face. She picks up her handbag and shopping basket and steps out onto the platform
Dolly:	It's almost 20 to 6.
Cinematic AD:	Cut to Laura, hope fading from her face. She picks up her handbag and shopping basket, and the camera pulls back as we follow her progress to the door. Cut to the platform. Laura emerges from the Refreshment room.

Arguably, both types of AD convey the same narrative information. Yet in one we could be listening to an audio book; in the other it is clearly cinema, not least because the cinematic AD brings with it a much stronger sense of movement, which is 'central in cinema' (Hirvonen, 2013: 103). In the cinematic version we are aware of the switch in the camera POV, such that Laura steps towards us as she *emerges from the Refreshment room*, rather than away from us as *she steps out on to the platform*. AN raises the question as to why we go to the cinema. Is it only to follow the story? Fryer and Freeman argue that it is for more than that (see Fryer 2010; Fryer and Freeman, 2013a; 2013b): we go to be entertained, to escape from the everyday by being 'transported' to other worlds; to be challenged intellectually and culturally; to share a social occasion with friends or family, and sometimes specifically to admire the camerawork or visual effects. If this is the case, then access not only to the visual elements but also to the visual style of the film is essential if the AD user is to be on the same footing as members of the sighted audience. Quantitative measures in the *Brief Encounter* experiment showed that participants reported a greater sense of presence when watching the film with cinematic AD, as compared to watching it with a 'standard' AD. Qualitative responses were mixed, as shown in Table 10.1, although they illustrate the desire of at least some members of the AD audience to be given information about camerawork. This opinion has been reinforced in comments made by delegates (of whom approximately 50 per cent had a visual impairment) at the Blind Creations conference (2013) at a session discussing the film *Across Still Water* (dir. Ruth Grimberg, 2014), which was screened with an AD that did little to convey the filmmaker's vision (Grimberg, personal communication), leading her to feel that she 'was watching a different film'.

134 *Accessible filmmaking and describing camerawork*

Table 10.1 Qualitative responses to the cinematic description of *Brief Encounter*

Against cinematic AD	For cinematic AD
I didn't notice any difference in the AD between this one and the cinematic clip, which means I can take it or leave it [the cinematic]. When I could see, I wasn't particularly enthusiastic about camera angles etc.	What you miss out on [with standard AD] is the cinematography.
The lack of 'shots' in the [standard] description left space for me to become more involved.	I think the [cinematic] AD of the movement when they came into the station was much more vivid, their expressions and describing the camerawork was much more dramatic – especially when she dashed out on the platform, it was terrific.
I found standard AD far more gentle in its handling of scene changes. In the change from the refreshment bar to the library, I found the use of 'at home, Laura . . . ' far more friendly than the use of 'cut to . . . '.	I enjoyed being able to understand what film shots were being used, perhaps because I do love and have an interest in film. I felt that the AD used when Laura might throw herself under a train added an intensity and urgency to the scene.
I didn't think the camerawork was important. It was more important to know that Laura was passing Alec a cigarette than that they were framed through a car windscreen.	It occurred to me that being framed in the windscreen of the car was a great image.
Because there was more information about the camera movement, initially I felt overloaded and a bit confused. I found 'cut to' irritating, but I feel I got more detail and maybe as a result it drew me more into the characters.	At the beginning I found the cinematic AD distracting but then it melted into the film.
I didn't like 'Laura's coming towards us'. It seems too technical. It's like an autopsy. It takes away the magic and the flow.	I was surprised by my interest in the camera views. I liked the sense of movement in this. The word 'cut' was really nice and useful, because my mind was already changing the image. It would have to be a particular film where I wanted that intensity of AD.
The increased detail about the way the film is shot means more detailed AD. This has the overhead of making the AD more distracting.	Ultimately I prefer the cinematic because it had more information. You can always filter information out, but you can't introduce it if it's not there.

In order to address this discrepancy there are two possible strategies. One is to provide an AI (see Chapter 12); the other, proposed by Elisa Perego (2014: 108), is 'Revisiting the guidelines to include a balanced use of cinematic terms.' Perego's arguments in support of this strategy include the impact of filmic techniques on audience reception and an improved opportunity for social inclusion, as they might offer a chance for 'the blind to be trained in film reading and in acquiring a mediated visual literacy' (ibid.). This view would be supported by a Late Blind American man who, when asked to describe what, for him, characterises quality in AD, replied:

> AD that uses adjectives, adverbs, and cuing description that helps me imagine specific and differentiated people, things, and places, as well as provides me with a sense of directorial choices (e.g., pans, close-ups, POVs, et al.).

A Late Blind English participant put forward a similar view:

> J: When I was getting stuff from the RNIB about the audio-description of film and television [mm] I thought I really ought to try this because at least I'm receiving information, ... and ... I found it hugely [cough] disappointing in comparison to my theatre experience.
> LF: Why?
> J: I ... er ... well ... that was the key question and I'm not sure I've found the answer to it ... but the only film I went to was *No Country for Old Men* umm ... and it left me completely cold. And then we got a new television set and I went to a lot of trouble to make sure we bought one where we could get audio description sort of as a built in feature [mm-hmm] and I tried two or three programmes that I knew had it ... and then ... I tried ... to be honest it didn't really make a lot of difference. Why you ask? [cough] I think the nearest I've got to it, is that it works for me extraordinarily well in the theatre because ... first of all I've had an introductory disc [an AI] which has given me an overall sense of the set within which the action is taking place, whether there's a proscenium arch or it's in the round or whatever – it gives me infinitely more detail than I ever need ... so ... what is it about film and television that didn't work for me? I think it was something to do with the fact that the logic of a film, and this is er ... where ... I'm really groping for language, is essentially visual, umm, and therefore, most of the audio description I've heard, all it's been concerned to do is to do essentially what is done in the theatre, that is to say, he moves towards her and gives her a passionate kiss ... not in the film I saw, but that sort of thing about just saying what is happening on the screen. What that gives me is not a film at all, what that gives me is ..., if you like, a spoken narrative consisting of the dialogue and sound effects of the film and any music, which is fine and I welcome that, and a voice that comes in and links together the narrative and provides any descriptive stuff, but it doesn't tell me about what I'm watching as a film, it tells me what I'm watching as a narrative, and [uh-huh] I found that very frustrating because I didn't have any feel of a film, it felt like a rather bad radio play.

136 *Accessible filmmaking and describing camerawork*

This is in direct opposition to the assertion of the ADC, which argues: 'We have established that we are watching a film or video, so repeated references to the screen are unnecessary' (ADC, 2009: 17).

10.4 AD and the artistic team

Where the describer feels cautious about their own film literacy and expertise, and to promote the likelihood of a director's having confidence that the translation is a good representation of his/her artistic product, Pablo Romero-Fresco (2013) has proposed the idea of accessible filmmaking, incorporating AD and subtitling strategies from a film's inception and facilitating the close working of the describer with the rest of the filmmaking team. This is the approach he took with his own film *Joining the Dots*. The author was involved in editing the AD script. Having direct access to the filmmaker meant that when there was no time to incorporate the words of the sign in Mags' garden, 'A grumpy old man lives here', the director agreed to extend the shot by a couple of seconds, which was enough to allow the AD, and therefore the user, to make sense of Mags' comments about Trevor with reference to the sign. It also helped Romero-Fresco to realise that the film, as a whole, would benefit from greater 'breathability'. Thus the collaboration was mutually beneficial. For *Notes on Blindness*, the author recorded the AD with the film's directors present, allowing them to make last-minute adjustments to the AD script. For example, at 06.28 the description identified 'motes of dust', which co-director, James Spinney, felt was too specific. It was replaced with the phrase 'white particles', which both director and describer felt captured the abstract image more effectively. If Ruth Grimberg had been able to work with the describer in such a way, she might have felt more comfortable with the end product.

It is obviously easier to have contact with film directors in small, independent companies, but in an email to the author Di Langford, the describer of the Harry Potter franchise, recalled fondly Warner Brothers' interest in the AD:

> My favourite memory of that one was turning up one morning in Leicester Square and being met by Richard Huhndorff, the charming technical director of Warner Bros UK, wearing a Gryffindor scarf. We then proceeded to sit in the echoing empty Odeon with a representative from the RNIB and the man responsible for the new AD technology, plus some people who were checking the subtitles and I listened to myself describing the film. I think there were probably six of us in this huge echoing auditorium. Luckily for me Warner Brothers were pleased with it and decided they wanted the same voice and style of description for them all.
>
> So that was the first experiment. We were then able to get the rest of the films in advance as they were made, so that the AD was available in cinemas on the day the film opened. One memorable day, Richard, the technical director, who works in a state of the art office in Theobalds Road, arrived at the door of my humble, one bedroom, basement flat in Brighton with a plastic carrier bag containing I think it must have been the second film, which had not yet

been released. It was on 7 short videos. The film had been separated between these, and each screen had written 'spoilers' all over it in large white letters – WB in the middle, and my initials and Richard's initials so if anything went missing they would know who was responsible.

I use my bedroom as an office and had moved the TV in there so that I could work at the computer while watching the films. We decided it might be a good idea to make sure that my Heath Robinson [what Americans call Rube Goldberg] arrangements were going to work so I will never forget the day I had the technical director of Warner Brothers UK sitting on the end of my bed, drinking coffee and watching Harry Potter!!!

10.5 Auteur description

Szarkowska calls this approach 'auteur description', as it 'incorporates the director's creative vision in the AD script . . . and thus gives the audio describer the artistic license to depart from the dictate of objectivism' (Szarkowska, 2013: 383). Szarkowska acknowledges that direct communication with the artist, be that author or director or producer, is not always possible and suggests alternative sources for accessing their inner thoughts, such as the screenplay, citing Almodóvar's description of the character Raimunda in the screenplay of his 2006 film *Volver*:

> Raimunda, of an astounding and racial beauty, is firmly grounded by her luscious rounded bottom and her bosom, which one can hardly take one's eyes off. Uncompromising, resolute, exuberant, courageous and fragile at the same time.

Such a description surely goes beyond the bounds of objectivity, but is funny, vivid and accurate. Objectivity is discussed in Chapter 12.

As a describer, the author has enjoyed being drawn in more closely to the artistic process. Similar situations have occurred in live events – for example, shared discussions about the approach to describing *Like Rabbits*, with the choreographer/co-director Ben Duke. In an interview for the evaluation of the project for Arts Council England the benefits of this way of working were explained as follows:

> The choreographer/director can be helpful in outlining their vision. With contemporary dance there is often no established vocabulary for particular steps, lifts, movements. Sitting in on rehearsals allows you to eavesdrop on the kind of language the dancers themselves use – often this can be very graphic and evocative – perfect for description. I've sat in on a rehearsal and a run-through and chatted to Ben about the kind of approach I'd like to take. He's very open, and we explored possibilities of making the dancers themselves more audible through the use of stage microphones, so it's easier to understand the physical effort by hearing their breathing, and locate them within the space by hearing footfalls, etc. This may not materialize in this production, but looks like a good thing to work into future shows.

138 *Accessible filmmaking and describing camerawork*

At the National Theatre of Great Britain, access to the company manager and/or the stage manager gives an opportunity to walk the set, noticing elements and details about materials and textures that may be hard to see from the stalls under stage lighting. Understanding the mechanics of how an effect works may lead to a more accurate or more effective description. Some theatre companies that integrate able and disabled performers, such as Extant and Graeae, have incorporated the describer into the action. For example, in Graeae's Rhinestone Rollers (their wheelchair dancing troupe), the describer, Willie Elliott, complete with rhinestones of his own, takes the role of the line-dance caller, effectively describing by calling out the moves the performers are about to make. Although this then begs the question of the need for a meta level of AD, whereby the describer is himself described in relation to the troupe, it has the advantage that the AD is not just an add-on or afterthought. Udo and Fels (2009: 5) reported on a similar approach in theatre when:

> Andrea Wasserman, director of Hart House Theatre's production of *Hamlet*, worked with Paul Leishman, the audio describer, to create, develop, and perform an alternative audio description strategy that would remain true to the director's initial vision, entertain the audience, use stylistically similar dialogue, provide an additional avenue for audience members (sighted and visually impaired) to access meaning, and be seamlessly incorporated into the entertainment experience.

10.6 Conclusion

Students of AD need to know the guidelines of the country in which they are working and be aware of when and why they might feel the need to break them. Evidently, description that is developed from the beginning with the artistic team not only liberates describers from the fear of subjectivity, but also has the possibility of greater coherence when it is no longer merely an afterthought. Not all films would benefit from an auteur description approach; for example, Hollywood 'romcoms' are designed such that the camerawork is deliberately unobtrusive. By contrast, films by directors such as Alfred Hitchcock, Pedro Almodóvar and Quentin Tarantino are sometimes celebrated more for their camerawork than for the stories their films portray.

10.7 Exercises and points for discussion

1. Watch a film by an auteur director, for example Michelangelo Antonioni, Pedro Almodóvar, Luis Buñuel, Ingmar Bergman, the Cohen brothers, Alfred Hitchcock. Choose a scene where you think the camerawork is important. Discuss why that might be. Write and record two descriptions. First, describe it in a way that makes the filmic language explicit. Describe it again so that the information is implicit.
2. Listen back. Which do you think works better?
3. Offer to describe a student film. Discuss AD choices with the director. Reflect on the (dis)advantages of this type of collaboration.

References

ADC (2009). Standards for Audio Description and Code of Professional Conduct for Describers'. Retrieved from www.audiodescriptioncoalition.org/adc_standards_090615.pdf [accessed 19.09.15].

Austin Community College (n.d.). 'Five C's of cinematography'. Retrieved from www.austincc.edu/sfarr/online/3dls/Camera-5Cs.pdf [accessed 19.09.15].

Benecke, Bernd and Elmar Dosch (2004). *Wenn aus Bildern Worte werden – durch Audio-Description zum Hörfilm* [When images become words: through audio description to audiofilms]. Munich: Bayerischer Rundfunk.

Branigan, E. (1992). *Narrative comprehension and film*. London: Routledge.

Chaume, Frederic (2004). 'Film studies and translation studies: two disciplines at stake in audiovisual translation'. *Meta: Journal des traducteurs/Meta: Translators' Journal* 49, no. 1: 12–24.

Fryer, L. (2010). 'Directing in reverse'. In I. Kemble (ed.) 'The changing face of translation'. In *Proceedings of the 9th Annual Portsmouth Translation Conference*. ISBN 978 1 86137 616 9.

Fryer, Louise and Jonathan Freeman (2013a). 'Cinematic language and the description of film: keeping AD users in the frame'. *Perspectives* 21, no. 3: 412–426.

Fryer, Louise and Jonathan Freeman (2013b). 'Visual impairment and presence: measuring the effect of audio description'. In *Proceedings of the 2013 Inputs–Outputs Conference: An Interdisciplinary Conference on Engagement in HCI and Performance*, p. 4. New York: ACM.

Hirvonen, Maija (2013). 'Sampling similarity in image and language – figure and ground in the analysis of filmic audio'. *SKY Journal of Linguistics* 26: 87–115.

ITC (2000). ITC Guidance. Retrieved from www.ofcom.org.uk/static/archive/itc/itc_publications/codes_guidance/audio_descripion/index.asp.html [accessed 4.04.15].

Kim, Jieun, Jihoon Kim and Hokyoung Ryu (2014). '"Heart-to-feel": a new audio description coding scheme for the visually impaired on affective cinematography and emotive vibration'. Retrieved from http://rise.hanyang.ac.kr/4.%20Conference%20papers/2014/TVX2014/BBC_JH%28jihoon%29.pdf [accessed 30.12.15].

Kruger, Jan-Louis (2010). 'Audio narration: re-narrativising film'. *Perspectives: Studies in Translatology* 18, no. 3: 231–249.

Perego, Elisa (2014). 'Film language and tools'. In Anna Maszerowska, Anna Matamala and Pilar Orero (eds) *Audio description: new perspectives illustrated*. Amsterdam: John Benjamins, pp. 81–102.

Rai, Sonali, Joan Greening and Leen Petré (2010). 'A comparative study of audio description guidelines prevalent in different countries'. London: RNIB, Media and Culture Department.

Romero-Fresco, Pablo (2013). 'Accessible filmmaking: joining the dots between audiovisual translation, accessibility and filmmaking'. *Journal of Specialised Translation* 20: 201–223.

Snyder, Joel (2014). *The visual made verbal: a comprehensive training manual and guide to the history and applications of audio description*. Arlington, VA: American Council for the Blind.

Szarkowska, Agnieszka (2013). 'Practice report'. *Journal of Visual Impairment and Blindness* (September–October): 383–387.

Udo, John Patrick and Deborah I. Fels (2009). '"Suit the action to the word, the word to the action": An unconventional approach to describing Shakespeare's Hamlet'. *Journal of Visual Impairment and Blindness* 103, no. 3: 178–183.

Film references

Across Still Water, R. Grimberg (2014).
Brief Encounter, D. Lean (1946).
Joining the Dots, P. Romero-Fresco (2013).
Volver, P. Almodóvar (2006).

References to live events

Like Rabbits, dirs. B. Duke and L. Kirkwood (Lost Dog Productions http://lostdogdance.co.uk/) (2013). Almeida Theatre, London (describer Louise Fryer).
Oresteia (a new version of Aeschylus' original, created by Robert Icke), dir. R. Icke (2013). Almeida Theatre, London. AD by VocalEyes (describers Louise Fryer and Veronika Hyks).
. . . Some Trace of Her, dir. K. Mitchell (2006). National Theatre of Great Britain, London. AD by in-house team (Roz Chalmers and Tony McBride).
The Master and Margarita, dir. S. McBurney (2012). Barbican Theatre, London.
Waves, dir. K. Mitchell (2008). National Theatre of Great Britain, London. AD by in-house team (Roz Chalmers and Bridget Crowley).

11 Audio description and censorship

11.1 Introduction

Given that the purpose of AD is to make AV material accessible, it might seem odd to include any mention of censorship, but it is surprising how often describers seek to 'protect' their audience from the harsh realities of what is shown on screen or stage. Officially there is general agreement that censorship should be avoided. In their comparative study of AD guidelines, Rai et al. (2010: 77) state:

> Within the constructs of quality description, describers must convey all of the visual elements of the material being described. Describers must not censor information for any personal reason such as their own discomfort with the material or a political belief, i.e., describers must relay objectively the visual elements of nudity, sexual acts, violence, etc. Our constituents have the right to know the critical visual material that is evident to sighted people and we have the obligation to convey that material. If a describer feels that describing particular material will make him/her uncomfortable, s/he should not accept this assignment.

Yet theory does not always translate into practice. One Englishman who lost his sight as a child asks describers

> Not to skirt round stuff like sex . . . I know it must be awful for you sometimes but it must be awful for the audience not to realise stuff like that, not to have it in too much detail but not to be . . . you shouldn't actually be squeamish. You've got to be very sort of blatant and down to earth.

A blind American AD user complains about

> being dismissed as some kind of crackpot when I tried to engage . . . in a serious dialogue about how poorly most AD deals with sex and nudity. I realize that the Blind Industry has had a long history of squeamishness when it comes to blindness and sexuality, but it was particularly galling to encounter this squeamishness in such a setting and realizing that censorship in the

142 *Audio description and censorship*

Blind Industry is alive and well. AD should grow up, engage in a mature and constructive dialogue with its blind viewers and provide better description of nudity – description that actually lets the viewer know how this 'naked woman' appears vis-à-vis just a generic 'woman who happens to be naked'.

11.2 Language

In reference to translation in general, José Santaemilia (2008) notes:

> While censorship is an external constraint on what we can publish or (re)write, self-censorship is an individual ethical struggle between self and context. In all historical circumstances, translators tend to produce rewritings which are 'acceptable' from both social and personal perspectives ... translating is always a struggle to reach a compromise between one's ethics and society's multiple constraints – and nowhere can we see this more clearly than in the rewriting(s) of sex-related language.

The ITC Guidance (ITC, 2000: para. 4.11) states:

> Describing sexually explicit material has to be sensitively handled. Just as in works of literary fiction some sex scenes work better than others, the same applies to the audio description of such scenes. If handled insensitively they may be embarrassing, crude or just very dull.

Sexual terms, possibly more than any others, would seem to be culture specific such that they have a different strength and emotional valence in one culture, as compared with the corresponding term for the same action or body part in another. There may be similar 'cultural' differences between their iconic and verbal representations. This is an area ripe for research.

One reason why describers might hesitate to go 'full frontal' is the difficulty of choosing the right language and the difference in impact between language that is read visually, processed silently in your head and language that is received aurally, often through headphones, and so received directly in your ears. A case in point is a play called *The Motherf**ker with the Hat* by Stephen Adly Guirgis. It is described as 'a high-octane verbal cage match about love, fidelity and misplaced haberdashery' (Broadway.com). While the asterisks used in the pre-show publicity, prior to its performance at the National Theatre of Great Britain, presented no problem to the eye, the title instantly raises the question of how to vocalise it. One possibility is to use the urban slang MoFo, which sounds less offensive and is appropriate to the tenor of the play, but it is a word with which a UK audience may not be familiar and that does not convey the way the title has been censored by the use of asterisks for the sighted audience (this is also the reason behind not just saying 'Motherfucker' straight out). An alternative solution, at least for the recorded AI, would be to say the word F**ker, masking the first syllable with a bleep. As this would mask the potentially offensive word while making the censorship audibly explicit, it would directly replicate the written form used in the publicity for the show (posters, advertisements etc.). This was the approach taken at the National Theatre of Great Britain, but by not making it explicit that the visually presented title contained asterisks, it still provoked the irritation of one young blind man, who, on hearing the bleep exclaimed 'We're adults!' (Roz Chalmers, personal communication.) Head of Access at the National Theatre of Great Britain, Ros Hayes, adds that the decision to bleep out the word 'F**ker' in the AI originated in the theatre's strategy for the recorded season brochure, which is produced in an audio format for BPS users, where Guirgis's play was mentioned as one of around fifteen productions. The title was bleeped because, according to Hayes: 'the recording could potentially be heard by other people in the room, the car, wherever BPS are listening. The season, for instance, included a couple of children's/family shows.'

AD is not a unique mode of AVT to experience translation censorship. Subtitling and dubbing are equally prone. Santaemilia (2008: para. 8) points to the high incidence of

> partial translation, minimisation or omission of sex-related terms. For example, Karjalainen (2002) documents the systematic elimination of insults, blasphemies and taboo words (goddam, damn, hell, bastard, sonuvabitch, for Chrissake, for God's sake, Jesus Christ) in two translations of J. D. Salinger's *The Catcher in the Rye* (1951) into Swedish. Similarly, the Spanish translation of the same book is also a moral product – a catalogue of omissions and reductions. *El guardián entre el centeno* (1978) deprives [Salinger's] original from most of its colloquial traits, such as blasphemies or sex-related expletives.

Bucaria (2007) points out that censorship of AV products happens even before the translation process begins, in that they are edited differently 'depending on whether they will be viewed at the cinema, on TV or on planes' (ibid., 135–136). Beyond this they will also be edited differently for TV broadcast, depending on what time they are shown, i.e. before or after the watershed.

11.2.1 Expletives

Adamou and Knox (2011) note that 'Conventional practice dictates that Greek subtitling omit expletives not central to textual meaning'. This is not necessarily a decision taken in consultation with the audience. As Gabriela Scandura (2004) reports:

> When watching subtitled material, audiences often feel they are being cheated because they realize that what was said could not have been what was written in the subtitles, since images which are quite 'hot' are matched with words that seem to have been taken from children's books. 'The feedback-effect from the original – whether that consists of recognizable words, prosodic features, gestures, or background visuals – may be so strong that (. . .) the friction between original and subtitle causes noise, and the illusion of the

translation as the alter ego of the original is broken' (Gottlieb, 1994: 268). After all, a person who does not understand a certain language might know a few words in that language. Moreover, even if viewers do not understand the language of the original, the images are so obvious that they will consider any 'proper translation' wrong (if you see two criminals fighting, you know they will not be polite when shouting at each other!).

As we have already noted from Kruger (2012), AD is unusual in that other modes of AVT mostly translate dialogue. For dubbing, the potentially offensive words to be translated are mostly expletives. In AD, the need to verbalise swear words is rare, except in the case of audio subtitles, or the title of the play already mentioned. Other instances include expletives sprayed on walls as graffiti or perhaps appearing in a book title. Otherwise, describers will need to generate the words themselves in order to describe images of a sexual nature or gestures that accompany or articulate swear words. One example of this was the play *Tribes* by Nina Raine, performed at London's Royal Court Theatre (2011) and directed by Roger Michell. The play is about a hearing family with a deaf son, Billy, who meets Sylvia, who was born as a hearing child into a deaf family and now, in her twenties, is becoming deaf. Billy wears hearing aids and is used to lip-reading, while Sylvia signs, a skill that Billy starts to learn. For the benefit of the hearing audience, their signed conversations were translated and projected as surtitles onto a gauze screen that was also a wall, dividing the rear from the front of the stage. Much like providing audio subtitles (see Chapter 9), the AD had to incorporate the words on screen as well as describe those the signs, which provoked laughter from the sighted audience as they graphically portrayed Sylvia's colourful vocabulary, for example: 'Sylvia forms a well with her left hand, inserts her right forefinger and screws it round.' In this case the AD strategy was easy. It was a simple case of saying what you see: the description of the sign made its meaning obvious.

11.3 Sex and AD

In UK English, saying what you see can be problematic in sex scenes, as there would seem to be a paucity of acceptable sexual terms, leaving describers a choice between the anatomical specifics and playground obscenities. There are also differences according to gender. There are many words for penis that might be deemed acceptable; far fewer for female sexual organs. Again, this challenge is not unique to description. Bucaria (2007: para. 11) points out:

> When translating sex, what is at stake is not only grammatical or lexical accuracy. Besides the actual meanings of the sex-related expressions, there are aesthetic, cultural, pragmatic and ideological components, as well as an urgent question of linguistic ethics. Eliminating sexual terms – or qualifying or attenuating or even intensifying them – in translation does usually betray the translator's personal attitude towards human sexual behaviour(s) and

their verbalization. The translator basically transfers into his/her rewriting the level of acceptability or respectability he/she accords to certain sex-related words or phrases.

This can lead either to euphemism or to dysphemism, minimising or heightening the valence of the original. This is an example from the AD of *Young Adam* (Mackenzie, 2003), the story of an amoral drifter, Joe, who finds work on a river barge and has an affair with the bargee's wife:

00:15:49
AD: Down below, Ella's sitting darning.
Ella: Where's Les?
AD: She stares up at Joe.
Joe: He's found someone to play darts with.
AD: He takes a few paces towards her.
Joe: He'll be at least an hour.
AD: He stands over Ella whose face is lit by the lamp hanging from the ceiling. She stares at him timidly, almost scared. Joe's face is firm and resolute, wisps of his brown hair fall over his forehead. He places a hand on Ella's shoulder.
Ella: [whispers] You'll waken the boy.
AD: She looks towards Jim's bed.
Joe: [whispers] Why don't we go up on deck?
AD: [long pause] . . . Ella's eyes are fixed on the young man in front of her. She lowers her head then places her darning on the table. Ella rises to her feet and checks Jim's asleep. On the towpath they walk in the opposite direction from the pub. [*sounds of footsteps which stop*]
Ella: I'm not going any further.
AD: The barge is still in their sights. Ella is standing up against a low embankment wall. Joe takes a quick look along the moonlit towpath then steps in towards her. He starts to slowly unbutton the coat she's now wearing. Ella stands stock still. Joe opens the coat then slips his hands inside. His hands caress her breasts. He steps closer and forces her back [*rustling noises and a breath*]. He frantically pushes up her skirt. She lies back on top of the embankment wall and places her arms behind her head, her bare legs are apart, her knees bent, Joe kisses her thigh and runs a hand down towards her groin. He bends down and places his head between her legs. Her breathing quickens and her hips begin to squirm . . . His right hand gently strokes her stomach. He raises his head and watches her. Joe moves his hand up to her breast and gently squeezes it. He lowers his head then sinks back down to bury it between her legs.
Ella: No Joe.
AD: [*describer's tone hardening and pace quickening*] Joe raises his body up. His hand goes to his crotch and he unfastens his fly. He semi

146 *Audio description and censorship*

crouches on top of her [*involuntary gasp from Ella*]. Her heels dig into his back as he presses down on her knees and thrusts into her. Her head is stretched back, her mouth open as their love-making continues. 18:21–18:23 [*rhythmic yelping and panting*]. Afterwards, Ella's sitting on the embankment wall, Joe beside her, smoking a cigarette.

As you can tell from the AD, this is no romantic love tryst. Tender words such as 'gently', 'stroke' and 'caress' sit uncomfortably alongside the anatomical 'groin'. By using such clinical terminology (groin is more commonly associated in English with sports injuries), the describer reflects the hard-heartedness of Joe, who is opportunistic, taking advantage of Ella's desire to escape the harsh realities of her impoverished life. The AD leaves the soundtrack to do much of the work, which is to be recommended, yet the describer appears to run out of steam with the phrase 'the love-making continues' – love-making a rather delicate term for the short, urgent, semi-brutal act presented, and 'continues' unnecessary as the continuing pants and groans make abundantly clear.

11.3.1 AD of porn

For most of that scene from *Young Adam* the describer's strategy also seems to have been WYSIWYS. The difficulty is that what you are seeing is a simulation of a sexual act, the actors carefully positioned to imply actions, rather than actually carrying them out. Much is implied but actually we see little. Clearly, this is not what you should say. The exception to this is in a porn movie, where you do generally see what you think you see. I am indebted to Veronika Hyks for giving me access to the script for the AD of one such movie. The AD was written for an experiment implemented by what was then called the Department of Media, Sport, Arts and Culture. According to Hyks, 'They asked us [the facilities house IMS] to set out the parameters for the description of sex. We took a piece of film, and described it according to the time of transmission. Pre 9.00pm ... post 9.00pm' (Hyks, personal communication).

Here the language is much more robust, as befits the 'no holds barred' visual content:

18 11:03:28: 00–11:03:41:03 A flashback to the killing. A girl with red highlights, Yvette, snorts some coke, then joins Donna's husband Marcus and a brunette on the marital bed. Donna, sees them through the open bedroom door.

19 11:03:50:09–11:03:53:00 one sucks his cock; the other his thumb.

20 11:04:01:24–11:04:06:08 Yvette and Marcus kiss: Both with silver studs in their probing tongues.

21 11:04:07:11–11:04:11:00 He bends down to suck and lick her breast.

22 11:04:18:17–11:04:24:15 He leans down to kiss the other girl. Donna watches stock still as Yvette sucks her husband off.

23 11:04:34:18–11:04:41:12 Yvette on top grinds her body into his as he lies back on the bed, their tongues flicking in each other's mouths.
24 11:04:48:14–11:04:56:06 The brunette lying by them, spreads Yvette's bottom, and with the tip of her tongue, licks it as it rises and falls on Marcus' stiff cock.
25 11:05:07:13–11:05:11:03 Marcus' long brown shaft pumps Yvette's pussy.
26 11:05:17:18–11:05:26:06 He slows his pace, teasing his cock in and out of her cunt, her round white ass held open by her playmate's long caressing fingers.
27 11:05:36:11–11:05:41:08 Yvette tickles Marcus's chest with her pendulous breasts as she rides up and down.

Here, the linguistic tricks discussed in Chapter 3 are out in force. AD 25 combines rhythm and alliteration. Hyks says 'Describing heavy sex is all about punctuation! As with comedy, timing is everything.' The vocal delivery is also key. For the experiment, IMS used the American Desiree Lush to voice the AD, rather than Hyks herself, even though she is a consummate voice-over artist as well as a describer.

The difference between the two examples is to do not only with explicit versus implicit content but also with the function of the scenes within each film and the audience's motivation for watching them.

Young Adam is rated an 18 by the British Board of Film Classification. According to its website (www.bbfc.co.uk/about-bbfc/who-we-are):

> 18 works are for adults and can contain strong issues such as:
>
> - very strong violence
> - frequent strong language (e.g. 'f***') and/or very strong language (e.g. 'c***')
> - strong portrayals of sexual activity
> - scenes of sexual violence
> - strong horror
> - strong blood and gore
> - real sex (in some circumstances)
> - discriminatory language and behavior.

In *Young Adam*, the sex scene facilitates the story; it is part of a larger narrative. The reasons for watching the film are many but it is unlikely to be watched for the sex scene alone. By contrast, in any porn movie the story is secondary to the graphic depiction of sex. People watch porn for the purposes of titillation, to provoke sexual excitement. The AD should strive to create a similar response in its audience. Hyks says: 'In porn, each new "position" merits a mention; in drama, only insofar as it serves the overall dramatic narrative.' Other examples

148 *Audio description and censorship*

of sexually explicit scenes come from the AD for *Borat* (Charles, 2006). Here the describer uses colloquial, lavatorial language – for example 'stark bollock naked' and 'fat arse' – in tune with the images and humorous intention of the scene. The describer also coins his own innuendo: when a naked Borat and his producer burst in on a conference of mortgage advisers and the protagonists are described as 'waving their "endowment policies" about', the describer makes a neat and witty association between endowment mortgages and a person with large genitals being commonly described as 'well endowed'. As humour is the purpose of the scene, this uncensored description style is entirely appropriate – but it would possibly draw criticism if broadcast before the watershed. (Although the film itself is unlikely to be broadcast until after the watershed.)

However as with the *Motherf***ker* example above, the images in Borat have their own visual censorship – a black rectangle obliterates Borat's genitals. Humorously, it is much larger than one assumes it needs to be. Unfortunately, there is no mention of this in the AD.

11.4 Blood and gore

Another area where describers may be tempted to self-censor is in scenes of violence or images full of blood and gore. The ITC Guidance draws a parallel between describing sex and describing violence, advising (ITC, 2000: para. 4.11):

> Scenes of violence require the same level of sensitive consideration. Many viewers, sighted and visually impaired, find violence more shocking than explicit sex scenes and whereas sighted people can look away if they cannot bear to look at what is being shown, the visually impaired viewer listening to the audio description cannot protect himself from a terrifying image. The rule, if at all possible, is to find a form of words to conjure up the intention of the scene, without undue discomfort.

One research participant who is partially sighted discussed watching *Casualty* (a BBC TV series set in the accident and emergency department of a hospital):

> And there's this surgeon Andy and . . . I hate watching it if I'm eating my tea, my dinner and there's always somebody being sick, you know – obviously I hate all the blood and guts and all that and you're thinking, you're just about to crack into her head or something, so I close me eyes but obviously they tell you, then there's blood gushing out – oh [jokey scream]. And so I'm sitting there, closing my eyes and he's telling me like he's just cracked into her scalp or something like that and there's blood oozing out and like ooooh, I'll have to turn the sound off as well.

However, another participant recalled watching the film *127 Hours* (Boyle, 2011). Here the AD does not shy away from giving the visual detail in full. Again, it is the interaction with the soundtrack that makes the AD effective.

It's the one where the guy goes climbing and he falls and gets trapped and ends up having to cut his arm off. It was brilliant because, had it not been for AD that film would have been completely inaccessible to me because most of the time there was only him, so there was no dialogue. There was his thoughts from the past or when he thought he was going to die, his thoughts about what he thought was going to happen in the future to his family, so it had like images and a little bit of sound about what his thoughts were, but there weren't really other characters, but like, when he was cutting through his arm, there was music and there was him cutting through his arm, and there was the audio describer and I thought they all worked perfectly together and I had a real sensation of [sharp intake of breath] ooooh, this is really nasty and horrible and I thought the sound that they used when they actually got to his nerve, it was like a kind of twanging painful sort of sound and like the describer and him screaming, they all worked really, really well together, so yeah, I thought that was really, really good.

11.4.1 Blood, gore and live events

In the theatre, a classic example of simulated violence must be the blinding of the Duke of Gloucester in Shakespeare's *King Lear*. There are two aspects here. The describer needs to convey reasons for the disgust that may be audibly expressed by the sighted audience, as well as simultaneously conveying how it is achieved. In the production directed by Michael Attenborough at London's Almeida Theatre in 2012, the actors were so positioned that the act of blinding was not visible at all. The description read solely:

> *AD:* Cornwall leans over [Gloucester]
> *Gloucester:* O cruel! O you gods!
> *AD:* blood streams down Gloucester's face.

A similar strategy was used for the blinding in the production at The Donmar Warehouse, directed by Michael Grandage (2011):

> *Gloucester:* Give me some help!
> *AD:* They surround Gloucester, Regan punches him. His face is hidden from view. Cornwall steps back – something in his palm. Blood streams down Gloucester's face. Cornwall throws down the eyeball and stamps on it.
> *Gloucester:* O cruel! O you gods!

In this version the mystery object becomes an eyeball once the implication is made clear by the nature of Gloucester's injuries. Explicitly naming it as an eyeball is possibly unnecessary and certainly inaccurate, yet, as the object at that moment clearly became an 'eyeball' for the sighted audience, naming it as such helped to synchronise the decisive point of recognition for the sighted and sight-impaired audiences, while reinforcing the obscenity and inhumanity of Cornwall's action.

It is interesting to note the subtle difference in stagecraft between the two productions that hinges not so much on the action but in the positioning of Gloucester's exclamation. In the first example it coincides with the blinding, indicating that the blinding is taking place; in the second, Gloucester cries out in response to the act. It is another example of the interaction between the audio and the visual and how timing affects our response to it. It is also an example of the contribution AD can make to theatre/film studies by making such subtle differences apparent.

11.5 Positive aspects of censorship

Having shown that censorship in AD is roundly denounced, there is, however, one aspect where it should be welcomed: namely, in censoring personal opinion. It can be tempting for a describer to express their disgust or frustration with a production or performance: 'she gestures unnecessarily in a hideous blue dress' – but the describer should desist. It is not the role of the describer to act as critic but, rather, to give BPS users sufficient information that they are in a position to do so. Marzà Ibañez (2010: 147) stresses that 'clearly biased or personal interpretations should be avoided'.

11.6 Political correctness: describing race and disability

Kowal and colleagues, in their paper on diversity training (2013: 323), cite Marques (2009), who defines political correctness as the desire to 'avoid all expressions or actions that could possibly be perceived to exclude, marginalise or insult people who are socially disadvantaged or discriminated against (Marques, 2009).' In AD such issues are especially sensitive, as AD users are likely to fall into such a category themselves and describers often work – for example – with theatre practitioners, who are likely to be particularly alert to issues around political correctness. Elaine Gerber (2007: 27) pertinently asks 'What is culturally salient in the visual field?' In order to find out, she carried out a telephone survey with thirty-nine American AD users to discuss whether there was a need for race to be described. She adds that anthropologists are clear that 'race is a cultural construct . . . not a biological phenomenon'. Accordingly, the American standards advise (ADC, 2009: 6), 'Sighted audience members don't see a character's race, ethnicity or nationality rather, they see skin color and facial features. Accordingly, the describer should simply describe each person's skin color and, if time allows, facial features.' Gerber points out that difficulties arise in the instance of 'people who visibly do not fit into a single specifiable "race" . . . (for example Cubans, Dominicans, Puerto Ricans and others)'. Moreover, 'racial categories used in the United States are significant for blind people, whether or not they can see those differences for themselves' (Gerber, 2004: 31–32). Gerber found that 'Overwhelmingly, the blind people participating in this study wanted to know races of characters in film, on TV, in the movies and cast in theater. These participants argued for the need for race-based knowledge as an important part of cultural literacy' (ibid., 32). This attitude is not limited to the American blind population, although the importance of race is likely to vary from one culture to another and even from one individual to another. In the UK, current advice from the AD company Mind's Eye is to reference a multi-racial cast without necessarily describing the skin colour of each actor individually (A. Hornsby, personal communication, 15.10.15), although the blind playwright and theatre director Maria Oshodi says, 'I grew up through the disability arts movement and before that I worked in black theatre, so it was identity politics which pushed my agenda' (Oshodi, 2009). Maria is always keen to be told which of the actors is black; otherwise, she says, she spends the performance trying to guess, and that distracts her from the play.

Obviously an actor's race and appearance are more important in some plays than others, especially in a theatre company that follows a policy of 'colour blind' or 'integrated' casting. Yet, much as Ralph Berry (1997: para. 1) complained that, because the press did not mention that Declan Donellan had cast Nonso Anozie as King Lear, 'The issue was silenced', so too, by not mentioning what is, after all, visible to the sighted audience, the describer is excluding the BPS audience from appreciating a conscious artistic decision. As one of Gerber's participants pointed out,

> I want to know that. It's important culturally how roles are cast. It says something about the changing of our cultural norms. If there is a person, for example, who uses a wheelchair for mobility, where that doesn't play a part in the character. It's significant that that person is in a wheelchair because, wow, another barrier is down. If they are playing a white man and a black woman as a couple, where the race does not enter into the play, it nonetheless says something about the theater, the director, and the culture.

In a production of *Carousel* (dir. N. Hytner, 1992), actor Clive Rowe was cast as Mr Snow. In this case, the describers did mention the actor's skin colour, if only to explain the laughter of the sighted audience when a black 'Mr Snow' walked out on stage. The casting decision also caused some discussion in the newspapers; it would have been socially excluding for AD users not to understand what prompted the debate, whether or not they agreed with the strategy. Daniel Rosenthal (2013: 65) explains that Hytner wrote an article wondering why detractors 'had been "horrified by the unreality of a black Enoch" and yet "seemed unconcerned by . . . the odd propensity of these particular New Englanders to break into song at the drop of a hat, or to employ ballet as a regular means of discourse."'

The describer's default position is that, if race is important to mention because of its relevance to the plot, then it should not be assumed that most of the cast is, by default, white, i.e. the race of all cast members should be specified, not just those who are (or are assumed to be) in the minority. In the theatre, this is usually accomplished in the AI. In a film it might be necessary, for example, to include it in the dynamic description. Sometimes the dynamic description can be used to reinforce or remind the AD users; for example, in the film *The Last King of Scotland* (MacDonald, 2006) it will come as no surprise that the role of Ugandan dictator Idi Amin is played by a large, powerfully built black actor (Forest Whitaker) and the Scottish doctor by a pale, lanky Scottish actor (James McAvoy). But it makes

152 *Audio description and censorship*

for a poignant moment when the dictator has an accident and the doctor is called upon to splint his wrist and takes the dictator's huge black hand in his small white one. The doctor's lack of concern about any possible racial taboo says much about his character. Forest Whitaker also has a drooping eyelid, caused by an inherited condition called ptosis. This is not mentioned in the AD, presumably because it is of no relevance to the plot, although it might be of interest to the BPS audience.

Like race, disability is also often 'overlooked' (or more literally 'silenced') on the grounds of political correctness. One reason is that naming someone's medical diagnosis does not always tell you much about its visual manifestation or the effect (if any) on an actor's performance. Describing a person's physical impairments seems distasteful. Again, as with sex, we have a paucity of language at our disposal, with little between the clinical and the playground. A list of acceptable terms has not been included, as language deemed to be politically correct is notorious for frequently changing. Often there is a discrepancy between the disability of a character and the actor portraying the role. Georgina Kleege (1999: 45) says: 'Movies about the blind generally display such a distressing array of negative stereotypes that I find it hard not to run screaming from the theatre. The movie blind are a pretty sorry lot; they are timid, morose, cranky, resentful, socially awkward and prone to despair. Actors represent blindness with an unblinking zombie stare, directing their gazes upward to give the face a supplicating look of helplessness.' The author was asked recently to improvise an ad hoc description of an episode of *Little House on the Prairie*, the one where Mary Ingalls, recently blind, arrives at the blind school in Iowa in the USA. The (largely blind) audience asked with glee whether she had 'started groping yet'. And they howled with recognition when she (inevitably) did. This is a case for describing the portrayal of disability, no matter how inaccurately or ineptly done, so that blind people can celebrate the day that it starts to change.

On a more practical level, possible strategies are omission, which equates to censorship, and naming with explication (and ideally, with sensitivity). Ultimately the describer must feel comfortable saying the words they have written, which comes from knowing that the actor is equally comfortable with the description. Here 'accessible filmmaking' takes on another important role, as the chance to ask an actor or a director about the portrayal of a particular character can supply appropriate language such that the BPS user can comfortably access what the sighted audience is absorbing implicitly.

11.7 Conclusion

The injunction to describe the visual elements of a production applies to all types of content, regardless of the prejudices of the describer. Whether it be text on screen or explicitly portrayed sexual or violent acts, blind people want to hear about it 'warts and all'. Censorship is not exclusive to AD; other areas of AVT are also prone. In terms of AD strategies, omission is not an option and the soundtrack often becomes of pre-eminent importance. WYSIWYS can be a helpful maxim as long as you remember that rarely do you see as much as you think you see; your brain is working overtime to fill in the gaps. On describing minorities, Gerber cites three reasons why skin colour and disability should be included in a description, rather than AD becoming a social utopia where visually based discrimination is left behind. First, because race or disability may be central to the plot; second, because it is socially relevant in terms of theatre policy; and third, and perhaps most important, because 'it serves as a foundation for cultural fluency about race ([BPS] people need to understand the world the same way as sighted people, even if it is a racist world). It is an issue of equality' (Gerber, 2004: 38).

11.8 Exercises and points for discussion

1. Find the AD for a sexually explicit or violent scene of your choice. Discuss the language employed in the AD. How well does it capture what is shown on screen? What would you change, if anything? If you are not a native English speaker, can you find appropriate terms in your native language?
2. Alternatively, find and describe a sexually explicit or violent scene of your choice. Seek feedback from your colleagues. Did they flinch or did the earth move for them?
3. Watch the film *Joel* on the accompanying website. Discuss any sensitive issues around language that you may encounter in an AD for this film.

References

Adamou, Christina and Simone Knox (2011). 'Transforming television drama through dubbing and subtitling: sex and the cities'. *Critical Studies in Television: An International Journal of Television Studies* 6, no. 1: 1–21.

ADC (2009). *Standards for Audio Description and Code of Professional Conduct for Describers*, 3rd edn. Retrieved from www.audiodescriptioncoalition.org/adc_standards_090615.pdf [accessed 30.12.15].

Berry, Ralph (1997). 'Shakespeare and integrated casting'. Retrieved from http://www.francisbennion.com/pdfs/non-fb/1997/1997-002-nfb-black-casting.pdf [accessed 30.12.15].

Bucaria, Chiara (2007). 'Humour and other catastrophes: dealing with the translation of mixed-genre TV series'. *Linguistica Antverpiensia, New Series – Themes in Translation Studies* 6: 235–254.

Gerber, E. (2007). 'Seeing isn't believing: blindness, race, and cultural literacy'. *The Senses and Society* 2, no. 1: 27–40.

ITC (2000). ITC Guidance. Retrieved from www.ofcom.org.uk/static/archive/itc/itc_publications/codes_guidance/audio_descripion/index.asp.html [accessed 4.04.15].

Karjalainen, Markus (2002). Where have all the swearwords gone? An analysis of the loss of swearwords in two Swedish translations of J.D. Salinger's *Catcher in the Rye*. Unpublished 'Pro Gradu thesis', University of Helsinki, Finland.

Kleege, G. (1999) *Sight unseen*. Newhaven, CT: Yale University Press.

Kowal, Emma, Hayley Franklin and Yin Paradies (2013). 'Reflexive antiracism: a novel approach to diversity training'. *Ethnicities* 13: 316–337, doi: 10.1177/1468796812472885.

Kruger, Jan-Louis (2012). 'Making meaning in AVT: eye tracking and viewer construction of narrative'. *Perspectives* 20, no. 1: 67–86.

Marques, Joan F. (2009). 'How politically correct is political correctness? A SWOT analysis of this phenomenon'. *Business & Society* 48, no. 2: 257–266.
Marzà Ibañez, A. (2010). 'Evaluation criteria and film narrative: a frame to teaching relevance in audio description'. *Perspectives: Studies in Translatology* 18, no. 3: 143–153.
Oshodi, Maria (2009). '13 questions'. http://www.bbc.co.uk/ouch/interviews/13_questions_maria_oshodi.shtml [accessed 30.12.15].
Rai, Sonali, Joan Greening and Leen Petré (2010). 'A comparative study of audio description guidelines prevalent in different countries'. London: RNIB, Media and Culture Department.
Rosenthal, D. (2013). *The National Theatre story*. London: Oberon Books.
Santaemilia, José (2008). 'The translation of sex-related language: the danger(s) of self-censorship(s)'. *TTR: Traduction, terminologie, redaction* 21, no. 2: 221–252.
Scandura, Gabriela L. (2004). 'Sex, lies and TV: censorship and subtitling'. *Meta: Journal des traducteurs/Meta: Translators' Journal* 49, no. 1: 125–134.

Film references

127 Hours, D. Boyle (2011).
The Last King of Scotland, K. MacDonald (2006).
Young Adam, D. Mackenzie (2003).
Borat, L. Charles (2006).

References to live events

Carousel, dir. N. Hytner (1992). National Theatre of Great Britain, London.
Tribes, dir. R. Michell (2010). Royal Court Theatre, London. AD by VocalEyes (describers Louise Fryer and Jo Whitfield).

12 Audio introductions

12.1 Introduction

Throughout this book, there have been frequent references to audio introductions (AIs). You can access a written and spoken example on the accompanying website. AIs have been defined by Fryer and Romero-Fresco (2014: 9) as 'pieces of continuous prose, spoken by a single voice or combination of voices lasting between five and fifteen minutes . . . to provide a framework by which to understand the play'. They go on to say that AIs for film must 'engage the listener's attention, whet their appetite and, most importantly, enable them to appreciate the film's inherent cinematic qualities' (ibid., 12). AIs were introduced into the UK through the live AD model that in the 1980s was imported to the UK from the practices of the Washington Ear in the US (see Chapter 2). AIs are now an established feature of audio-described performances for live events, not only for theatre but also for opera and ballet, as outlined by York (2007). Their use has been advocated for film (Romero-Fresco and Fryer, 2013) following the positive reception of AIs by BPS users in research at Roehampton University. This experiment has since been replicated in Italy (di Giovanni, 2014) and in Poland (Jankowska, 2013), also with positive results, although more for feature films (drama) than for documentary. Bavarian TV broadcast an AI for the German film *Die Wand* (*The Wall*, Pölsler, 2013). This AI was delivered live at the Berlin Film Festival and included with the AD version of the film on DVD (Benecke, personal communication).

12.2 Audio introductions and timing

AIs have the advantage of being free from the timing constraints contingent on most types of AD, with the exception of the typhlofilm described in Chapter 6, in which the film is paused for the duration of the description. AIs are perhaps all the more relevant now that scheduled broadcast systems are being replaced by VOD (see Chapter 2), as they can be hosted on a website and accessed at any time before, after or even during streaming of the programme. Another advantage of AIs is that the AI itself can be relatively cheaply translated into multiple languages. The AI for *Die Wand* was written in English and translated into German. Although currently the AD is available only in German, a version of the AI can be downloaded as a text file

156   *Audio introductions*

or listened to as an mp3 in English from a stand-alone website, www.audiointros.org, that was set up for the Roehampton experiment. The same site hosts AIs in English for *Slumdog Millionaire* (Boyle, 2009) and *Man on Wire* (Marsh, 2008).

AIs provide an opportunity to describe the visual aspects of a production in more detail than can be fitted within the soundtrack. This might include the AD of a complex set, and more detailed descriptions of characters and locations, or even of an action sequence or repeated patterns of movement that will be encountered in the dynamic AD. They are particularly useful for explaining visual style, whether of camerawork or stagecraft, as in this example from a production of *Beauty and the Beast* (dir. K. Mitchell) at the National Theatre of Great Britain in 2010:

> A short flight of steps leads down off the front of the stage. Cecile comes down to talk us or to operate a shadow puppet show. Immediately in front of the people in the first row, there's a long low wooden chest with shallow drawers. It's a light box. Set into the top of it is an A4-sized sheet of glass with a brass frame. This can be illuminated from below. The shadow puppets are cut out of black paper. Cecile and her helper take them out of the drawers and slide them over the glass. The red velvet stage curtains open and the black shapes of the puppet characters are projected onto a white safety curtain behind. They're all rather long and thin – a queen with a tall headdress like an upside-down ice-cream cone, a dragon with a snake-like neck and sharp teeth, a young prince with big innocent eyes. There's also a fairy – but not the sort of delicate, fragile fairy you might imagine. This one's a dumpy, round little thing with short, stubby wings, buzzing around like an angry bee.
>
> Helping Cecile with the shadow puppets is Rabbit. A general dogsbody, Rabbit wears a caretaker's brown coat, with pin-stripe trousers that stop well above her scuffed workman's boots, revealing bare legs. She has a pale face partly hidden under a shock of wild, tangled white hair. Rabbit is hunched over, shy and nervous. She never speaks and looks about with an expression of permanent surprise like . . . well . . . like a Rabbit caught in the headlights. Sometimes Rabbit operates a gadget called a thought-snatcher, which she wears like a wooden backpack. It has an extendable arm, coiled with tubes and wires, ending in a brass bowl. When Rabbit extends the arm and places the bowl over people's heads we can hear their most secret thoughts.

As you can see, this section of the AI combines the *What* and the *How* of the production. Although it might be said to be giving the game away, that is not an issue for at least one man who has been blind since birth, who feels that an AI eases the cognitive load:

> C: I think it's quite nice to have a bit up front, hooks to hang the play on if you like. I quite like that, I quite like not having surprises, I sort of like to know there's going to be a wicked stepmother, there's going to be a tempestuous daughter, I mean these things are good and they're hooks for you to hang it on.

Audio introductions 157

> L: Mmm, so that makes the whole process of watching the play easier?
> C: Absolutely, because sight helps you, because if someone walks in you're getting information in a flash, in the span of a flash bulb you can see the expression on their face, their clothes, I mean it's just so quick. And of course you can't do that with AD as well so the up-front information is very good. And it helps you to understand the play, definitely.

In answer to the question 'What does AD mean to you?' a VocalEyes patron had this to say:

> A few years ago I was lucky enough to attend the audio-described production of *Les Mis*[*erables*] in London and although I thought I knew the story well as I had the CD at home and listened to it many times, it really brought it to life in a completely new way. The description of the costumes before the start of the production was delightful and really helped my mum, who usually has to try to explain the plot and stuff to me. She also enjoys programmes with audio description and finds that it brings them alive in a new way as you are a step ahead of the action and so it is much easier to follow a complicated plot. . . . if I was ever able to attend another audio-described production I would jump at the chance as I know how much more it brings to the enjoyment for anyone, with a sight problem or not.

AIs are not completely free from timing constraints, depending on context. At live events the AI is usually read out live, fifteen minutes before the start of the performance. As members of the audience are unable to take their seats in the auditorium before clearance has been given by the front-of-house staff, the AI cannot last longer than the span between the house's being opened and curtain up. On the rare occasion that the house opening is delayed, the AI might need to be truncated. Occasionally, the AI has been delivered not in the auditorium but elsewhere, such as in the theatre bar, to ease this problem or to overcome technical difficulties with the transmission system. In any case, brevity is to be recommended, lest the notes overwhelm the BPS audience before the show has even begun.

The difficulty of timing the ending of the notes and the beginning of the dynamic AD can be resolved by the providing the describers with a cue light, such that, along with the rest of the company they are given a thirty seconds' cue before curtain up by the stage manager. On rare occasions, such as in those cases where the play has only an AI rather than a complete AD, the stage manager has been known to delay the start of the performance until the AI is finished.

Partly for these reasons, the AI is usually recorded and sent to AD users when they book their tickets so that they can listen in the comfort of their own homes. Alternatively, they may be able to download the AI from the AD provider's or the theatre's website (see Vocaleyes.com). This is particularly beneficial in those theatres that use an infra-red system to 'broadcast' the AD/AI. This system requires an uninterrupted 'line of sight' between the infra-red radiators and the headset worn by the user. At the time when the AI is being delivered live in the auditorium this 'line of sight' is frequently interrupted by other members of the audience as they take their seats. This not a problem in those theatres where the AD is delivered by a radio system that can usually be heard in any part of the building. A recorded AD may be longer than its live counterpart, containing elements that are dropped for the described performance – for example, interviews with the cast and longer extracts from articles in the printed programme.

12.3 Sensitive material

The increasing availability of AIs means that describer must be sensitive to the fact that the actors they describe may listen to the AI, or at least may be told by an AD user how they have been described in the notes. It is possible for an actor to take offence at a description. That said, remember that it is the character you are describing, rather than the actor.

12.4 The *What* of audio introductions

In addition to detailed descriptions of characters and sets, the AI for live events will also include functional information, such as the duration of the performance, number and lengths of intervals, and warnings of, for example, strobe lighting, smoke effects or gunshots, conveying the type of information that may be displayed in the theatre foyer. The names of the describers may also be included, together with a list of cast and production credits. Informal feedback from AD users suggests that they like to have the name of the actor mentioned at the same time as the description of the character they're playing, as in this extract from the AI for the production of Eugene O'Neill's *Anna Christie* (dir. R. Ashford, 2012) at London's Donmar Warehouse:

> The production lasts for approximately 2 hours and 30 minutes with an interval of 20 minutes. Please note that the second half is only 35 minutes long. During the play there are loud noises and some use of strobe lighting. . . .
>
> . . . Finally, we meet a brawny stoker, Mat Burke, played by Jude Law. Mat is a tall shaggy-bearded Irishman in his thirties, with wild dark hair, a braggart's tongue and a dangerous twinkle in his piercing blue eyes. Mat arrives bare-chested with a filthy singlet knotted around the waist of his beige cotton trousers. A silver crucifix dangles on a chain around his neck. His hands unconsciously ball into fists, even as he stoops to look into people's eyes, beaming at them with boyish wheedling charm.
>
> Later, squeezed into a blue suit at least two sizes too small, and wearing a pale grey bowler hat, Mat's muscular body threatens to force its way through the seams. He's clean and scrubbed, but the black coal-dust is too ingrained into his bitten fingernails and his swaggering, rolling seafarer's gait too entrenched for him ever to pass as a city boy.

The characters are described in whichever order seems most appropriate for the production. Sometimes it will be in order of appearance, at others the most important character will be described first, or possibly last so as to be more memorable. Usually they are grouped according to relations in the story, for example in Nicholas Hytner's production of *Hamlet* in 2010, the character section began with a summary sentence so that the AD users knew what to expect: 'There is a mixed-race company of 27 actors' (for views on describing race, see Chapter 11), followed by a detailed description of Hamlet, played by Rory Kinnear. After Hamlet, came a description of his friend, Horatio, then Old Hamlet (his father's ghost), then the three soldiers who meet Horatio when the ghost is first seen, followed by Claudius, brother of Old Hamlet and uncle to young Hamlet, then Gertrude, who is married to Claudius and is Hamlet's mother, Osric, who is Claudius's right-hand man, etc. The idea of incorporating the web of relationships is to avoid AD users' having to remember an abstract list of characters and appearances. An alternative method is to link the characters with their locations. For example, in the AI for *The Lion King* (Taymor, 1994–), the meerkat Timon and the warthog Pumba are described in their jungle setting, in contrast with the characters from the plains. As 27 is a huge number of actors to keep tabs on, some (such as soldiers, actors or courtiers) will be grouped together, and their descriptions kept to a minimum. For example, in Hamlet:

> Ambassadors come to both Claudius' and Fortinbras' courts, all immaculately dressed in grey suits and the men sometimes wearing heavy, expensive dark-blue overcoats.

12.4.1 Technical language

In some cases the AI can also be used as a kind of glossary, explaining technical terms in advance, allowing the strategy of naming without explicitation to be used in the dynamic AD. This might be especially useful in description of camerawork, or for ballet with reference to particular dance steps.

12.5 The process

The type of content that should be included in an AI for film has been described at length in Fryer and Romero-Fresco (2014) using the example of *Inglourious Basterds* (Tarantino, 2009). Below is an outline of the process, concentrating on creating an AI for live events.

The AI is the first element of an AD that needs to be produced by the describer(s), as BPS people like to be able to access it as soon as they book for the AD performance. For this reason, when first seeing a show, describers should always take with them a notebook and pen (not a scratchy pencil that might be audible and annoying to other members of the audience). As the play unfolds, they need to make detailed notes about the set for each scene, the costumes and characters, as well as aspects of the performance that will be difficult to make out on a poor-quality DVD, such as facial expression, or stage business involving small objects. Where possible, describers should arrange to walk the set in the company of the stage manager in order to understand how it works, as well as to see fine details. Notes should also include anything about the general style of the piece that will help provide clarity for AD users. For example, a play that is very dialogue heavy, with little time for description, can benefit from a note to that effect, to avoid the AD user worrying that the AD system has broken down, as in this example from David Hare's play *The Permanent Way* (dir. M. Stafford Clark, 2004):

> Please note that throughout this production, description will be kept to a minimum as the dialogue is very dense and, for the most part, characters introduce themselves. But please keep your headsets switched on as there are some moments when a brief description is necessary and, we hope, helpful.

It is also useful to include information about the audience position and perspective in relation to the stage, and perhaps about the conceit behind the design. For example, in the production of Eugene O'Neill's *Anna Christie*, the AI explained:

> O'Neill was a seaman and a ferocious drinker who spent much of his time in down-at-heel waterfront saloons, experience that he draws upon for this play. *Anna Christie* is set on the eastern seaboard of America, a place where immigrant workers from all over the world mingle in a stew of different accents, faiths and cultures. The Sea is almost another character in the play and at the moment we could be on, or perhaps below deck.

As the BPS audience members are likely to attend a touch tour (see Chapter 3), it is important to distinguish between the appearance of something and what it is really like. Again from *Anna Christie*:

> the stage floor is made of decking – closely-spaced wooden boards stained black with graining reminiscent of ripples of water. The back wall is panelled with wider boards, lapped horizontally to just above head height where they meet a narrow walkway. The boards are roughly textured as though weatherproofed with pitch.

This is also important in order for the AD user to understand the *How* of the production. As a partially sighted man explained:

> S: In [the musical] *Chitty Chitty Bang Bang* there's a car and you think so it's a car then.
> L: Right. Are you sometimes left in doubt as to whether it's a real thing or a . . .
> S: Often. Yeah sometimes there is that, because it could be just a cardboard cut-out which people see and I wouldn't. And to me a cardboard cut-out can look real . . . so it is important to know.

Where two describers are working on the production (see Chapter 2), it is common for one to concentrate on writing the description of the set, the other on costumes and characters. Once a preliminary AI has been drafted, each describer will comment on the notes written by the other and one will undertake to weave the two sets of notes together, possibly incorporating part of an article from the printed programme and a cast list at the end. When both describers are happy that the AI reflects the production, best practice dictates that the AI script will be sent to a third describer, who has not seen the play, for editing. Their task is to check that it is vivid and clear, with no unintentional ambiguity. As you have already seen what you are describing it is easy to believe you have made everything clear, while in practice you may have introduced unintentional ambiguities. Further informal checks occur, when the AI script is recorded, often by a different describer who will probably also be unfamiliar with the production. Last-minute alterations are sometimes made in the studio, ideally after consulting with the AI's author(s).

12.6 Cross referencing

Lines of description from the AI may be woven into the dynamic AD, particularly at the change to a new setting, to act as a reminder of the more detailed description with which AD users will already be familiar. Consistency of names of characters and locations is especially important. Where a character is referred to by more than one name, this should be stated so as to avoid confusion; for example, in *Landscape with Weapon* (Penhall, dir. Michell, 2007) at the National Theatre of Great Britain, the AI stated: 'Ned is visited by his boss, Angela Ross – called Ross in the printed programme, she's only ever referred to by the other characters by her first name.' As the character is referred to as Angela for the rest of the AI, it was left implicit that this was also how she would be referred to during the dynamic AD.

The visuals can be reinforced through choice of language. For example, in *Anna Christie*, the sea-faring setting having been established, marine references were made throughout, so: 'The stage floor is made of *decking* – closely-spaced wooden boards stained black with graining reminiscent of *ripples of water*. The back wall is panelled with wider boards, *lapped* horizontally.' Instead of lamps, the space was lit by storm lanterns. These are obviously deliberate choices on the part of the designer (Paul Wills) and, as such, should be reflected in the AI and AD.

12.7 Synopses

Whether or not to include a synopsis in the AI is contentious, as it could be regarded as patronising. The rule of thumb for VocalEyes and the National Theatre of Great Britain description team is that a synopsis will be included in the AI whenever one is included in the printed programme. This is most likely to be the case for a classic such as a play by Shakespeare. The following example comes from the AI for *The Alchemist* by Ben Jonson, directed by Nicholas Hytner (2006):

162 *Audio introductions*

The printed programme contains this synopsis of the play: The scene – London. Subtle, a con-artist and pimp, and his associate Dol Common, a prostitute, have teamed up with Face so that they can occupy the house in Blackfriars that Face is looking after in his employer's absence. (Lovewit, the employer, has left London to escape an outbreak of the plague and is not expected to return until the city is entirely free of it.)

The three use the house as the centre of a scam that presents Subtle as an Alchemist, on the verge of discovering the Philosopher's Stone – the elixir that can turn base metal into gold, cure disease, and grant its possessor eternal youth.

Face – disguised as 'Captain Face' – hangs around pubs and street corners looking for the gullible and the greedy, to whom he advertises the virtues of Subtle – the 'Doctor' – in several different disguises. Their richest mark, Sir Epicure Mammon, is convinced that the Doctor is on the verge of 'projection' – the final process in the production of the elixir. Face also brings in the occasional client for Dol Common.

As the play starts, Subtle and Face are arguing about which of them is more responsible for the success of their Enterprise.

In the recorded version, the synopsis may be included on a separate track, so that the AD user can choose whether or not to listen. A less formal type of synopsis might be implied in the AI by the way the characters and locations are linked, such as: 'the next place they visit is . . . Where they encounter X, Y and Z.' Certain elements or events should be kept vague, avoiding explicit phrases such as 'after X is shot', so as to avoid ruining the show with a spoiler. The synopsis acts as a contextual frame, facilitating the user to follow the AD, especially at the beginning, where there is lots of information to absorb.

12.8 Conclusion

In this chapter we have explored the way in which an AI can integrate with the AD to assist the description by allowing more time for explicitation and descriptive detail, as well as incorporating functional information to help the AD user prepare for the performance. In the future the move toward theatres using virtual programmes may lessen the need for the functional information in AIs for live events.

12.9 Exercises and points for discussion

Prepare an AI for one of the short films on the accompanying website, working with a partner. Test it out on a third person before they see the film. What did they find helpful, or confusing? How well did it match what they eventually saw?

References

Di Giovanni, Elena (2014). 'Audiodescription meets audio introduction: an Italian experiment'. In *TRAlinea Special Issue: Across Screens Across Boundaries*, ed. Rosa Maria Bollettieri Bosinelli, Elena Di Giovanni and Linda Rossato. Retrieved from www.intralinea.org/specials/article/2072 [accessed 30.07.15].

Fryer, Louise and Pablo Romero-Fresco (2014). 'Audiointroductions'. In Anna Maszerowska, Anna Matamala and Pilar Orero (eds) *Audio description: new perspectives illustrated*. Amsterdam: John Benjamins, pp. 9–28.

Jankowska, A. (2013). 'Taking a British idea to Poland: audio introductions for voiced-over films'. Paper presented at *Advanced Research Seminar on Audio Description (ARSAD) 2015*, Barcelona (March).

Romero-Fresco, Pablo and Louise Fryer (2013). 'Could audio-described films benefit from audio introductions? An audience response study'. *Journal of Visual Impairment and Blindness* 107, no. 4: 287.

York, Greg (2007). 'Verdi made visible: audio introduction for opera and ballet'. In Jorge Díaz Cintas, Pilar Orero and Aline Remael (eds) *Media for all: subtitling for the deaf, audio description, and sign language*. Approaches to Translation Studies, vol. 30. Amsterdam: Rodopi, pp. 215–230.

Film references

Die Wand (*The Wall*), J. R. Pölsler (2013).
Inglourious Basterds, Q. Tarantino (2009).
Man on Wire, J. Marsh (2008).
Slumdog Millionaire, D. Boyle (2009).

References to live events

Anna Christie, dir. R. Ashford (2012). Donmar Warehouse, London. AD by VocalEyes (describers Roz Chalmers and Louise Fryer).
Beauty and the Beast, dir. K. Mitchell (2010). National Theatre of Great Britain, London. AD by in-house team (describers Bridget Crowley and Louise Fryer).
Hamlet, dir. N. Hytner (2010). National Theatre of Great Britain, London. AD by in-house team (describers Bridget Crowley and Louise Fryer).
Landscape with Weapon, dir. R. Michell (2007). National Theatre of Great Britain, London. AD by in-house team (describers Louise Fryer and Andrew Holland).
The Alchemist, dir. N. Hytner (2006). National Theatre of Great Britain, London. AD by in-house team (describers Roz Chalmers and Louise Fryer).
The Lion King, dir. J. Taymor (1994–ongoing). Lyceum Theatre, London. AD by VocalEyes (original describers Louise Fryer and Andrew Holland).
The Permanent Way, dir. M. Stafford Clark (2004). National Theatre of Great Britain, London. AD by in-house team (describers Louise Fryer and Andrew Holland).

13 Contentious issues and future directions in audio description

13.1 Introduction

This chapter looks at areas of AD that are controversial, such as subjectivity and describing facial expressions. Questions of redundancy and persistence are explored, along with other areas where more research in AD is required. An argument is proposed for making multisensory descriptions, less exclusively focused on the visual. It is argued that standards that pin down how AD is carried out are perhaps best avoided, as AD still needs to evolve if it is to provide access in its fullest sense.

13.2 Objectivity and subjectivity

Objectivity in AD is seen to be desirable in some quarters, notably in American AD (see Snyder, 2014); in others it is recognised as unachievable, not only for AD but for all categories of translation. Lawrence Venuti (1998: 4) describes the author Milan Kundera as naïve because 'He assumes that the meaning of the foreign text can avoid change in translation, that the foreign writer's intention can travel unadulterated across a linguistic and cultural divide. A translation always communicates an interpretation . . . '.

Simply by describing some products and not others we may be demonstrating some degree of selection bias, although such decisions are rarely in the audio describer's hands. In the original AUDETEL experiment the collaborating broadcasters aimed to test AD for a variety of programme genres, but choice was affected not only by what was available in the programme schedule during the pilot period but also by the describers' personal preferences. Similarly, the examples contained throughout this book are highly subjective, influenced by recall and selection bias. They were chosen specifically to illustrate and support the author's view of best practice in description. The author does not pretend to be objective, either in discussing AD or in her work as a practising describer. While wary of telling blind people what to think, the author does not want descriptions to be bland – leading to what one American AD user described as 'mostly a Cliff Notes experience'. He argues, persuasively, that:

AD should abandon the myth of objectivity, as well as the principles and practices that this false premise engenders – acknowledging, embracing, and valorizing subjective description should free describers to provide richer filmic experiences for blind viewers [through] better description of people, things, and places – providing details that actually describe this person, that thing, those settings – raising the AD experience up from the current rather generic and undifferentiated blandness – i.e., liberal use of adjectives and adverbs.

Guidelines in most countries caution against subjectivity (Rai et al., 2010). However, attitudes to this have gradually changed over time, at least in Europe. For example, in 2007 Andrew Salway wrote: 'It is stressed that care must be taken not to use subjective adjectives and adverbs' (Salway, 2007: 152). Seven years later, Mazur (2014: 183) cited Vercauteren and Orero (2013: 193), who suggest that 'the objectivity rule can be taken too far'. Mazur (2014: 87) cites Mazur and Chmiel (2012) in proposing that choices, for example between using a more objective or subjective description, should 'be perceived not as binary oppositions but rather as two ends of a continuum'.

The author has found BPS users to be pragmatic with reference to subjectivity. Asked specifically 'Do you mind a subjective description?' one congenitally blind man responded:

> No, no I mean I'm not too precious about it. I mean, if someone says an attractive young girl walks in the room, I guess most of the population would say she's attractive . . .

A partially sighted woman said:

> I would like to build up an image similar to what other people do but I think that's difficult to quantify . . . and I've noticed, even with colours, because I have PAs [personal assistants] that help me get dressed and stuff, and like I'll ask them what tops are in the wardrobe at the moment, and everyone sees colours differently and they all describe them differently and I think it's quite personal and . . . everyone sees things differently.

However, the reasons given for striving for objectivity are good ones, i.e. to avoid forcing a single (and necessarily) sighted person's perspective onto the user and to confer autonomy by offering the visual evidence and giving the user the satisfaction of drawing their own conclusion(s). These are generally traded against concision (e.g., it is quicker to say 'he looks bewildered' than to describe the particular contractions of a number of facial muscles that betray this), and it involves more cognitive effort to decode a set of muscle contractions into a recognisable expression, especially as blind people are likely to be less familiar with that non-verbal code.

According to Orero (2008: 180), 'drafting an audio description script is still a practice performed largely by intuition, with the authors following exclusively their own practice as a guideline'. This suggests that the whole practice of AD is subjective, not simply the word choice for individual utterances. The purpose of AD guidelines is to limit such subjectivity, but, as we have seen, guidelines themselves are often open to interpretation and vary in content and implementation from country to country. Vercauteren and Orero (2013: 197) conclude: 'As research into audio description starts to develop, it becomes ever more clear that existing guidelines, valuable and indispensable as they may be, should not always be taken at face value. They leave some basic questions unanswered and . . . taking them too literally could result in descriptions that are far from ideal.'

Another way to guard against an over-subjective viewpoint is by collaborating and having more than one person involved in the process of developing a description. By listening to and commenting on the dry run in a live AD, or taking part in script and recording checks for screen AD, it is possible to guard against the worst excesses of subjectivity. The other solution, as proposed in Chapter 10, is to accept that the view put forward will not be the subjective view of the describer, but that of the creator, given voice by the describer who is working hand in hand with members of the artistic team.

13.3 Describing facial expression

Iwona Mazur (2014) points out that most guidelines (American, Spanish, French, German, Polish and British) are in favour of describing facial expression. The question of how to do so brings us straight back to the objective/subjective divide. The advantage of describing the physical characteristics of a gesture can be an educational one for blind users. For one congenitally blind man, description of facial expression came near the top of the list of what he wanted from AD:

> The most important thing I guess for me is explaining the silent passages, knowing looks, people walking into rooms, walking out of rooms, I mean in sheer practical terms that's the bit that you need most. I mean, I've had, I've watched films without [AD] and then watched it with it and it's almost like a different film. Because I'm trying . . . my imagination's trying to plug the gaps. But of course maybe occasionally it's better, but usually it's not better, I mean you actually want to watch the real film, so . . . as it was meant to be, so . . . you want the AD and you miss things, you miss clues. The second thing, um – I guess knowing looks and knowing gestures would be for me more important than descriptions of the people because I think that's more pertinent to the, to the – not always but often more important to the plot. If someone scowls or looks happy that's more important than whether or not they're wearing a red dress or blue shirt. All AD's good; all AD of people, what they do, their gestures – it's quite amazing because actually I learn things about people generally about their gestures because I don't know what gestures are like, or looks, like in literature I learn a lot about how people behave, how the sighted world behaves and how it works in terms of visualisation.

However, describing facial expression would seem to be particularly open to charges of subjectivity, perhaps because expressions are not always easy to read. Many a time even experienced describers have been reduced to utterances such as 'an enigmatic expression' or, in a frank admission of defeat, 'his face is hard to read'. This is more common in screen AD, when the camera cuts to a close-up reaction shot, than in live events, when there is usually some other aspect you can describe, such as body posture. Descriptive utterances such as 'his head droops, his shoulders slump' may tell us as much about a character's emotional state as the contraction of his facial muscles.

Psychologists Ekman and Friesen (1978) developed the Facial Action Coding System (FACS) in order to systematise the visual expressions of internal states of mind. However, they noted forty-six action units that alone or in combination account for visible facial movements. The combined effect of these units can result in some several hundred thousand distinct expressions. FACS allows precise specification of the morphology and the dynamics of facial movement. But the FACS is rarely used because it is so time consuming to learn to recognise them. McCloud (2006: 92) attempted to simplify the system, identifying twelve facial muscles – some of which have wonderfully descriptive names, such as the squinter, the brow lifter, the corrugator and so on – the combinations of which denote the basic emotions. However, psychologists are not even in agreement as to what those basic emotions might be (Burkeman, 2015). Igareda and Maiche (2009: 21) conclude: 'we can find that many emotional expressions are synonyms or convey different connotations of particular emotions and that the number of expressions conveying emotional meanings is much greater than researchers thought, but it is smaller than the number of possible expressions'.

Vercauteren and Orero (2013) argue that describing facial expressions is important because they indicate emotions, and emotions are so often responsible for driving a film narrative, giving a character motivation for their subsequent actions. Whereas a novelist can take as much time as they like describing an emotion, a screen actor must make it evident in the duration of a close-up that often lasts no more than a few frames.

Feng and O'Halloran have attempted to define what they call 'a systemic functional lexico-grammar' for analysing meaning-making in visual imagery (Feng and O'Halloran, 2012: 2068). Although their focus is on visually expressed emotion in comic-book illustrations, they argue that their 'social semiotic lexico-grammatical approach is not only effective in explaining the emotion resources in nonverbal behavior, but also useful for investigating cultural differences in the visual depiction of emotion'. Feng and O'Halloran emphasise that facial expressions are only part of a multimodal code and need to be seen in the context of other information, such as dialogue and narrative, in order to be interpreted correctly. A classic illustration of the importance of context comes from the Soviet silent filmmaker Lev Kuleshov, who showed the same shot of an actor with a neutral expression after different emotive primes. After a shot of a bowl of soup, the neutral face was said by viewers to express hunger; after a shot of a child's coffin, sadness; after a shot of a seductively dressed woman, lust, although in

168 *Contentious issues and future directions*

fact the expression did not change. The describer must be aware when describing an expression that their own interpretation has been similarly manipulated by the narrative. Descriptions of facial expression were included in the AD for *Avenue Q* (dir. J. Moore, 2006), before the describers remembered that the show featured Muppet-style puppets who could have no facial expression, or only a single (fixed) expression. The describers were in fact describing the expression and physicality of the in-vision puppeteers who, for the sighted viewer, merged almost indistinguishably with the cloth puppet they were operating so that puppet and puppeteer became one and the same. Similarly, the life-sized horse puppets in the stage version of *War Horse* (2007, dir. M. Elliott) had glass eyes that caught the light and leather ears that could swivel, but appeared to betray a series of complex emotions, despite a limited range of facial movement. Whether the characters are puppets, computer-generated images or real humans, an action or expression will be described differently at different points in the story. Feng and O'Halloran (2012) argue that comic books depict only partial representation – for example, a curved line depicts a smile, which signifies happiness or pleasure. In AV scenarios, as in real life, a whole bunch of other muscles are involved. The US guidelines suggest that describers should describe these muscles so that the main signifier (the curving mouth) and the consequent emotion may be deduced. The ADC Standards (2009: 3.1) suggest: 'For instance, instead of "Johan likes the chocolate milk," say, "Johan sips the chocolate milk, then licks his lips." Arguably, that could equally imply that Johan is fastidious about keeping his lips clean.

The UK's ITC Guidance (ITC, 2000) suggests that it is acceptable to ignore the more complex physical manipulations and simply announce the main part of the message: 'she smiles', or even build on the indexical signs and explicitly declare 'she smiles happily' or, more tellingly, 'her smile fails to reach her eyes'. However, even UK describers would want some visual evidence presented and feel uncomfortable with a simple statement such as 'she is happy'. The key question to ask yourself as a describer is 'How do I know that?' Interrogate your conclusion in order to expose the visual evidence, which, as we have seen, will be only one aspect of the evidence presented, together with narrative inference, character motivation, audience reaction, etc. The balance between these different types of evidence may help you to decide whether the expression needs description at all (for a discussion of reinforcement/redundancy, see below).

Mazur (2014) offers a number of possible strategies for describing facial expression and gesture: literalness; explicitation; generalisation; omission; or any of the previous four in combination. However, literalness is itself a continuum rather than a single fixed point. To use Mazur's own example, some people might consider it literal to say 'She is waving'. Others would view this as deductive, preferring the potentially more objective utterance 'She raises her right arm and moves it from side to side'. The real problem of the subjective/objective divide, even when it is presented as a continuum, is that deciding which position a descriptive utterance occupies on that continuum is itself subjective. As ever, the strategy of naming and explicitation has much to recommend it, such as 'She lifts a hand in farewell' or 'She circles her thumb and forefinger: "perfect"', giving voice to the meaning of the expression. 'She rolls her eyes in an "I told you so" fashion' is another example.

Chmiel and Mazur (2011) tested 'subjective' descriptions such as 'She has dreamy eyes and smiles softly' versus more 'objective' ones: 'Her lips are slightly apart and her pupils dilated. She lowers her eyes, squints them and raises her lip corners slightly.' And the majority of their blind Polish participants preferred the subjective ones. Although these descriptions came in the context of a scene rather than a complete film, which may alter the cognitive load in favour of more succinct AD, Mazur (2014: 184) points out that 'the results do point to the fact that the blind did not mind such detailed descriptions all together, though making any generalisations about the processing of such elaborate ADs would definitely require more extensive testing'.

13.4 Reinforcement, repetition and redundancy

As we have seen, people whose sight and hearing is unimpaired expect information to be presented bimodally. When what we see is complemented by what we hear the two modes strengthen and reinforce each other, increasing reaction times and rates of learning (Bahrick et al., 2002). A sighted viewer's sense of pathos during the funeral speech in *Four Weddings and a Funeral* (Newell, 1994) for example, is heightened by seeing the actor John Hannah's bleak expression. Incongruent facial expression is of course the most important to describe (Mazur (2014: 185) calls it 'discourse-conflicting'), as the dialogue says one thing while the expression or gesture says another, such as one character saying 'Pleased to meet you' while failing to shake the other's hand or look him in the eye, or smile. It can be a rare moment of describing what is not happening: 'he doesn't smile.'

As for congruent expressions, people with sensory loss are used to receiving information unimodally, and the advantage of supplying information to compensate for the impaired sensory mode remains to be demonstrated. BPS users may consider it patronising or simply unnecessary. A man who lost his sight in later life expressed extreme frustration at being given what he felt to be redundant information:

> J: Just occasionally in the AD in the theatre I do find stuff that's superfluous- because given the sort of build up in a dramatic scene you can more or less tell what's likely to happen and then if somebody tells me there's a really angry expression on his face . . .
>
> LF: . . . you can hear it . . .
>
> J: Of course you can bloody hear it! I mean I spend all my life doing it and maybe it's a slight underestimation of the skills acquired by people with sight loss over time.

However, there is always the difficulty that if you omit visual information on these grounds, the AD user will assume that you have 'missed a trick'. A blind woman once took a describer to task, saying, 'You told me the first time she dropped the cigarette lighter but not the second.' To which the describer responded, 'I thought you would hear it.' Evidently she had heard it, otherwise she could not have pointed out the omission. Yet she was a seasoned AD user, who had become familiar not with bimodal redundancy but with unimodal redundancy. She liked the security that the AD afforded in confirming her own powers of deduction.

13.5 AD and persistence

For the sighted viewer, vision, as noted in Chapter 1, allows viewers to remain in one spatio-temporal setting, even though the soundtrack makes a pre-emptive move to another or comes from a totally different place altogether. Further, it has been claimed that persistence of vision is necessary for a series of static images to be viewed as dynamic. This infuriates film scholars such as Joseph and Barbara Anderson, who claim that such an argument presupposes a 'passive viewer upon whose sluggish retina images pile up' (Anderson and Anderson, 1993: 3). Yet, from a cognitive perspective, persistence is important in the sense of object persistence. As Mitrov and Alvarez (2007: 1199) explain:

> An important component of successful visual perception is the ability to keep track of information as belonging to the same entities from one moment to the next. As an observer moves about the environment, and the environment about the observer, objects need to somehow be linked into persisting representations . . . While this process of object persistence is critical, it is not obvious how best it should be accomplished. On one hand, it would be too taxing on our visual system to remember every detail from one view of the world to the next, such that each view can be compared with the previous one. From what is known of attentional processing and memory, even a limited version of such a system is just not feasible.

The question relates to AD in the sense of how a describer can ensure that an object or action persists in the 'mind's eye' of the user. It is possible that this is automatic, as suggested by the Assumption of Normality and frames discussed in Chapter 3. So, once we have described Agamemnon as undressing, BPS users will not need a reminder unless the process is taking inordinately long or he is having difficulty unpinning the brooch that holds his garments together. We have seen that repetition of a character's name is helpful because a memory for character voices is difficult to establish. But what of a mute character or an eavesdropper who perhaps hides at the start of a scene. Does the AD user need frequent reminders that they are still there? Is it different if they are visible rather than hiding? Or is it sufficient to state it once, at the outset?

13.6 Topics for future research

Such questions might best be answered by reception studies, qualitative interviews and other forms of empirical research with describers and AD users. Other

Contentious issues and future directions 171

possible research projects might centre on density. How much description is too much? Given that visual information may not always mean much to people who have never seen, would it be better to present information by way of non-visual modalities? For example, would it be better to describe skin as dry and papery rather than as translucent and pale?

This book has endeavoured to capture at least part of the process a describer goes through when faced with an AV text. Research specifically using the Think-Aloud Protocol might reveal more about different describers' ways of working. One danger in studies purporting to compare difference in AD styles between countries is that there may be as much disparity between scripts written by two describers from the same country as between describers from different countries. Other aspects that have yet to be considered in AD have already been dealt with in interpreting, such as power relations and how AD is affected by the contextual frame. This would be particularly appropriate for comparing AD in museums, delivered face-to-face, with recorded AD. There is also room for more quantitative data documenting the social benefits of AD, so as to complement the sizeable amount of qualitative evidence. As pointed out in Chapter 4, potential increases in social presence from the use of the first person plural for description, as opposed to using a third-person perspective, need to be tested.

Among potential audiences for AD, more work is needed on whether AD benefits other target groups, such as the elderly and those who find it difficult to follow the narrative thread. Also, people who suffer from severe prosopagnosia (an inability to recognise faces, also known as face blindness) might be expected to benefit from the frequent naming of characters. As mentioned in Chapter 9, the guidelines are silent on the subject of translating lyrics, and research is needed to discover ways in which the lyric content of foreign songs can be conveyed without masking the music.

AD has much to offer researchers in other areas, such as biological and cognitive neuroscience, artificial intelligence and scientists interested in sensory substitution. The describer is limited by the fact that the AD user cannot read the describer's facial expression, movements and gestures. Another question to be answered is the extent to which such paralinguistic content is audible, releasing the describer from (potentially patronising) explicitation.

There are new areas into which AD is only just beginning to expand. For example, presentations at conferences should be made accessible, with speakers incorporating AD into their slide presentations; the British Blind Community on Facebook recently pleaded with its members to include AD when uploading video and photographs. Will these informal settings yield a different style of AD? Describers themselves might be a useful resource as subjects for psycholinguistic studies. How do describers organise their mental lexicon? Do they differ in this from other professionals for whom words are a fundamental part of their working lives? Do describers working monolingually show similarities with bilingual translators? Or are they more akin to those with highly developed visual skills, such as artists and architects?

One area of accessibility still to be explored relates to people who are both deaf and blind, such as those with Usher's syndrome. It remains to be seen whether tactile innovations can be harnessed for AV translation for the benefit of a group of people currently completely excluded from mainstream media. As more is understood about mirror neurons and the role of embodied cognition (e.g. Arbib, 2005), such as that language develops from commonly experienced actions rather than observation, it will be interesting to see whether description incorporating multimodal references will be more effective than AD that concentrates on visual properties in what might be thought of as multimodal AD. There is a need for validated measures in order to compare alternative styles of description. Existing presence measures are helpful, but need to be refined for use in low-immersion media and taking account of sensory loss.

13.7 Conclusion

The pursuit of objectivity in AD would appear to be doomed. Sight is inherently subjective: we look for longer at an object that we like. When an object is presented that we do not like our pupils contract, we shut our eyes or turn our heads away. In order to increase engagement and immersion in AV products, describers need to accept and move towards subjective description, authorised where possible by the work's creator

13.8 Exercises and points for discussion

1. Take a short scene and describe it as objectively as you can. Describe it again subjectively and compare the difference.
2. Find examples of subjective description. What do you make of them? Find some still images of faces and try to describe them. Is this harder than describing expressions in a film? Why might that be?
3. Take the AD script for *Notes on Blindness*. Re-work the AD, substituting multisensory descriptions for visual ones.
4. Try recording your own approach by 'thinking aloud' as you prepare the AD for a short scene of your choice, or review a script you have already written as part of a previous exercise. Compare your way of working with a colleague. Does this help you to avoid some of the common scripting errors? (See Chapter 6.)

References

Anderson, Joseph and Barbara Anderson (1993). 'The myth of persistence of vision revisited'. *Journal of Film and Video* 45, no. 1: 3–12.

Arbib, Michael A. (2005). 'From monkey-like action recognition to human language: an evolutionary framework for neurolinguistics'. *Behavioral and Brain Sciences* 28, no. 2: 105–124.

ADC (2009). Standards for Audio Description and Code of Professional Conduct for Describers. Retrieved from www.audiodescriptioncoalition.org/adc_standards_090615.pdf [accessed 19.09.15].

Bahrick, Lorraine E., Ross Flom and Robert Lickliter (2002). 'Intersensory redundancy facilitates discrimination of tempo in 3-month-old infants'. *Developmental Psychobiology* 41, no. 4: 352–363.
Burkeman, Oliver (2015). 'What is an emotion?' *Guardian*. Retrieved from www.theguardian.com/lifeandstyle/2015/aug/14/oliver-burkeman-what-exactly-is-an-emotion [accessed 14.08.15].
Chmiel, Agnieszka and Iwona Mazur (2011). 'AD reception research: some methodological considerations'. Retrieved from https://150.254.65.83/bitstream/10593/8710/1/Chmiel_Mazur_Emerging Topics.pdf [accessed 31.12.15].
Ekman, Paul and Wallace V. Friesen (1978). *Manual for the facial action coding system*. Consulting Psychologists Press.
Feng, Dezheng and Kay L. O'Halloran (2012). 'Representing emotive meaning in visual images: a social semiotic approach'. *Journal of Pragmatics* 44, no. 14: 2067–2084.
Igareda, Paula and Alejandro Maiche (2009). 'Audio description of emotions in films using eye tracking'. In *Proceedings of the Symposium on Mental States, Emotions and Their Embodiment*, pp. 20–23. Retrieved from http://citeseerx.ist.psu.edu/viewdoc/download?doi=10.1.1.160.4581&rep=rep1&type=pdf#page=21 [accessed 31.12.15].
ITC (2000). ITC guidance on standards for audio description. Retrieved from www.ofcom.org.uk/static/archive/itc/itc_publications/codes_guidance/audio_description/index.asp.html [accessed 22.12.15].
Mazur, Iwona (2014). 'Gestures and facial expressions in audio description'. In Anna Maszerowska, Anna Matamala and Pilar Orero (eds) *Audio description: new perspectives illustrated*. Amsterdam: John Benjamins, pp. 179–198.
Mazur, Iwona and Agnieszka Chmiel (2011). 'Audio description made to measure: reflections on interpretation in AD based on the Pear Tree Project data'. In Aline Remael, Orero Pilar and Mary Carroll (eds) *Audiovisual translation and media accessibility at the crossroads*. Media for All 3. Amsterdam and New York: Rodopi, p. 173.
McCloud, Scott (2006). *Making comics: storytelling secrets of comics, manga and graphic novels*. New York: Harper.
Mitroff, Stephen R. and George A. Alvarez (2007). 'Space and time, not surface features, guide object persistence'. *Psychonomic Bulletin & Review* 14, no. 6: 1199–1204.
Orero, Pilar (2008). 'Three different receptions of the same film: the Pear Stories Project applied to audio description 1'. *European Journal of English Studies* 12, no. 2: 179–193.
Rai, Sonali, Joan Greening and Leen Petré (2010). 'A comparative study of audio description guidelines prevalent in different countries'. London: RNIB, Media and Culture Department.
Salway, Andrew (2007). 'A corpus-based analysis of audio description'. In Pilar Orero and Aline Remael (eds) *Media for all: subtitling for the deaf, audio description, and sign language*. Approaches to Translation Studies, vol. 30. Amsterdam: Rodopi, pp. 151–174.
Snyder, Joel (2014). *The visual made verbal: a comprehensive training manual and guide to the history and applications of audio description*. Arlington, VA: American Council for the Blind.
Venuti, Lawrence (1998). *The scandals of translation: towards an ethics of difference*. New York: Taylor & Francis.
Vercauteren, Gert and Pilar Orero (2013). 'Describing facial expressions: much more than meets the eye'. *Quaderns: revista de traducció* 20: 187–199.

Film reference

Four Weddings and a Funeral, Mike Newell (1994).

References to live events

Avenue Q, dir. J. Moore (2006). Noel Coward Theatre, London. AD by VocalEyes (describers Louise Fryer and Jonathan Nash).

War Horse, dir. M. Elliott (2007–2016). National Theatre of Great Britain, London. AD by in-house team (describers Louise Fryer and Andrew Holland).

14 Afterword

14.1 What is audio description, revisited

Now that you know something about the art of AD, let us return to the question posed by Alicia Rodríguez at the Advanced Research Seminar on AD 2015. 'What is Audio Description?' VocalEyes put the question to some of its users, in the form 'What does AD mean to you?' Audio description provides social benefits such as equality, inclusion and community integration. It makes a huge difference to the lives of people with sight loss. The following is a selection of their comments.

- For me, audio description means being able to really enjoy a play. No longer do I have to miss any of the action or nuances, or put up with long gaps in the dialogue after which the story is often impossible to pick up again. Friends and family are also able to relax and fully enjoy the performance too, without having to worry about describing the action, very often to the irritation of other theatre-goers!
- Audio description brings programmes alive for me. It means I can fully understand what is going on during a soap or a film or documentary as a recorded voice tells what is happening during quiet parts or parts with music. I would never know what is happening fully in a programme without audio description. It gives me information on the parts most sighted people take for granted as they can see the screen. 'A man running down the street wearing a blue top and waving his hands.' I wouldn't have known that without audio description.
- Audio description means that, as a blind person, I can watch a film with my friends and laugh at the same time as they do. I can understand the story without having to pause the DVD so that they can describe the bit that I didn't understand. That my husband can relax beside me without having to make the big effort of describing the action to me.
- As a partially sighted person, I benefit from AD in two ways. It highlights things I would otherwise miss, and thus I am able to see them and possibly photograph them if it is a building. There are other objects and of course notices which I cannot see or cannot read, and so a description is particularly helpful. Well-trained describers make the experience interesting and entertaining.

- It doesn't just paint a picture and describe the action; audio description opens up a whole new world of enjoyment for me and my visually impaired family. How else would I know that Lightning McQueen sticks his tongue out or that *Lion King* the musical has such spectacular costume and choreography?
- An audio description is an inspiring way for me to learn about ways to experience something without having to use my eyes. Often what you see overpowers what you might experience if you allow yourself to become immersed in something and feel it across all your senses. An audio description provides a different dimension to an experience. It goes beyond a visual impression and gives depth to an experience by providing another perspective.
- I am not visually impaired but my 8-year-old son is, and I am always looking for ways to communicate about what is going on around him, so he can also see what he can't see with his eyes.
- An opportunity to expand and broaden horizons for the blind and partially sighted.
- Having audio description gives a voice to the visual arts and brings the experience to life in a way that promotes independence, participation and choice.
- Audio description enables me to continue to enjoy the theatre, whether it be drama, musical or ballet. I had given up attending performances, as I was missing so much and unable to understand what was going on, until I gave audio description a try. The touch tours can also be very helpful in giving something to attach the description to. I do not attend any performance now unless it is audio described.

14.2 Conclusion

And finally: what does AD mean to me? I have worked as a describer since 1993. It has been an extraordinary education in the psychology of sight. I have worked with interesting and skilled people, met BPS people full of courage, humour and insight and had the opportunity to work in some fascinating places, see some great performances and sit on my own in rooms full of ancient artefacts or priceless paintings, being paid to look at them long and hard while trying to capture their essence in words. I have learned to say less and listen more. I have learned how speech is so much more than words. AD has given me a career, an area of expertise. I have had the satisfaction of knowing that people found my work useful, interesting and that, like me, it helped them to regain some independence. It has brought me friendship and provided the subject matter for endless conversations. If AD is altruistic, I have been the beneficiary.

Appendix 1

Answers to Chapter 1, exercise 3

Question 1 (c); Question 2 (a); Question 3 (c); Question 4 (b); Question 5 (true); Question 6 (false; although this is contentious, see Cattaneo and Vecchi, 2012; Fryer, 2013); Question 7 (true).

Appendix 2
Like Rabbits AD script

Introduction

Welcome to the Almeida and this audio described performance of *Like Rabbits* – An Almeida Festival 2013 Commission for the award-winning company Lost Dog. Developed by choreographer Ben Duke and writer Lucy Kirkwood, and described as a work-in-progress, *Like Rabbits* is a dance piece for two performers, inspired by Virginia Woolf's short story: Lappin and Lapinova. The production website summarises the story like this:

A delicate woman, deeply in love, marries a man named Ernest. Every night the newlyweds slip away from their real lives and disappear over the moors into a world of their own creation. There, they are King of the Rabbits and Queen of the Hares. But as she craves to stay longer and longer in this fantasy world, she soon fears that her husband considers it only a game – one that has already begun to lose its novelty – and the couple hurtle towards quiet, devastating tragedy.

This production updates the tale to a contemporary setting. The stage is bare except for two black stools brought on by the performers and set one on each side, close to us. There's a microphone on a stand in front of the right hand stool. The woman, Eva, is perhaps 30 – tall, lean and long-limbed. Her body is strong but deceptively slim – her tiny wrists and ankles fragile-looking. There is something androgynous about her – her brown hair is cropped very short. She has sharp cheekbones, a neat nose, a well-defined jaw and a long slender throat. Her eyes are dark, bright but often wary. For much of the time her expression is hard to read – solemn, severe – but is transformed by an occasional smile. While the woman holds herself stiff and tense, the man, Chris, is relaxed and comfortable in his own skin. Of similar age and height to Eva, Chris has frizzy, light brown hair, pulled up into a top-knot and an unkempt beard. His arms hang loosely from his shoulders. He ambles rather than walks. His brown eyes are warm, curious, intrigued.

Both the man and the woman are dressed casually.

Dynamic AD script

The houselights dim. Onstage, the lights brighten. On a stool to the right a woman sits – legs crossed, barefoot – a pouch of tobacco in her hand. As she rolls herself

Appendix 2 179

a cigarette, a young man spots her from the back of the space. Stands, hands in pockets, staring. She stiffens, noticing, but continues with her task.

He steps closer, body turned away, feigning disinterest. Strokes his beard and watches her covertly. She gives no sign but he walks towards her. Stops. Cups his neck in his hand rolling a lazy shoulder, elbow lifted. The pose gets no response. He marches forwards, raises his arms, biceps bulging in a strong-man stance . . . can't resist a glance to see if she's impressed. She licks the cigarette paper. Three quick steps and he's right beside her. She continues unconcerned. He leans back, rolling his fists as if winding her in. He pads backwards still winding. She puts the cigarette to her lips . . . He winds with his whole body, chest and hips circling . . . eyes fixed on her. She picks up a bottle of water. His shoulders dip and weave – fluid, rapid. He runs his thumb up his chest, to his mouth, pulls it sharp across his teeth. Runs it up and down his body. She allows herself a smile. He spins and slinks forwards – step, hip thrust; step, hip thrust – grabs his foot and pulls it up over his head, leg fully extended. Lets it drop, sinks low and retreats, body snaking, gyrating. Grinning now, she takes another drag, taking sly peeks over her shoulder. He reverses, making his way back, lithe, but purposeful . . . starts to skip from side to side . . . Lets the movement grow, legs swinging wide and low pulling him down to the floor, spinning on his knees and up; arms scything as he circles back to her – coming to a deep lunge, jazz hands spread in a clownish greeting. She sips her water, looking away. His whole body sighs. He straightens up, pauses momentarily, then trembles, little juddery movements running through him as she packs her things into a cloth bag. She softens just as he turns on his heel and walks away. She stands to go. He cartwheels back, sliding into the splits but she's gone. He kneels up [sigh] clambers up [sighs] chest heaving.

[clump] She's by the opposite stool.

[sit down] He comes over and sits, hopeful, nervous, meek. With an enigmatic smile, she walks towards the back of the space, stows her bag, and fixes her eyes on him. Steps a little closer. Stops, almost coy. Looks away and back. Rolls her shoulders slowly, flicks her head, toes curl up and she swivels first on heels, then toes, inching closer, edging away. Legs wide, strongly planted, she sinks into a deep squat, rolls back her shoulders, lifts her chest, thrusts it towards him, torso circling, rises up and sinks low. Arms spread – upper body yearning for him, feet fixed fast. She spins, lunging and the moves repeat. . . . She almost slides across the floor, turns away, arms hugged to her chest, protective. But she eases slowly back getting closer with each slinking step. He sits alert, hands on knees, and almost breathes her in. Her body ripples and writhes. She turns to face him and their gazes lock. He makes no move but still she's off. Body angular, twisting, uncertain . . . With great giant steps she picks her way across the floor, drawn to him but still resisting. He daren't move. Her foot plants itself between his, her chest inches from his face, her head bowed a little as her nose traces his hairline. She continues down one arm, as if sniffing every inch, and up the other – lips now level with his, hovering close but not touching. She steps back, arms winding him, drawing an unseen thread. She clasps the end close to her heart and slides her hands over her breasts, elbows circling. Her hands stroke up the back of her neck, ruffling her short, almost spiky hair and down over her face, her chest, her thigh, her leg. She picks up her foot and steps it forward, hands all over her body as if they would pluck off her skin. She lies back on the floor, spreads her legs wide, draws up her ankles and propels herself along. She convulses, sitting up – shoots out a leg towards him, pulls it back and up, knee raised, balancing on a single leg. She arches back, arms loose and abandoned; launches herself into a leaping run, legs flicking up behind. At the rear of the space she drops into a squat, hands stroking imaginary ears . . . she throws herself onto all fours, back arching up, head tucked in then thrown back to look him straight in the eye. Arch and up. She stands – he stands with her – they're 10 feet apart. She pulls off her top. Underneath a skintight leotard, pale pink. He watches, motionless. She eases her trousers down over her narrow hips. The pink legs of the stretchy fabric outline strong thighs, slender calves. She tosses her outer clothes aside. He pads slowly towards her. She runs to her bag, pulls out another skin-tight stretchy suit that matches her own. Lays it on the floor in front of him. He stares down at it. She waits. He looks from her to the suit . . . cautiously prods at it with his toe . . . bends down and picks it up. He takes it with him to the stool. Starts to pull down his trousers, stops, glances at her. She turns her back. He strips down to his pants, and hesitantly pulls on the suit (*she sings*). Covertly she watches him tug the suit over his chest, smooth the wrinkles. Like hers, it clings tightly, leaving only hands, feet and head bare. He struggles to zip up the back. She comes closer . . . pauses . . . steps in to help. He turns and kneels in front of her. She strokes his head (fixes rabbit ears to his head?) and backs away. 10 feet from him she lies down on her side, raised on one elbow, feet towards him – an Odalisque in a pink rabbit suit. Her gaze is frank, steady. Slowly he reaches forwards, til his hands take his weight. On all fours he creeps towards her – the predator invited by the prey. Reaching her, he slowly stands – hands hanging, his gaze tracing the curve of her hip. His bare hands quiver, inching closer, itching to touch – she does not move and he makes contact, hands press down on her hip and thigh. He pushes her forward and back, her body rippling with his movement . . . up . . . and push . . . up . . . and she swivels beneath him, he grabs her leg and swings her up and against him, down into a squat. He squats directly behind. She smiles. He springs her high, taking her weight, down, up, lifting her up, down – she's flat on her back on the floor. He stands, she looks up at him, sweeping her legs up and over, into a shoulder stand, her hands behind her back lifted like paws. He slides to the floor, pulls her legs down and over him, rolls beneath the arch of her back, flipping her up. He kneels, weight to one side, she kneels beside him, nestling into him, head against his shoulder . . . Her hand caresses the back of his neck, he leans away, pulling her with him, swivels and pushes her to her feet. Hands clasped, she tugs him up to join her, he spins her in against him, taking her weight. Edges back and lifts her – her legs scamper mid-turn, he sets her down, kneels, she puts one foot on his shoulder, forcing him into a roll. On her backside she scoots past. He straightens; she dives at him; head between her legs, he lifts her up, down. She walks, catching her with his arm he spins her, they turn together. She ducks under his arm – he grasps her around the chest, lifting, turning her. She faces him – foot to his torso. He seizes it, raising her

Appendix 2 181

high as he spins. Down. He almost falls. She traps him beneath her, together they roll across the floor. On his knees, facing her, he clamps her ankles wide – yanks her close – she folds into him . . . he thrusts her onto her back, feet against his chest, she shoots him to vertical – taking his weight as he leans in – she arches up. He pulls her into a squat. He squats, facing her. They spring together. Down – he on his back, legs bent up – she held above him, shin to shin. They stand. She turns away, sits proud. He grabs her from behind, lifts . . . she turns the tables, pulling him as he sets her down. He steps over her, raises her onto her knees and vaults, his feet hook on her shoulders; his weight on his hands. She steps forwards on her knees, he – hand-walking with her – a curious single beast. . . .

She lies back, he straddles her, pulls her up to stand close. With the back of his hand, he presses her cheek, flips her onto her side, one leg horizontal, he pivots her round. She pushes him to the floor, pinning him with her foot – he clasps her ankle, sits up, his face between her thighs, swivels her leg over his head and brings her down to the floor. She places his hand to her cheek. Presses it against her neck. Stands, pads urgently backwards pulling him with her – momentum reversing he swings her up horizontal across him and runs with her. Down. They half tussle to the floor . . . He lies face down, she – spread along his back – she lifts and he arches up beneath her [exhale] arch up [exhale] arch up [exhale]. She slips from his back to the floor. He stands and she's up and behind him, taking his weight as they both sink into a wide legged squat. His hands on her haunches – her paw beneath his nose for him to sniff . . . He pulls her over his thigh to lie flat on the floor, he at right angles, arched back over her, his legs spread wide. He rolls himself onto one side, she tucked in against his back, exhausted, eyes closed . . .

She eases herself free, leaving him sleeping. Never taking her eyes from him, she pads back towards the stool and sits by the microphone. Only when she speaks does he stir.

[Hey, hey, rabbit . . . more like a lapin?] he sits up [lapin is soft . . . maybe Lappin?] she picks up the mic and steps towards him, [that's perfect, come with me?] He stands and slips his arm around her waist. [pre-empt] They stroll forwards and embrace, the microphone pressed between them. [music] they explore each other's bodies . . . the buck lifts his doe, his muzzle in her belly, her hindlegs clamped around him in a tight ball; she nuzzles down his chest, to his crotch . . . he scrabbles down her back . . . nibbles her neck . . . a tangle of urgent limbs, haunch against flank, forepaws scrabbling, teeth biting . . . he lifts her as she squats and spins her round. . . . he noses at her soft underside, pulls her up onto his chest, her rump level with his shoulder, his face buried between her hind legs. He sets her down. They straighten, stand entwined, smiling. She squats. Pulls him down with her. He listens. Alert [King Lappin . . .] she hands him the mic. [. . . and the friendly rabbits . . . above all, there's the something?] He puts away the mic as she leaps and scampers behind him. He comes to face her. They join in a series of bounds – limbs stretched and extended – enjoying the space – now high, now kneeling up and spinning; they roll together, rise, facing, forepaws high; he twirls as she whips past him; both lift a hind leg, drop into a crouch . . . canter on all fours, sway to be pulled into a spin – hers high, his low to the ground. They pause. She looks down at him, he up at her, and she's off – he in pursuit; they turn – he falls to the ground, she sprawls over him, raised on splayed paws, nose to nose. She skitters away and he follows. They move together. Forepaws crossed and hugged in as they turn, skate backwards, launch forwards at a run, zig-zagging across the open space, grinning. He traps her knees, easing them towards him so she sinks into her squat . . . echoing his . . . He lifts his arms into forepaws, hands dangling. Hers the same, she straightens her back, looks at him anew, head twitching. Looselimbed they rise, shoulder to shoulder, bodies twist and spiral to the ground . . . From low squats they leap high, and squat again, noses lifted, catching a scent. They tumble over and away, with corkscrew frisks of the body – barely breaking eye contact – they come to rest, sitting facing each other – a sound and they bolt, racing to the back – her paw touches his chest and slips around him, his neck arching, he bounds after her and they rest on all fours, take a breath but she's off, he follows, forepaws planted, a hindpaw swung up and over. Happy bunnies, side by side, roll back and waggle their legs in the air – the buck head over heels, the doe swept up onto her hindlegs, she dives over him, and ducks under, as he ducks then dives. She jumps and he rolls under the narrow gap beneath. They pause, crouched, neck to neck and breathe each other in. She retreats, he gives a two-footed leap and she's back, bodies rippling . . . they're off again. A whirl of limbs, bunny hops . . . She exhilarated, he sinks, wearily trying to match her spring for spring. He pulls up, struggling for breath. [phew . . . give me five mins] he rubs the muscles of his thighs. She stands sober, expression cold [doesn't it hurt your legs] she turns on her heel, marches back to the stool. Sits with her back to him. He slumps on the floor. . . . [long pause]

 She picks up her tobacco pouch, takes out a rizla, rolls herself a cigarette. He lifts his head, watching her tense back, propping himself up on his arms. He sits up, wary, arm resting on his raised knee, chin resting on his arm [stuff about hare, what was her name?] She looks round at him [Lapinova: Lapinova]. She softens a little, turning towards him, stands, turns back to us, cigarette between her lips. Slowly her knees part and bend, her shoulders round forwards and hunch, belly contracts, chest clamped between powerful haunches as she crouches, hands dangling like paws. The lighter slips from them. [noise] She looks at it, surprised. Her head twitches. Curious, she nudges the lighter with her paw . . . Sweeps it away. Back straight, back hunched, head ducks towards it. She tries to trap it between her paws, lifts it up, inspects it, fumbles. [clatter] She frowns, loses interest, her head jerks this way and that. She bats the cigarette from her lips, her gaze darts here . . . there . . . The man stands and walks towards her, she stays crouched, twitching . . . He places his hands under her arms to raise her up, straightening her. She slips through his grasp and back to crouch. Her gaze darts, uncomprehending. He retrieves the lighter and the cigarette . . . puts the mic back on its stand. He sits on the stool. Lights the cigarette for himself. She extends an arm as though the limb might not be hers. Brings the paw back up to her chest, rubs one knee against her shoulder, easing an itch. Edges round on her hind paws, her forepaws held in front of her and glances at him. [my sister called today . . . email her that recipe?] She spreads elbows and knees, with ungainly twisting and reluctant effort regains a two-legged posture and stands. [which reminds me . . . I can do that] She quivers, sinks back into a squat, head slumping. Not looking at her, he smokes [some words . . . butter] She stands by him, runs her hand over his shoulders [. . . bread] he doesn't respond. [some chicken] She withdraws, limbs flex, she slides to the ground [yeah well have you tried the plunger . . .] she rolls on to her back and up. [the plunger . . . direct debit] slowly she skitters and frisks. [defrost it on the weekend . . . this is my mother]. She stands, looks around, and with a faint smile, comes towards him. Perches politely beside him on the stool, her hand on his knee. She glances at him, a smile hovering. One then both hands lift and dangle. With a smile to the unseen mother, he catches the incipient paws, and pushes them down into her lap. They lift again. His hold is forceful. With a wicked smirk, she leaps up, pulls him with her launching into a run, zig-zagging across the open space, grinning. They back and turn, in unison. . . . racing, chasing . . . she darts forwards, pads slowly back and spins, squatting in front of him, squatting behind, her hands on his haunches, his hands thrust forwards to become her paws. The paws reach up to scratch her ear . . . she wriggles free, they canter on all fours, up and spin. She dives at him; head between her legs, he lifts her up, down. He spins her, they turn together. She ducks under his arm – he grasps her around the chest, lifting, turning. She faces him – foot to his torso. He seizes it, raising her high as he spins. Down. He almost falls. She traps him beneath and they roll across the floor. She waits in vain for him to clamp her ankles wide – she tugs his knees forcing him to squat – facing her. He rolls back, legs bent up – she above him, shin to shin. She jumps up, pulling him. He grabs her from behind, lifts . . . flips her onto her side, one leg horizontal, he pivots her round. She shoves him to the floor, pins him with her foot – swivels her leg over his head and sits facing him. Desperate, she presses his hand to her cheek. Stands, pads backwards dragging him with her – flings herself at him. He stands unmoved, eyes cold, manipulating her body, pulling her to the floor. He lies on his side, she flops over him . . . He's face down, she along his back – he arches up [exhale] arch [exhale] arch [exhale]. She slithers from his back to the floor. He stretches out, she on one side, tucked against him, exhausted, eyes closed . . . her arm, draped across his chest . . . his eyes open. He slips from her sleeping grasp and gets to his feet, dazed. Chest heaving he looks down at her. Then at himself. He unzips the rabbit suit, freeing his shoulders, arms, chest, legs, wriggling free, skinning himself. She stirs, sits up, watching. She stands. He drops the suit on the floor . She looks from the suit, to him standing in his underpants – her face forlorn. [I need a piss] He marches off. She stands very still. Slowly her knees part and bend, her shoulders round forwards and hunch, belly contracts, chest clamped between powerful haunches as she crouches, hands dangling like paws. The doe raises her head, looks down at the suit, curious. Jerks her gaze to one side, up, down, bunny hops and stays crouched. He returns, flossing his teeth. She hops closer to us, forepaws raised, head twitching, eyes uncomprehending. . . .

As the lights fade?

All rights whatsoever in this play are strictly reserved and application for performance etc. of the text by Lucy Kirkwood must be made before rehearsal to Casarotto Ramsay & Associates Limited, 7–12 Noel Street, London W1F 8GQ. No performance may be given unless a licence has been obtained.

Index

127 Hours 148–149
4oD 21

accents 88–89
accessibility 5
accessible filmmaking 49, 109, 136, 152
Across Still Water 133
action 56, 58, 60, 104, 107
actors 37, 124, 127, 158
Adamou, Christina 5, 143
Addington, David W. 96
adjectives 23, 60–61, 67, 69, 70, 135, 165
Advanced Research Seminar on Audio Description (ARSAD) 7–8
adventitiously blind (AB) people 57
adverbs 60, 135, 165
affordances 56
age 42, 43–44
Agost, Rosa 7
Albee, Edward 16
The Alchemist 161–162
alliteration 67
Almeida Theatre 1, 62; *King Lear* 149; *Like Rabbits* 38, 54; *Oresteia* 125, 130; touch tours 37
Almodóvar, Pedro 137, 138
Alvarez, George A. 170
ambiguity 62–63, 82, 161
American National Association of the Deaf 20–21
amplification 61
Anderson, Joseph and Barbara 170
Anna Christie 158, 160, 161
Anozie, Nonso 151
aphasia 87
apologies 94

appearance 56
apps 18
Arma, Saveria 54, 55, 59, 65, 69, 70
articles 65–66
artistic team 136–137, 166
Aslam, Mubeen M. 69
Assumption of Normality 35, 65, 83, 170
Attenborough, David 111
Attenborough, Michael 149
attractiveness of characters 104–105, 165
AUDETEL project 9, 17, 19, 22, 164
audience responses 38
audio cues 30
audio description (AD): camerawork 130; cinematic 132–136; cognitive model of 46–48; definitions of 7–9; delivery 87–101; facial expressions 166–169; future research 170–172; genre 102–118; guidelines 22–23; history of 15–19; introduction to 1–2; legal background 19–20; meaning making 4–6; objectivity and subjectivity 164–166; persistence of vision 170; presence 6–7; redundancy 169–170; script preparation 75–86; users' views 175–176; within audiovisual translation 2–4
Audio Description Association (ADA) 81, 88
Audio Description Coalition (ADC) 8, 131, 136, 168
audio introductions (AIs) 36–37, 54, 94, 98, 134, 155–163
audio narration (AN) 132
audio subtitles 122–124
audiovisual translation (AVT) 2–4, 7, 51, 61, 144

auditory information 26, 27–29, 123
Australia 19
'Auteur Description' 54, 137–138
authenticity 94
Authority for Television on Demand (ATVOD) 21
Avenue Q 168

Bakkhai 62
Bal, Mieke 8
ballet 155, 159, 176
BBC: *In Touch* 16; iPlayer 21, 45; nature documentaries 111; News Channel 19; Parliament Channel 102; Radio 3 45; Radio 4 1
Beauty and the Beast 156
Belgium 20, 22
Benecke, Bernd 3, 114
Benjamin, George 32
Berry, Cicely 96
Berry, Ralph 151
Berry, Wendell 59
Bertelsen, P. 47
Billy Elliot 17, 22
Biocca, Frank 6
Bistricky, S. L. 45–46
blind or partially sighted (BPS) people 2, 7, 8, 42–53; accessible filmmaking 152; age 43–44; audio introductions 155; children 5; definitions of blindness and partial sight 42–43; feedback from 19, 36, 38; images in the mind 57; live events 85; social inclusion 49; touch tours 37; views on audio description 175–176; visual processing 44–46
Blockbusters 103
blood and gore 148–150
body language 8, 167; *see also* facial expressions
Borat 89, 122, 148
Bosseaux, Charlotte 3
Bourne, Julian 55, 61
Braille 33, 43
brand names 57
Braun, Sabine 1, 3, 7, 112, 123, 124
Breaking Bad 59–60, 61, 119–120
'Breaks in Presence' (BIPs) 48
Brief Encounter 28, 133, 134
Britten, Benjamin 109

Brown, B. 68
Brown, G. 35
Bucaria, Chiara 143, 144–145

Cámara, Lidia 60, 110–111
camerawork 1, 18, 89, 130–140; audio introductions 159; horror films 106; nature documentaries 111; *Notes on Blindness* 49
Campbell, D. Grant 102
Canada 19
captions 58, 95, 112, 123
Carmichael, A. 9
Carousel 151
cast lists 58
Casualty 148
The Catcher in the Rye 143
Catchphrase 103
censorship 83, 141–154
Channel 5 21
Channel Entertainment 21
characters: attractiveness of 104–105, 165; audio introductions 156, 158–159, 161; naming 23, 28–29, 83, 170, 171; soaps and serials 113
Chaume, Frederic 131
Chevalier, Tracy 45
Chicago 126–127
children 5, 22, 31
children's programmes 88, 114–115
China 20
Chion, Michel 26, 94, 95
Chitty Chitty Bang Bang 160
Chmiel, Agnieszka 165, 169
Chocolat 69
choreographers 137
cinemas 18, 26; *see also* films
Cirque du Soleil 18
The Clock 34
Closer 125
Coco Before Chanel 122, 123, 124
Code on Provision of Access Services 42, 94, 102–103, 113
cognitive load 29–30, 169
Cohen, Sasha Baron 89
coherence 82, 112
Collins, Ross 114
colour 23, 68–69, 165
comedy 88, 104, 115

186 Index

Communication Acts (1996, 2003) 19
comprehension 6, 9, 50, 77–78, 91
Computational Auditory Scene Analysis 33
condensation 124
congenitally blind (CB) people 7, 28, 57, 68
conjunctions 70, 82
corrections 94, 97
costume dramas 107, 108
Cousins, Geoff 88
credits 58, 119, 124, 127, 128
cross referencing 161
The Crystal Maze 103
C.S.I. 88–89
cues 48, 70–71; audio 30; verbal 79
cultural references 61–62, 69
The Curious Incident of the Dog in the Night-Time 125–126
curtain calls 127
Cutler, Anne 88, 90, 92

dance 22, 38, 62, 63, 67, 137, 159, 178
A Daring Daylight Burglary 1, 54
Dávila-Montes, José 57, 58, 59
De Gelder, B. 47
De Rijk, A. E. 29
deaf and hard of hearing people 2–3, 171–172
A Delicate Balance 16
delivery 87–101; listening back 97–98; live 98; prosody 87–96; recording strategies 97; text on screen 122–124; voice preparation 96–97
Derrida, Jacques 4–5
describers 2, 4, 19, 39; attractive characters 104–105; audio introductions 159–161; biases of 46, 150; censorship 141; continuity of 115; future research 171; improvisation 22; incorporation into action 138; mental models 45; use of two 112–113
description 58
dialogue 27, 28–29, 38, 47, 80, 144
Díaz Cintas, Jorge 15
digital television 17, 19
directors 136–137, 138
disability 151, 152, 153
documentaries 89, 92, 95, 110; nature documentaries 110–112

dogs 85
Donellan, Declan 151
dramas 95, 103; costume dramas 107, 108; movie genres 104; soaps and serials 112–113
'dry runs' 36–37, 166
dubbing 3, 4, 143, 144
Duke, Ben 137, 178
DVD 17, 46, 126–127, 155
dynamic AD 1, 151, 157, 159
dynamic range 87
dysphemism 145

Eckert, Pete 131
Ekman, Paul 167
elderly people 9, 43, 171
electronic scripts 80–81
electronic voices 89, 91, 92; *see also* text-to-speech
The Elephantom 114
Elizabeth 108
Elliott, Willie 138
ellipses 71
Emmott, C. 35
emotions 27, 32, 34, 93; delivery 88; facial expressions 167; music 121
end credits *see* credits
Engstrom, Erika 96
Equality Act (2010) 19
equivalence 4–5, 6
errors 94, 96, 97, 98
Espasa, Eva 60, 110–111
euphemism 145
European Audiovisual Media Directive 19–20
Evans, Elizabeth Jane 102, 103, 109
excess description 83
expletives 143–144
explicitation 60–61, 62, 152, 171; audio introductions 162; documentaries 110, 111; facial expressions 168–169; over-explicitation 82
eye-gaze 46

Facial Action Coding System (FACS) 167
facial expressions 27, 48, 58, 128, 159–160, 166–169, 171
factual programmes 109–112
fades 76

Fels, Deborah 54, 88, 138
Feng, Dezheng 69, 167, 168
Fernald, Anne 90
films: accessible filmmaking 49, 109, 136, 152; artistic team 136–137; audio introductions 155, 159; 'Auteur Description' 54, 137–138; children's 115; cinematic audio description 132–136; genres 104–107; historical 107, 108–109; history of audio description 15; language of cinema 130–132; music in 33; position of voice 94–95; silent movies 15, 119; *see also* screen audio description
Finland 20
The First Action Movie 1, 54
first-person perspective 65, 94, 114, 171
fluency 96
Foley 30
Four Weddings and a Funeral 169
Fox News 110
frames 35–36, 119, 170
France 29, 69, 77, 89
Frazier, Gregory 16
Freeman, Jonathan: *Brief Encounter* study 28, 133; emotive music 121; presence 6; speaking over music 34; TTS versus human delivery 91, 92, 93; words and shapes 66
Friel, Brian 45
Friends 60
Friesen, Wallace V. 167
Fryer, Louise: audio introductions 155, 159; *Brief Encounter* study 28, 133; emotive music 121; images in the mind 57; presence 6; speaking over music 34; TTS versus human delivery 32, 91, 92, 93; users' views on quiz shows 103–104; words and shapes 66

Gambier, Yves 2, 4, 5, 126
gaps 26, 33–34, 39, 79, 80, 81; *see also* pauses
gender 89–90
generalisation 168
genre 102–118; children's programmes 114–115; factual programmes 109–112; intertextuality 108–109; live performance 115; movies 104–107; soaps and serials 112–113; suitability of AD 102–104
Gerber, Elaine 2, 150, 151, 153
Germany 15, 19, 29; audio introductions 155; filmmaking 131; guidelines 22; legal background 20; *Valkyrie* 120, 121
gestures 27, 166, 168, 171
Gibson, J. J. 46, 56
Giovanni, Elena di 7
Girl with a Pearl Earring 90, 108, 124
Gloriana 109
The Godfather 47
Goodwin, Polly 33
Gottlieb, Henrik 4, 143–144
Grainge, Paul 121
grammar 82, 91–92
Grandage, Michael 149
Grease 31
Greece 29
Gregoras, Dan 120
Grellier, Frederic 60
Gricean maxims 66
Grimberg, Ruth 136
guide dogs 85
guidelines 22–23, 29, 56, 138; censorship 141, 142; children's programmes 114; documentaries 110–111; facial expressions 166, 168; filmmaking 131; music 31; subjectivity 165, 166; violence 148
Guirgis, Stephen Adly 142–143
Gunton, Michael 111
Gysbers, A. 6, 45

Halliday, M. A. K. 55
Hamlet 54, 138, 159
Hare, David 160
Harry Potter and the Sorcerer's Stone 121
Harry Potter films 113, 136–137
Hayes, Ros 143
headsets 17, 37, 85, 95, 157–158
Herbert, J. 91
Herman, David 35
Hill, Annette 109
His Dark Materials 115
historical films 107, 108–109
The History Boys 63
Hitchcock, Alfred 45, 48, 138
Holland, Andrew 17, 67

Hong Kong 20
horror films 106–107
The Hours 55
The House of Bernarda Alba 1
Hull, Diana 16
Hull, John 48, 50
human voice audio description (HVAD) 32, 91, 92, 93
humour 93, 148
Hurtado, Catalina Jiménez 55
Hybrid Broadband Broadcasting for All (HBB4All) 21
Hyks, Veronica 146–147
Hytner, Nicholas 159, 161

Iceland 20
Icke, Robert 130
Igareda, Paula 33, 167
images 57, 58, 102
improvisation 22
'In time' 77, 78, 83
In Touch 16
inconsistency 82, 83
The Incredibles 89–90
independence 50
Independent Television Commission (ITC) 22, 23, 29; camerawork 130; censorship 142; children's programmes 114; delivery 88; documentaries 89, 110, 111–112; facial expressions 168; lyrics 122; musicals 31; violence 148
indexicality 56
information processing 87
Inglourious Basterds 159
insertions 55
intersemioticity 3, 4, 82
intertextuality 108–109
intonation 90, 91, 92
introductions *see* audio introductions
iPM 1
Italian language 70
Italy 19, 155
ITV 21
'I-voice' 94

Jakobsen, Roman 3, 60
The James Plays 115
Jane Eyre 92
Jankowska, Anna 9, 20, 22, 54, 59, 61

Japan 15, 119
Jespersen, O. 66
Joining the Dots 30–31, 33, 37, 61, 128, 136
Jones, Matthew T. 6
Jones, Richard 109
Jonson, Ben 161

Kappur, Shekhar 108
Karamitroglou, Fotios 2
Karjalainen, M. 143
Kemmerer, David 70
Kill Bill 2 122–123
Kim, Jieun 131
King Lear 149–150, 151
Kirkwood, Lucy 178
Kisner, Jordan 33
Kleege, Georgina 46, 120, 152
Knox, Simone 5, 143
Korea 20
Kowal, Emma 150
Kreifelts, Benjamin 27
Kruger, Jan-Louis 3, 62, 132–133, 144
Kuleshov, Lev 167–168
Kundera, Milan 164
Kurz, Ingrid 91–92

Lambert, Mary 16
Landscape with Weapon 161
Langford, Di 113, 136–137
language 7, 54–55; audio introductions 159; censorship 142–144; children's programmes 115; cinematic terminology 131, 133; *Landscape with Weapon* 161; learning 8; linguistic processing 5; multilingualism 126; nature documentaries 111; political correctness 152; structure 70; tense 64; translation 4, 122, 124–125
The Last King of Scotland 151–152
legal background 19–20
Lehmann, C. 54
Leishman, Paul 138
Les Miserables 157
Leung, Dawning 20
lexico-grammatical approach 167
Life Story 111
light 34, 42, 68, 106

Like Rabbits 38, 54, 56, 67, 137; cues 70–71; cultural references 61–62; metaphors 69; pronouns 63; repetition 70; script 178–183
linguistic processing 5
The Lion King 17, 105–106, 159, 176
listening back 97–98
literalness 168
Little House on the Prairie 152
live events 3–4, 18, 21–22; audio introductions 155, 157–158, 159–161; blood and gore 149–150; curtain calls 127; delivery 98; genres 115; lack of guidelines 23; musical 31–32; process for the AD user 85; proximity of voice 95; scripts 75, 80–81, 84; sound 37–38; text 125–126; timing 36–37; *see also* theatre
LiveDescribe 75, 79
locations 36, 161
logos 34, 46, 58, 121–122
Lorca, Federico García 1
Lury, Celia 121
Lush, Desiree 147
lyrics 122, 171

Macfarlane, Robert 58–59
Magee, Bryan 7
Maiche, Alejandro 167
Maiworm, Mario 27
Major Barbara 16
Mamma Mia! 115
Man on Wire 156
Mangiron, Carme 61
The Manhattan Project 120
March of the Penguins 111
Marclay, Christian 34
Marques, Joan F. 150
Marzà Ibañez, Ana 58, 81, 150
The Master and Margarita 130
Maszerowska, Anna 3, 61, 68
Matamala, Anna 105, 113
Matilde 27–28, 29, 34, 35–36
Maupassant, Guy de 45
Mazur, Iwona 165, 166, 168, 169
Mazzie, Claudia 90
McAvoy, James 151–152
McCloud, Scott 167
McKechnie, Kara 108

meaning 4–6, 7; ambiguity 62–63; images 102; prosody 87, 88, 92; segmentation 90; stress 90
memory 29, 30
mental models 6, 45
metaphors 69, 110–111
metonym 106
Metzger, Melanie 4
Michalewicz, Irena 106
Michell, Roger 144
microphones 78, 96–97
A Midsummer Night's Dream 123
Miller, G. A. 29
Milligan, Martin 7
Millions 46
Mind's Eye 21, 151
mise en scène 108, 109
Miss Marple 88–89
Mitchell, Katie 130
Mitrov, Stephen R. 170
mobile phone apps 18
modes of meaning 3
Monk, Claire 107, 109
Monsters Inc. 115
Moos, Anja 77
Morpurgo, Michael 126
*The Motherf**ker with the Hat* 142–143
The Mottershaw Burglary 60
movements 8, 58, 61, 67, 70
movies *see* films
multilingualism 126
multimodality 172
multisemioticity 4
Munro, Rona 115
Murder in the First 47
music 3, 27, 31–33, 39; emotive 121; *Matilde* 28; translation of lyrics 122, 171
musicals 31, 105, 115, 127, 176
'myth of neutrality' 4

names 125, 170; actors 124; audio introductions 161; documentaries 95; pronunciation 79
naming with explicitation 61, 110, 111, 152, 168–169
narration 58, 132
National Geographic 111
National Theatre of Great Britain: access to company and stage managers 138;

audio introductions 156, 161; children's programmes 114; *Closer* 125; *His Dark Materials* 115; *The History Boys* 63; history of audio description 16, 17; in-house team 21; mixed media 130; *The Mother F**ker with the Hat* 142–143; *Peter Pan* 38; *A Taste of Honey* 67; touch tours 37; *Under Milk Wood* 115; *Waves* 89
nature documentaries 110–112
'The Necklace' 45
Netflix 20–21
Netherlands 15
neuroscience 5
'neutrality, myth of' 4
news programmes 103, 109–110
Ng, H. K. 30
No Country for Old Men 33, 135
non-broadcast television 20–21
non-verbal signals 27, 47
norms 94
notes 71
Notes on Blindness 48–49, 54, 60, 64, 67, 91, 136
nouns 59, 63, 69, 70

objectivity 164–166, 169, 172
Ofcom 77, 123; children's programmes 115; Code on Provision of Access Services 42, 94, 102–103, 113
offensive material 77, 142–143, 158
O'Halloran, Kay L. 69, 167, 168
Olivola, Christopher Y. 109
omission 83, 110, 128, 152, 168, 169–170
O'Neill, Eugene 158, 160
onomatopoeia 66
opening titles 34, 58, 119–121, 123, 124, 128
opera 22, 109, 125, 155
Orero, Pilar: audio subtitles 123; audiovisual translation 7; brand names 57; children's programmes 115; eye-gaze 46; facial expressions 167; Gricean maxims 66; multisemioticity 4; narration and description 58; opening titles 124; subjectivity 165–166; visual links between scenes 59
Oresteia 64, 125, 130

Oshodi, Maria 36–37, 151
'Out time' 77, 78, 83, 97

pace 93, 98
pantomime 115
partial sight, definition of 43
patronising information 29, 62, 82, 161, 169, 171
pauses 33–34, 87, 98; *see also* gaps
Pearson, Roberta 102, 103, 109
Pedersen, Jan 61, 62
Peli, Eli 9
perception 46, 47
Perego, Elisa 134–135
The Permanent Way 160
persistence of vision 170
Peter Pan 38
Petrilli, Susan 45
Pfanstiehl, Margaret 15–16
photography 131–132
Piety, Philip 47, 55–56, 63–64, 65, 69, 79, 131
Pimsleur, P. 77
Pinchbeck, Daniel M. 45
pitch 87
The Play that Goes Wrong 66
poetry 67
point of view (POV) 18, 49, 133
Poland: audio introductions 155; children's programmes 115; gender of voice 89; legal background 20; mixed describing teams 19; objectivity and subjectivity 169; talking newspapers 109–110; TTS versus human delivery 92; typhlofilms 80; voice-over 124–125
political correctness 90, 150–152
Ponzio, Augusto 45
porn 146–147
Porter, James E. 108
Portugal 20
position 56
The Powerpuff Girls 114
pragmatic transfer 82
presence 6–7, 48, 133, 171, 172
Pring, Linda 66, 114
The Private Life of Henry VIII 107
pronouns 63, 82
pronunciation 79, 88, 95–96, 98
prosody 27, 29, 87–96

Psycho 45, 48
Pullman, Philip 115
punctuation 70, 78–79, 87
puppets 168

qualities 56
quiz shows 103–104

Rabbitt, P. M. A. 9
race 150–152, 153
radio 1–2, 54, 109
Raffray, Monique 16
Rai, Sonali 88, 130, 141
Raine, Nina 144
Rasheed, Z. 104, 106, 107
reading 56
Ready, Steady, Cook 104
recaps 113
recording 97–98
redundancy 169–170
register 82
'rehearse' mode 78
relevance theory 7
Remael, Aline 7, 105, 113, 126
repetition 70, 81, 114, 170
representations 55
Rhinestone Rollers 138
rhyme 67
rhythm 66–67
The Riot 89
Rodenberg, Patsy 96
Rodero, Emma 77, 78
Rodríguez, Alicia 8, 175
Romero-Fresco, Pablo 136, 155, 159
Rosenthal, Daniel 151
Rowe, Clive 151
Royal National Institute for Blind People (RNIB) 9, 17, 88–89, 135; children's programmes 114; definition of audio description 8; genres 102; guidelines 22; music 31; Working Party on Audio Description 16
Royal Shakespeare Company 21

Sacks, Oliver 87
Said, Edward 119
Salinger, J. D. 143
Salway, Andrew 60, 68, 69, 87, 165
Santaemilia, José 142, 143

Sargeant, Amy 107, 109
Scandura, Gabriela 143–144
scene sympathy 88
schemata 44–45
Scherer, Klaus R. 93
Schindler's List 44
Scotland 15
screen audio description 17, 18, 21; facial expressions 167; script software 75–80; scripting process 84; soundtracks 37; text on screen 122–124; *see also* films; television
scripts 2, 71, 75–86; audio introductions 161; common faults 81–83; live scripting strategies 80–81; marking up 97; pronouns 63; screen software 75–80; script development process 84; script exchange 22; translation of 4; *see also* writing
segmentation 87, 88, 90–91, 93, 97
semiotics 82
sense making 82
sensitive material 158
sentences 55
serials 112–113
setting 58
sex 67, 83, 105, 107, 125, 141–142, 144–148
Shah, M. 104, 106, 107
Shakespeare in Love 107
shapes 66
Shevchenko, Tatiana 77
The Shining 32, 106
Shriberg, Elizabeth 92
Sightlines 21
sight-specific references 68–69
sign language 21
signs 131
silence 33–34, 39; *see also* gaps
Silverman, Kim E. A. 87–88
simultaneity 126–127
Singin' in the Rain 31
Sky 19, 21
Skyfall 57
Slumdog Millionaire 156
smiling 93
Smith, Greg M. 27
Snyder, Joel 3, 46, 58, 60, 77–78, 87, 88
soaps 28, 112–113
social inclusion 49, 65, 134–135, 175

Softel 75
software 75–80, 83–84
... Some Trace of Her 130
sound 27, 37–38, 58
sound effects (SFX) 3, 27, 30, 39, 76, 93
sound symbolism 66–67
soundtracks 18, 37; action movies 107; emotion elicitation 93; nature documentaries 112
source text (ST) 3, 34, 35, 39
Southbank Centre 32
Spain: children's programmes 114, 115; documentaries 110; guidelines 22; history of audio description 15; legal background 20; pre-recorded audio description 17–18; speech rate 77
spectacle 105–106
speech 5–6; delivery 87–99; information processing 87; speech rate 77–78, 79
Sperber, Deirdre 7
spilling the beans 83
Spinney, James 136
stage directions 80
Starfish Technologies 75
states 56
Stepping Out 16
Stevens, Brett 45
stress 87, 88, 90–91, 93
style 82, 88, 91
subjectivity 164–166, 167, 169, 172
subtitles, audio 122–124
subtitling for the deaf and hard of hearing (SDH) 2, 3, 4, 19, 21, 143
Sunday in the Park with George 108
suppression 83
Sutcliffe, Tom 27, 45
swearing 77
Sweller, J. 29
synopses 161–162
Szarkowska, Agnieszka: AD as product and process 2; 'Auteur Description' 54, 137; gender of voice 89; multisemioticity 4; naming plus explicitation 61, 62; TTS versus human delivery 92; voice-over 124–125

tablets 80–81
Tarantino, Quentin 138
Tartter, Vivien C. 93

A Taste of Honey 67
Taylor, Christopher 62, 67, 108
Taymor, Julie 123
telepresence 6
television (TV) 2, 9; audio cues 30; children's programmes 114, 115; Code on Provision of Access Services 42; end credits 127; factual programmes 109–112; history of audio description 15, 17; legal background 19–20; non-broadcast 20–21; position of voice 94–95; preparation stage 19; responses to early AD broadcasts 47; soaps and serials 112–113; titles 120; *see also* screen audio description
tempo 87
tense 63–65
terminology 107, 113, 131, 133
text 34, 58, 91, 119–129; *see also* credits; titles
text-to-speech (TTS) 2, 32, 91, 92, 93, 123; *see also* electronic voices
textual faults 82
Thailand 20
theatre 16–17, 23, 85, 138, 176; audio introductions 155, 156, 157–158; delivery 98; genres 115; incorporation of describer 138; proximity of voice 95; scripts 80; use of two describers 112–113; video recordings 81; *see also* live events
Think-Aloud Protocol 171
third-person perspective 65, 171
Thomas, Dylan 115
Thompson, Hannah 7
Thuis 113
time 58
timecode 48, 75–76, 77, 79, 85
timing 34–37, 83, 155–158
titles 34, 58, 119–121, 123, 124, 128
To Die For 128
Todorov, Alexander 109
Toms, Elaine G. 102
tone 91, 92–93, 115
tongue twisters 83
Toolan, M. 35
touch tours 31, 37, 160, 176
translation 4, 122, 124–125, 155, 164, 171
Translations 45

Trelawney of the Wells 16
Tribes 144
Trouvain, Jürgen 77
trust 95
Tsay, Chia-Jung 32
typhlofilms 80, 155

Udo, John Patrick 54, 88, 138
Uglova, Natalia 77
Umwelt 44–45
Under Milk Wood 115
United Kingdom: accents 88; audio introductions 155; definitions of blindness and partial sight 42, 43; facial expressions 168; genres 102; guidelines 22, 29; history of audio description 16–17, 21; legal background 19; news channels 110; race 151; scripts 80; speech rate 77; theatres 81; use of two describers 112–113
United States: definition of blindness 43; facial expressions 168; filmmaking 131; legal background 20; low vision 42; news channels 110; pre-recorded audio description 17–18; race 150
University Challenge 103
usability 5
Usher's syndrome 171
utterances 55; body language 167; information processing 87; recording strategies 97; screen software 76

vagueness 23, 82
Valkyrie 120–121, 122
venues 16–17, 31–32, 37
Venuti, Lawrence 7, 164
verbs 60, 65, 68, 69
Vercauteren, Gert 8, 22, 23, 35, 165, 166, 167
video on demand (VOD) 21, 155
video recordings 81
viewpoints 56
Vilaró, A. 46
Vimeo 119
violence 77, 83, 107, 141, 148–150
visual acuity 42–43
visual information 26–27, 123
visual processing 44–46
vocabulary 82, 110

VocalEyes 17, 21, 38, 105, 157, 161, 175
voice-over 124–125
voice preparation 96–97
Volver 137
Von Uexkul, Jakob 44
Vygotsky, Lev S. 108

Wadensjö, Ceclia 3–4
The Wall 155–156
Die Wand 155–156
War Horse 126, 168
warming up 96
Warner Brothers 121, 136–137
The Washington Ear 16, 155
Wasserman, Andrea 138
Waterlow, Eleanor 15
Waves 89, 130
Weisen, Marcus 16
Weston, Kurt 131
What You See Is What You Say (WYSIWYS) 46, 56, 146, 152
Whitaker, Forest 151–152
Wig Out! 69
Williams, James 17
Wilson, Dan 7
The Wizard of Oz 94
Woch, Andrzej 80
Wolf Hall 108
women 43
Woolf, Virginia 67, 178
words 55; choice of 58–66, 71; segmentation 87, 88, 90–91, 97
words per minute (WPM) 77–78, 79
working memory (WM) 29, 30
Wright, Nicholas 115
Wright, Tracy 21
writing 54–74; creative use of language 70; cues and notes 70–71; sight-specific references 68–69; sound symbolism 66–67; word choice 58–66; *see also* scripts

York, Greg 155
You Describe 75, 79–80
Young Adam 145–146, 147
YouTube 80
Yule, G. 35

Zombieland 106–107

eBooks
from Taylor & Francis
Helping you to choose the right eBooks for your Library

Add to your library's digital collection today with Taylor & Francis eBooks. We have over 50,000 eBooks in the Humanities, Social Sciences, Behavioural Sciences, Built Environment and Law, from leading imprints, including Routledge, Focal Press and Psychology Press.

Choose from a range of subject packages or create your own!

Benefits for you
- Free MARC records
- COUNTER-compliant usage statistics
- Flexible purchase and pricing options
- All titles DRM-free.

Benefits for your user
- Off-site, anytime access via Athens or referring URL
- Print or copy pages or chapters
- Full content search
- Bookmark, highlight and annotate text
- Access to thousands of pages of quality research at the click of a button.

Free Trials Available
We offer free trials to qualifying academic, corporate and government customers.

eCollections
Choose from over 30 subject eCollections, including:

Archaeology	Language Learning
Architecture	Law
Asian Studies	Literature
Business & Management	Media & Communication
Classical Studies	Middle East Studies
Construction	Music
Creative & Media Arts	Philosophy
Criminology & Criminal Justice	Planning
Economics	Politics
Education	Psychology & Mental Health
Energy	Religion
Engineering	Security
English Language & Linguistics	Social Work
Environment & Sustainability	Sociology
Geography	Sport
Health Studies	Theatre & Performance
History	Tourism, Hospitality & Events

For more information, pricing enquiries or to order a free trial, please contact your local sales team:
www.tandfebooks.com/page/sales

www.tandfebooks.com